TREES

FOR YOUR GARDEN

Populus nigra ' Plantierensis '. *An imposing column*

ROY LANCASTER

TREES
FOR YOUR GARDEN

Aidan Ellis

Acknowledgements

In revising this book I acknowledge the help and advice of several friends and colleagues in the horticultural profession, in particular Brian Humphrey OBE, Harry J. van de Laar and Michael Warren. Others who have helped in various ways include Bill George, Jane Bayes, John Bond and Kenneth Lorentson. I am especially grateful to my wife Sue for typing the manuscript.

The author and the publisher would also like to express their appreciation in being allowed to take photographs at the following gardens:
Abbotsbury Subtropical Garden, Dorset
Arboretum Kalmthout, Belgium
Bressingham Gardens, Norfolk
Domaine de Courson, Courson Monteloup, France
Dunloe Castle Gardens, Killarney, Co Kerry
Earles Mede, Ampfield, Romsey, Hampshire
Exbury Gardens, Hampshire
Falkland Palace, Fife
Gardini Hanbury, La Mortola, Ventimiglia, Italy
Green Farm, Mendlesham, Suffolk
Harlow Carr Gardens, Harrogate, Yorkshire
The Sir Harold Hillier Gardens & Arboretum, Romsey, Hampshire
Knightshayes Gardens, Tiverton, Devon
Little Park, Flowton, Suffolk
Longstock Park Gardens, Stockbridge, Hampshire
Research Station for Nursery Stock, Boskoop, The Netherlands
Royal Botanic Gardens, Edinburgh
Royal Botanic Gardens, Kew
Royal Horticultural Society, Wisley, Surrey
Saling Hall, Saling, Essex
Savill & Valley Gardens, Windsor Great Park
Sharpitor, Devon
Sheffield Park, Sussex
Talbot Manor, Fincham, Norfolk
University Botanic Garden, Cambridge
University Botanic Garden, Oxford
Westonbirt Arboretum, Gloucestershire

This edition first published in the United Kingdom by Aidan Ellis Publishing, Cobb House, Nuffield, Henley on Thames, Oxon RG9 5RT

First edition 1993

Copyright © Roy Lancaster 1993
The right of Roy Lancaster to be identified as author of this work has been asserted by him in accordance with the Copyright Designs & Patents Act 1988

A CIP catalogue record for this book is available from the British Library

Book design by Craig Dodd

Filmset by Contour Typesetters, Southall, Middx UB2 4BD
Printed in England
by J H Haynes & Co Ltd, Sparkford, Somerset BA22 7JJ

imprint page
half-title: Quercus robur, the English Oak
page 6: Fraxinus excelsior 'Jaspidea'

Contents

The Importance of Trees

Few of us would deny that of all the plants that we grow in our gardens the tree has perhaps the greatest impact and appeal. Be it for flower, fruit, foliage, habit, or for its shade, the tree forms the kingpin in most landscapes and a focal point in gardens large and small. Whatever the size of a garden and however colourful its flowers, there is something special, vital even, in having a tree or trees there. Some trees add another dimension to gardens, that of sound. Who hasn't heard the furious rustling of poplar leaves in a breeze or the rushing sound of a beech canopy in a high wind? Nor should we forget the seasonal activities of trees, particularly those of a deciduous nature: the long cavalcade of buds swelling and bursting, leaves expanding, flowers and fruits developing, and so on to the final leaf colouration and fall. Even the movement of different branches in the wind can be interesting, especially to those of us with time to stand and stare.

A tree can be a public attraction, enjoyed by everyone or, alternatively, a personal, individual pleasure. It is many things to many people. Whenever I see an ancient oak or horse chestnut I think of my boyhood days; and anyone who, as a child, ever climbed into the branches of a large tree will know that detached and independent feeling experienced in sitting aloft, legs dangling, watching the comings and goings of life beneath.

Turning to the practical aspects of a tree, I cannot stress too strongly the necessity of the growing tree to man's health and survival. The trees of parks, gardens and streets are often described as the lungs of a city or town, and it is a fact that during daylight hours leaves impart life-giving oxygen to the air while soaking up carbon dioxide. Trees also act as barriers, protecting us from excessive noise, filtering sounds which might disturb or prevent rest, enjoyment or concentration. Trees temper strong winds, their foliage absorbs dust, and their roots consolidate the soil, preventing erosion. The ugliness of many buildings and industrial developments can have as telling an effect on our health and day-to-day living as the noise and fumes of traffic; and here again, trees planted as screens are playing an important role in combating this danger.

The economic importance of trees is well known: only the bamboos approach them in variety of usage. However, after hundreds of years of felling and planting for felling, woodlands are once again being allowed, even encouraged, to develop for amenity and recreational purposes. Perhaps, after all, this green and pleasant land will still be fact and not fiction for generations to come, though we must not weaken in our resolve to make it so. Ironically, it takes a disaster, such as that caused by the Great Gale in south-east England in October 1987 and others since, to make many people realise the importance of trees in our lives. Remembering its long term nature, planting a tree is an investment which can be enjoyed by succeeding generations. Too often these days when considering what to plant in place of trees lost by man's activities or natural causes, large trees are replaced by those of potentially small stature. A cherry replaces an oak or a crab instead of a beech. If our children are not to inherit toytown landscapes, then we must encourage those who would plant to replace wherever practical like with like. Whilst there are undoubtedly places in our gardens and parks for small ornamental trees, nothing can replace the status and presence of a large tree nor its significance to future generations.

Finally (though nothing is final in nature), an aspect of the tree not so well known or appreciated is the "micro-life" it supports. Every tree is, in effect, a world of its own: a world populated by birds, beetles, moths, caterpillars, mosses and lichens, to mention a few. The larger and older a tree, generally the more prolific and varied the life it supports. This is especially true of native trees and here it must be stressed that, contrary to popular opinion, not all insects found on or around a tree are necessarily harmful to it. As in many other communities it is the harmful minority which claims the limelight.

How a Tree Grows

Without delving too deeply into its life-history, a few simple but essential facts are worth bearing in mind if we are to understand the needs of a tree and therefore its successful cultivation. From a growth point of view, the tree comprises four main parts: roots, stem, branches and leaves.

ROOTS

The roots of a tree have two functions – anchorage and feeding. The popular misconception, in Britain certainly, that most trees have a central tap root deeply anchoring the tree into the ground was cruelly exposed during the great October Gale of 1987, when people in south-east England surveyed the countless trees, including oaks, lying on the ground with their unbelievably shallow root systems revealed. This disaster only rein-forced scientific knowledge that the main root system of a tree, under average conditions in Britain, is a lateral one: it spreads outwards through the surface layers of the soil. Only in the seedling stage do some trees, especially oaks, produce a vertical taproot which, however, changes in character as the tree matures.

Some roots are capable of delving deeply into the soil but these are an exception and the root system, even of a large tree, under average conditions is restricted to the upper 30cm of the soil, though its spread will normally extend further than the branches. It is easy to understand, therefore, how careless excavation or similar activities in the ground beneath a tree can cause instability if not the death of the tree.

All roots have the ability to absorb water from the soil; this essential process is mainly carried out, however, by tiny root hairs which are situated towards the tips of the finer (fibrous) roots.

The essential food elements (raw materials) required by the tree are carried into the roots dissolved in the water. This explains why trees which are transplanted with a good fibrous root system stand the best chance of success. Generally speaking, trees whose root systems have suffered heavy damage establish themselves only with difficulty. Some trees, how-ever, such as thorns (*Crataegus*), are naturally coarse-rooted and rarely produce a close-knit root system. These trees need special care in transplating and are best planted small or as container-grown specimens.

STEM

The main stem or trunk of a tree has several important functions. First of all, it is a support for the branches, enabling the leaves to be carried up and above the competition from lower-growing vegetation. Secondly, it carries, just beneath its bark, channels (rather like microscopic pipes) along which water and food elements (sap) pass between roots and leaves. The main bulk of the stem is composed of sapwood and heartwood. The former is still living and stores nutrients and transports sap. The heartwood is in effect dead (though not rotten) material, serving mainly to strenghthen and support. The heartwood is a repository for the tree's waste matter, and only decays when exposed to the air and elements as happens when a stem is badly damaged. In this connection, it is worth pointing out that the success of the tree stem as a support lies as much in its elasticity as in its rigidity – notice how it moves in a wind or bends towards the light.

The bark which covers the stem protects the vital food and water channels from the extremes of cold and heat, and from pests and diseases. Thus it is easy to understand why stripping or otherwise damaging the bark of a tree can lead to serious disorders, permanent injury, or even death.

BRANCHES

The branches of a tree are the aerial extensions of the main stem, and are generally arranged in such a way that most of the leaves have an equal chance to catch the light. Their structure is similar to that of the main stem. Damage to major branches may result in their death and, if further neglected, may attract disease, which in turn may threaten the health and possibly the life of the tree itself.

LEAVES

From a utility point of view, the leaves may be regarded as the factories of the tree. Water, carrying nutrients, arrives from the roots and, in the presence of light and assisted by chlorophyll, energy (in the form of sugars and carbohydrates) essential for growth is produced and carried away, again by water, to all parts of the tree's system. During this process, carbon dioxide is consumed by the leaf and oxygen is released into the atmosphere. Through the leaves excess water is released via tiny pores (stomata), which are mainly situated on the undersurface.

If we bear in mind the above facts, it is easy to understand why most trees need to be planted where their leaves can catch the maximum amount of light. Few ornamental trees actually prefer the shade, though some will tolerate it better than others.

While discussing the functional side of a tree, it is perhaps worth mentioning that the flowers are solely concerned with the production of seed. Their varied forms, colours and scents are intended to attract principally insect pollinators, except in the case of catkins and other wind-pollinated flowers.

How Trees are Produced

Most people planting trees buy them from a nurseryman – often through a garden centre. The present chapter, therefore, explains the nurseryman's methods of propagation; relatively simple methods, such as the use of seeds and cuttings, are easily practised by the amateur, though on a more modest scale.

The nurseryman produces trees by one of several methods, depending on the type of tree and its likely sale. Trees which are in great demand need to be produced by the quickest and cheapest means possible. This does not mean, of course, that quality is necessarily sacrificed for quantity; on the contrary, the nurseryman's specialised skills – techniques both old and new – plus the acquired experience, often of several generations, enable him to propagate and to grow a wide range of hardy trees. At the other end of the scale are trees which are difficult to propagate, and their production is necessarily a slow, patient and often expensive operation.

Of the various methods employed by nurserymen to propagate trees, the following are the ones most generally favoured.

SEED

Seed is generally the easiest, most reliable and most satisfactory method of propagation. In certain cases, e.g. *Eucalyptus*, it is the only reliable method. Seed is also the most convenient method of raising many trees for the amateur.

As a general rule, fresh seed gives the best results: that is to say, seed should be sown as soon as gathered. This is particularly true of such trees as maples, chestnuts, walnuts, oaks and to a lesser extent hickories, hazels and beech which are fleshy or succulent and soon dehydrate. Immediate sowing is essential in the case of willow and poplar seed which is tiny and has a brief viability. Fruits should be gathered when ripe, just as they are ready to fall naturally from the tree. Some fruits, such as the fleshy, berry-like fruits of *Sorbus*, are best netted before ripening commences. This gives some protection against hungry birds.

Large quantities of large seeds, such as oaks, maples, chestnuts and beech, are best sown in prepared beds, either by broadcasting the seed or, better still, evenly distributing it along shallow drills drawn with the edge of a hoe. A general guide to sowing depths is to sow seed to a depth of approximately two to three times its own size, i.e. oaks 4–6cm, beech and maples 2cm etc. Very fine seed, such as that of eucalypts, which should be sown in containers, requires very shallow sowing, i.e. 1–2mm. When germination occurs, the seedlings may then be thinned out or, alternatively, left and then transplanted at a later date when further established. Fleshy fruits, such as those of *Davidia*, *Crataegus*, holly, cherry, and also ash, are best stratified first. To do this, the fruits are mixed with moist sand and a little peat (four to one) and placed in a pot, box or some other container, and plunged in a bed of ash or sand outside, preferably at the foot of a north-facing wall.

A good tip gleaned from a propagator friend of long experience is to add to the above mix ordinary garden soil, say 15–20% of mixture. The reason for this is that peat and sand are sterile; therefore, by adding garden soil one is introducing bacteria which in turn help break down the seed coat – although, incidentally, it will also produce weed seedlings. Germination usually takes place during the second spring, though an occasional seed may germinate the first spring or, in the case of holly, sometimes several years later. Seeds of *Sorbus* invariably germinate the first spring.

Seeds of *Sophora, Gymnocladus, Gleditsia, Cercis* and similar members of the pea family (*Leguminosae*) with very hard, woody coats are usually scarified or, with small quantities, chipped to enable water to enter more easily and quickly, thereby assisting germination.

When seed of a particular tree is only available in small quantities, and this is normally the case with rare or difficult-to-grow trees, it is best sown in a prepared compost in a pot or other small container. The container should then be placed in a closed frame until germination occurs. Small quantities of large seed such as oak, walnut and chestnut may conveniently be sown individually in pots. Propagators in most up-to-date nurseries now employ other aids, such as chemicals and refrigeration, in an effort to assist or quicken the germination of certain "difficult" seeds, while various machines are sometimes employed, both for cleaning and sowing seed.

Remembering that some seeds germinate sooner than others, it requires constant and careful checking to spot the first signs of this having taken place. Care must be taken to protect seed sown outside from rodents and birds (a piece of fine wire mesh, firmly secured, is normally sufficient), and the seedlings from snails and slugs. Early emerging seedlings outside may need protection against frost. Whether seed is sown in pots, containers or in prepared beds, the resultant seedlings require transplanting and "lining out" or containerizing at some stage in their development.

VEGETATIVE PROPAGATION

For a variety of reasons, not all trees produce fruit in cultivation. Some trees which do, produce fruit which develop in the normal way but contain useless (infertile) seed. This state of affairs is particularly common in some species of *Acer* and *Sorbus*, for example few specimens of *Acer griseum* in cultivation in England produce good seed. Other trees produce fruits with good (fertile) seed but the resultant seedlings are so variable that only a small proportion resembles the parent. This is often a result of hybridization with other trees of the same genus growing nearby.

Many of the most ornamental trees in cultivation have arisen as seedling or branch "sports" or, alternatively, are seedling forms which have been specially selected for their improved qualities. In the former category are found many ornamental cherries, also trees with variegated or otherwise coloured foliage, such as *Acer cappadocicum* 'Aureum' and *Acer negundo* 'Elegans' (variegated), and those of unusual habit, such as *Liriodendron tulipifera* 'Fastigiatum' (upright) and *Fraxinus excelsior* 'Pendula' (weeping). The second category accounts for some of our finest autumn-colouring trees, such as *Acer rubrum* 'Schlesingeri' and *Quercus coccinea* 'Splendens', as well as many large-flowered forms, e.g. *Prunus padus* 'Watereri'. Trees produced as a result of hybridization may or may not produce good seed. Those that do, normally result in seedlings varying greatly in ornamental merit. Faced with the above facts, the nurseryman must resort to methods other than seed to propagate these trees.

CUTTINGS

Many deciduous trees, especially willows and poplars, are still commonly propagated by "hard-wood" cuttings taken in winter and arranged in shallow trenches in the open ground. These cuttings normally root in time for planting or "lining out" the following autumn.

An even greater range of trees is propagated by "semi-ripened' cuttings taken in mid to late summer, (mid July-September), when the current year's shoots are reasonably firm and leaves still green. This is certainly the best time to propagate evergreens, such as holly (*Ilex*), *Laurus nobilis, Prunus lusitanica* and *Magnolia grandiflora*. Such cuttings are best placed in a closed frame, either inside or outside the greenhouse. The cuttings themselves may be inserted directly into a suitably prepared rooting medium in the frame, or first placed in prepared boxes or other suitable containers. The main points to watch are shading (during sunny weather) and spraying. In most nurseries, the rooting of "semi-ripened" cuttings is facilitated by the use of special hormone preparations and improved techniques, such as mist propagation. When sufficiently rooted these are "lined out" in the usual way or containerized.

A third type of cutting is known as the "soft-wood" cutting, taken from the young growth between June and early July according to species. These cuttings may be placed in a frame in the normal way, inside or outside. However, because of their fragile nature, attention to shading and spraying is even more critical than with semi-ripened cuttings.

GRAFTING

Grafting is the method by which a shoot (scion) of a desirable form is joined by means of a deceptively simple piece of knifework to the stem (stock) of a common type. Successful union will normally only result when stock and scion are of the same or a related species. For instance, scions of *Acer rubrum* 'Schlesingeri' may be successfully grafted on to stocks of *A. rubrum*, less successfully on to stocks of *A. pseudoplatanus*, and with no success on to stocks of *A. platanoides*, the latter belonging to a different group. Normally the first of these is the most satisfactory. After cuttings, grafting is the most common method of vegetative propagation practised by the nurseryman. It is a relatively skilled operation, a craft which is acquired only after a long and patient apprenticeship. It is a method of propagation which comes nearest to the art of the surgeon. An interesting fact which is often forgotten or overlooked is that by this method gardeners were successfully achieving the union of two individuals hundreds of years before the first successful human transplant operations.

By grafting, many of the most popular ornamental trees are produced in quantity – trees such as *Acer pseudoplatanus* 'Brilliantissimum', *Betula pendula* 'Youngii' and *Robinia pseudoacacia* 'Frisia'. Most coloured and cut-leaved forms of trees, weeping and fastigiate forms, and those specially selected for outstanding characteristics such as autumn colour, as well as slow-growing and difficult-to-grow trees, are generally propagated in this way.

BUDDING

This, in effect, is another form of grafting, usually practised with "easier" subjects, such as ornamental cherries and crabs, as well as many *Sorbus* and *Crataegus*. With this technique, a single bud replaces the multi-budded scion used in grafting.

LAYERING

This old and popular method of propagation is useful with certain trees which are difficult to root from cuttings. It is generally accomplished by bending a suitable branch down to the ground and wounding a small area by removing a small sliver of wood. The wounded area may then be dusted with a hormone powder and pegged into the soil. A sandy compost will encourage the formation of roots, and mulch of peat or leaf-mould is beneficial, particularly during warm weather. As a general rule, one-year-old branches are the best. After rooting has taken place and the "new plant" is established, it may then be separated from the parent plant with a sharp knife or secateurs any time during the following winter.

ROOT CUTTINGS

Certain trees, such as *Ailanthus*, *Aralia elata*, *Rhus*, *Robinia*, etc., may be propagated by preparing, with a sharp knife, 8–13cm long cuttings of the roots. Best results are more likely from roots taken from young trees (3–5 years) in late winter or early spring. The cuttings may then be laid 3–5cm deep in a peat and sand (fifty-fifty) compost, preferably in a box. When the cuttings are established, they are potted-on and later lined-out in the normal manner.

Choosing a Tree

Trees are grown by nurserymen in two ways: either in the open ground or in containers. The former is possibly the older and certainly the more commonly practised method, the trees being lifted from the ground and sold bare-rooted (i.e. roots without soil but with protective cover); or, in the case of large specimens of evergreens, with the roots balled (with soil) and wrapped with hessian.

The advantage of buying trees grown in containers is that they normally suffer little set-back when planted into the open ground. An even greater advantage is that they can be bought and planted at any time of the year, whereas trees grown in the open ground should be lifted and planted only during the winter months (November-March) or, in the case of evergreen trees, September or May when roots are most active. One disadvantage with container-grown trees is that not all trees are suited to this method and, as a result, one's choice is often limited. In addition, although this should not be allowed, many trees left too long in containers become root-bound and establish only with difficulty. This is especially true of fast-growing trees, such as willows and poplars. Eucalyptus species are also prone to this trouble, and a point worth remembering here is that these trees should be planted as small as possible. A 2m high ecualypt looks very tempting in a pot but it isn't the easiest of trees to re-establish in the open ground. Pot-bound trees are often found to have their roots spiralling to such an extent that it is unlikely they will ever recover and grow normally again. This root insecurity frequently results in the sudden collapse or blowing down of a tree after several years of apparently normal growth. If one buys from a reputable nurseryman or garden centre, however, the trouble outlined above should not occur and trees, by whatever method they are grown, should be of good quality.

Forms of tree

Although young ornamental trees for planting are traditionally considered in terms of a standard, namely with a tall clear stem and a distinct head of branches, they may also be obtained in other forms such as half-standard, feathered and whip. The standard tree will normally possess a clear stem of approximately 1.8m, though some nurserymen can supply certain trees with clear stems ranging from 1.5–2.5m or more. Half standards normally possess a clear stem of approx. 1.2m. The feathered tree is basically a 1.8–2.5m central stem with branches retained to near ground level, whilst whips are smaller (1–2m) younger versions of the feathered tree or sometimes merely a main stem without branches.

The form of tree one buys will depend on several factors, including the tree's natural habit, planting site and, of course, personal taste. In theory, the smaller the tree the better its chances of establishing. On this basis, feathered trees and whips are preferable to standards and half-standards. For a start, no real staking is required although the initial support of a strong cane may be necessary in some instances. Secondly, the transplanting of a small tree is (or should be) less fraught with difficulties. The root system is normally smaller and, provided that planting is effected with care, the chance of success is that much greater. A feathered or whip form of a strong-growing tree will eventually catch up on one planted as a standard. Many less common ornamental trees, such as maples of the "snake-bark" group, *Styrax*, *Stuartia*, *Nothofagus*, *Magnolia*, *Eucryphia* and *Embothrium* as well as fastigiate trees such as *Carpinus betulus* 'Fastigiata' and *Liriodendron tulipifera* 'Fastigiata', are normally grown and sold as feathered trees or whips.

Having said this, one has to concede that standard and half-standard trees have immediate impact and appeal to a great number of people, especially first-time gardeners and those in a hurry, not least the elderly. Not surprisingly therefore, standard and half-standard trees are still the most popular; and provided they are of good quality, are correctly planted and receive the necessary after-care, there is no reason why they should not prove satisfactory. A wide range of popular ornamental trees is readily available as standards. These include Japanese cherries, mountain ash (*Sorbus*), flowering crab (*Malus*) and the various forms of ash (*Fraxinus*), lime (*Tilia*) and horse-chestnut (*Aesculus*), as well as weeping trees such as *Pyrus salicifolia* 'Pendula' and *Prunus pendula* 'Pendula Rosea'.

Whichever form of tree one favours, there are certain important points one should always check out before buying. First of all confirm that the tree is suitable for the site you have in mind, that it will not grow too large, that the soil is right, and that it is hardy (given your local climate). Check for a well balanced shape, especially a good leader. Even trees which are eventually bushy-headed, for example thorns (*Crataegus*), should have an obvious leader when young, so too should trees of a weeping nature such as *Pyrus salicifolia* 'Pendula' which you may wish to continue training to a greater height.

Check, where possible, for a well balanced and healthy root system which has not been exposed to drying winds or sun. Check also for pests and diseases and excessive die-back. It is not always practicable to establish these by examination at the time of purchase and one must sometimes take it "on spec". Those who, for one reason or another, order "blind", without first seeing the tree, are advised to deal only with reputable nurserymen and garden centres, particularly those recommended by satisfied friends or neighbours.

Planting a tree

WHEN TO PLANT

Generally speaking, deciduous trees grown in the open ground should be lifted and planted any time after leaf fall in the autumn and before first flush the following spring. For most trees this means late October until late March.

Evergreens grown in the open ground establish best when lifted and planted between September and early October, or in late April to May when roots are most active. Having said this, I have to admit that, given certain precautions, it is possible to move young trees, especially evergreens, at other times; but the amateur is advised to stick to the above well proven periods if he is not to tempt fate.

Container-grown trees, of course, can be planted at any time of the year.

When planting from the open ground or from a container you should avoid periods of inclement weather such as frost, drought, strong drying winds or after heavy rain if the soil is wet and sticky.

On the subject of autumn versus spring planting, there is no doubt in my mind that hardy trees planted in autumn when the soil is normally moist and still relatively warm, will experience some root activity before winter sets in. With trees of borderline hardiness, however, late spring or early summer planting is advisable, especially in the case of container-grown eucalypts.

WHEN A TREE ARRIVES

As soon as the tree arrives from the nursery, it should be inspected to check that no serious damage has occurred, either in the lifting operation or while in transit – young leaders are especially subject to damage in handling. Should the condition of the tree give cause for complaint, this must be made as soon as possible and not left until the cause may prove debatable. If all is satisfactory and conditions are suitable, planting should commence. If not, then the tree should be carefully unpacked and heeled-in, its roots resting in a prepared trench and completely covered with soil. Trees tied in bundles should be unfastened and distributed along the trench. Roots wrapped in sacking or in plastic and similarly impermeable wrappers should be removed first before "heeling-in". **On no account must the roots be left exposed to sun or drying winds. Roots which are found to be dry on arrival should be soaked in water before planting or heeling-in.** Container-grown trees should be watered as soon as they arrive and, if they are not able to be planted for some time, these too are best plunged in the soil until required. Trees which arrive during a period of heavy frost, when the ground outside is hard, should be stood in a frost-free shed, garage or outhouse, their roots covered by moist sacking or a good depth of straw until conditions outside are favourable.

STAKING

It is important to provide the newly planted standard with a strong stake on its windward side to prevent the rootball from rocking. In normal circumstances, the stake is required only for as long as it takes the root system to become established in the new soil, usually one or two years. If the tree has not become self-supporting by then it it unlikely ever to do so. The length of stake required has been the subject of some controversy in recent years, differing opinions favouring either a short or the traditional long stake. The "short stakers" point out that the stem of a tree needs no restriction if it is to grow strong yet remain supple enough to support its expected crown. A long stake, they argue, only prevents this natural development of the stem. Using a short stake (up to a third the height of the clear stem) secures the rootball against rocking while allowing the rest of the stem to develop naturally. Whilst there is a lot to be said for this method (it really does make sense), I am of the opinion that a longer stake is still useful in the case of slender stems which might otherwise lean or bend. Some crabs (*Malus*) and cherries (*Prunus*) are inclined to this. Long stakes are also worth considering for standard trees on exposed sites or where vandalism is likely to be a problem.

In an ideal world, trees should be planted as "whips" or as "feathered" specimens without need for staking; but for reasons already outlined in the previous chapter, I can see no early demise in gardens of the standard tree and, be it long or short, a stake. The following instructions, therefore, take into accont the use of a stake as a temporary support. Traditionally, sweet chestnut or peeled larch make the best stakes; though, given their temporary use, other woods will suffice.

HOW TO PLANT

Most trees planted in gardens are given homes either in a bed or border, or in a lawn or rough-grassed area. Whichever it is, the actual mechanisms of planting are more or less identical. Let us assume then that the tree is to be planted in a lawn. The width and depth of the hole will vary depending on size of root system. Ideally the hole should be twice as wide as the container/rootball and at least as deep. The tree should be planted as far as possible to the original soil depth (when in the nursery ground or container). Plant too deep and the roots will be further away from oxygen and rainwater vital to growth which are most prevalent nearer the surface. Plant too shallow and the roots will be more easily exposed to drying and damage.

Having first removed and stacked the turf to one side, the soil should then be excavated to just above the required depth (try the tree in the hole to check this). Having first forked over the bottom of the hole, place the turves (grass down) over the broken soil and firm gently underfoot. Alternatively or in addition, compost, leaf mould or well weathered manure may be used. A growing body of opinion believes that trees should be planted direct into the native soil without any additives. If the soil is fertile, I can go along with this but if it is otherwise, I recommend some improvement be made.

It is important to provide a newly planted standard or half-standard tree with a strong stake on its windward side to prevent it from blowing over or rocking about in the wind. If a long stake is chosen then it should be 0.7–1m longer than the clear stem of the tree. The base should be pointed. When prepared, the stake should be placed near the centre of the hole and driven into the ground to the depth of approx. 0.3m. Some of the excavated soil should now be placed back in the hole to form a small central mound. In the case of a **short stake** this should be approx. 1.3m long, the base pointed. It should then be driven into the ground to a depth of 0.3m. All is now prepared for planting.

Trees grown in a container should first be thoroughly watered and then placed in the hole and the container carefully removed. Bare-rooted trees should be inspected and damaged roots, must be cut away cleanly with a sharp knife or secateurs. Damaged roots cleanly cut become the site of new root generation and allow the tree temporarily to absorb water directly into its structure. The tree should then be stood in the hole close up to the leeward side of the stake, in a position where its stem fits closely to the stake along most, if not all, of its length. With a long stake, mark the stake at a point just below the level of the lowest branch, and cut off its top at the point marked. Carefully replace the soil over the roots while, in the case of bare-rooted trees, shaking the tree gently up and down to allow the soil to filter through, thereby preventing air pockets. This process should be continued until the roots are well covered, then the soil may be firmed gently using the heel, continuing until the hole is filled and the soil is level with or just below ground level. In normal circumstances, some subsidence will occur but not enough to cause concern.

In **wet ground** the planting may be raised a little above the level of the surrounding area (mound planting). In **dry ground** the opposite method (basin planting) is sometimes practised to enable water to be applied in quantity should it be required. Either way, the final soil level around the stem must not be allowed to exceed the original planting level (when in the nursery or container). Planting trees too deep is a common fault and is the cause of many tree deaths in later years.

The tree must now be secured to the stake by two "tree-ties" in the case of a long stake and by one in the case of short stake. The best tree ties are normally of plastic or rubber and are specially made for the purpose. Avoid using string, rope, nylon stocking or other temporary and unsuitable ties, and on no account employ wire for this purpose. Ideally, with a long stake, one tie should be fixed towards the base of the stem and the other at a point just below the lowermost branch. With a short stake, the tie is positioned just below (5–6cm) the top of the stake. Most ties have a buffer which is positioned between the stake and the stem to prevent the bark being rubbed or damaged, while some ties achieve the same effect by twisting between the two.

Finally, the newly planted tree should be given a thorough soaking. This is particularly important with container-grown trees planted during spring or summer.

Trees planted as whips or feathered specimens should be planted as above except that the hole, of course, will be smaller; and a stake is not necessary, although a supporting cane may be useful, especially when training a weeping tree to a high crown, or when encouraging a multi-stemmed young tree to form a leader. Any ties used in this operation must similarly be safe and adjustable. Checking the ties of fast-growing whips and feathered trees is a crucial and regular operation and should not be neglected. Tight ties must be loosened or removed.

PLANTING IN "DIFFICULT GROUND"

Where trees are intended for planting in ground which is in any way compacted, especially on heavy clay, or where ground is rocky or otherwise difficult to dig, it is recommended that the general area around the planting position be cultivated. Trees planted in "pockets" of good soil or compost in such situations are liable to suffer, as the holes act as sumps in wet weather or as root "prisons" in dry conditions.

If necessary, a peat substitute or compost may be added to the soil during filling-in and a "dash" of a suitable granulated slow-acting general fertiliser can be beneficial if added at the same time. More important, however, is a suitable organic mulch after planting. If the "soil" on the site is in any way unsuitable, and I really mean unsuitable (very stony, gravelly, dry shallow chalk or heavy clay), it might pay to remove the excavated soil completely and fill-in with a more suitable topsoil from elsewhere, preferably nearby. Trees planted in

bare ground may have well rotted farmyard manure or compost spread in the bottom of the planting hole. The more care and attention given to the planting of a young tree, the better its chances of surviving and flourishing. Many young trees have been lost – and are still being lost – through insufficient preparation of the site, unnecessary and neglected damage to roots and branches, too deep or too shallow planting and bad staking. Always bear in mind that you are dealing with a living thing, like yourself: start it off with care and it stands a better chance of making a strong, healthy specimen.

PROTECTING THE NEWLY PLANTED TREE

Young stems are subject to damage from the claws of cats, teeth of rabbits and hares, or even deer. Chicken wire coiled round the tree's base gives some protection, but spiral plastic sheaths specially designed for the job are available from garden centres and are more easily applied. Another form of protection for the whip or small feathered tree is a plastic mesh guard which should be tall enough to prevent the animal from reaching the main stem.

TREE GUARDS

For larger trees, especially those planted in a paddock or on the periphery of gardens in rural areas, a more robust protection can be achieved with the use of large plastic mesh tree guards. These are particularly effective against browsing by animals; whilst for protection against browsing horses or cattle, a more substantial guard made from wood or metal is necessary.

TREE SHELTERS

Another form of protection for young trees is the tree shelter, basically a vertical translucent or transparent plastic tube commonly 1.2m long (longer ones are available), which is placed around the tree. Apart from offering protection against rabbits, squirrels and roe deer, the tree shelter creates a favourable microclimate around a tree by acting as an individual greenhouse, encouraging faster growth. It also makes the chemical control of weeds a lot easier with less risk of damage to the tree inside. Such shelters have a life span of about five years which is normally long enough for the tree it protects to become well established. Obviously, tree shelters are applicable to small specimens such as whips and feathered trees, especially when planted in rough grass.

AFTER-CARE

It is a sad fact that more young trees are lost through a lack of after-care than for any other reason. Many people, having carefully planted and staked a tree, then leave it to fend for itself expecting it to grow from strength to strength without any further attention. The majority of ornamental trees, however, benefit from attention to one or two important details. In fact, I would go as far as to say that, unless you are prepared to take care of a tree after planting, it would be better not to plant it in the first place.

ADEQUATE WATER SUPPLY

The most important requirement of a newly planted tree is an adequate supply of water. Even trees in large areas of bare soil will probably require frequent watering during the first summer after planting. When trees are planted in grassy areas, it is absolutely essential that the circle of soil at the base of the stem (a minimum of 1m diameter) be maintained for several years, until the tree is obviously well established. Not only does the circle of soil allow easy access of water to the roots, it also removes the need for grass cutters to approach too close to the stem. I have seen so many wounds caused by attempts to cut grass growing around the base of tree stems. The circle must be kept free of weeds, preferably by hand, or, where many trees are involved, spraying with a recommended herbicide. To prevent the soil in the circle from drying out during warm sunny periods a 5cm mulch of a peat substitute, shredded bark, leaf-mould (or other suitable organic material) or a sheet of black polythene or a "treespat" (special rubber or plastic mat) may be applied, taking care to keep the base of the stem clear. It also pays to check newly planted trees after periods of frost, when the roots become loosened and the soil lifted. Simply re-firm the soil with a gentle trampling.

Watering, when it is necessary such as in time of drought, should be applied slowly and thoroughly, an occasional bucket of water during an extended drought is simply not enough. Much better is a slow but continuous "dribble" or a series of buckets in an earth basin around the base of the tree so that every drop of water is held and can percolate gradually and deeply. Beware shallow watering which encourages a too shallow root system to become even more prone to stress. If it is a question of priority, I would recommend giving rationed water to *young* trees as they represent a long term investment.

PLANTING ROUND THE BASE OF AN ESTABLISHED TREE

An alternative and attractive method of dealing with a large circle of soil at the base of an established tree is to plant it in a lawn. You can either try an annual planting with such things as wallflowers, bedding plants etc, or achieve a more permanent effect with perennials (take care not to damage roots). If the latter is chosen, there is a wealth of plants worth considering including bulbs and ground cover. In my own garden I have found *Geranium macrorrhizum* in its various forms excellent for this purpose, forming a pleasant and attractive base to the tree as well as preventing weed seeds from germinating. Alternatively, small bulbs such as scillas, snowdrops, chionodoxas, winter aconites and crocus provide a colourful spring carpet beneath young trees, as do hardy cyclamen in autumn. The circle around newly planted trees, however, is best left unplanted in order not to impede the supply of water to the roots.

TREE STAKES AND TIES

Once a young tree has become established in its new site (usually 1–2 years), stake and tie(s) must be removed. Too often this is neglected, and with the increase in stem girth the tie bites into the tender bark causing strangulation and eventually death. Even in the first two years, ties must be regularly checked and loosened if necessary. So too must labels, especially those fixed by looping string, cord or wire around a branch. A stroll round even the best labelled arboretum or tree collection will invariably reveal some labels whose ties have become embedded in the bark of a branch due to normal growth. The more vigorous the tree, the more vigilant you need to be.

PROTECTION IN EXPOSED AREAS

Trees planted in very exposed sites are obviously more susceptible during the first few seasons than those planted in more sheltered positions. Thus evergreens, and even deciduous trees when "flushing" in the spring, should be given some form of protection against cold wind. This can easily be done by erecting a simple hessian or polythene screen to the windward side of the tree, or all round the tree if turbulance comes from several directions. This can be dismantled when more settled weather arrives and, in normal circumstances, may be dispersed with altogether when the tree is sufficiently well established to face the blasts alone.

Training and Pruning

Ideally, trees should not be pruned as pruning causes wounds and wounds can lead to disease, decay, even death. However, we do not live in an ideal world, and many trees planted in the garden can expect to be pruned in some way at some time in their lives. Minor pruning concerns small branches or shoots where the resultant wound is minimal. Major pruning involves larger branches where the wound is considerable.

A tree purchased from a reputable garden centre or nursery usually has the beginnings of its natural shape and habit (see note under "Forms of Tree"). That is to say, if it is naturally tall and vigorous it should have an obvious leader; but if it is naturally bushy and dense it will have several leaders, though in a small specimen such as a whip or feathered form there should, nevertheless, be a main leader with which to increase height. As young trees develop, it may become necessary to prune in order to reduce or eliminate the weaker of two or several competing leaders, giving the favoured leader a better chance of increasing its dominance.

Again, with whips and feathered trees, if a clear stem of any height is envisaged, it will be necessary first to shorten and then remove the side branches over the first few years following planting. This "formative pruning", as it is termed, concerns shoots and small or slender branches and is normally achieved with the aid of a sharp pruning knife or secateurs. Likewise, branches which threaten to cross and rub together and those which are damaged or diseased will require similar attention.

Trees which have been budded or grafted sometimes throw up suckers from the stock. These should be removed clean from the base as soon as they appear, when they are relatively soft, using a sharp knife. *Aralia elata* 'Variegata' is particularly prone to this. Then there are trees with coloured or variegated foliage that sometimes produce a branch which has "reverted", producing green leaves: this should be removed in the same way. Two of the most notorious offenders are *Acer negundo* 'Variegata' and *Acer platanoides* 'Drummondii'.

The secret of successful formative pruning is to carry it out sooner rather than later. The smaller the branch to be pruned the smaller the wound. With established trees, pruning may be necessary to deal with branches damaged or broken by accident, vandalism or by strong winds. Such was the case in October 1987 after the Great Gale when thousands of trees in gardens throughout south-east England were left in need of attention.

Branches too thick for secateurs or a knife should be removed with a sharp saw. There is a whole range of pruning saws available on the market, including some handy collapsible versions suitable for small branches. The larger the branch to be pruned or removed, the larger the saw and the greater the skill required in accomplishing the operation successfully. Whilst it is possible to remove reasonably sized branches with a good handsaw, using a ladder where necessary, there is a point beyond which it is safer and more satisfactory to employ a qualified tree surgeon, who has skill and experience on his side and is correctly equipped and insured as well. This is certainly to be recommended where large branches are involved, especially if they are in any way difficult to reach or are critically situated: for instance above a public right of way or above your own or a neighbouring property. In these circumstances, if one is not trained or experienced in such matters accidents can and do happen and the tree is often not the only casualty! If you decide to employ someone else to deal with your tree, do **consult the yellow pages for a professional who is also insured**. Do not at your peril accept the advice or help of itinerent "cowboys" knocking at your door.

When removing a branch, always be sure to **make the final cut proud of the branch collar**, never flush with the trunk or a major branch if one is removing a side branch. This is because the collar zone of a branch possesses a natural ability to seal off a wound. Cut beyond the collar (the swollen base) and the chances of the wound healing successfully are lessened considerably. All but the smallest branches are best removed in two stages, making the first cut some distance (1m or more) from the branch base, and then removing the resultant "peg" or stub. Before removing the main weight of the branch, it helps to make an initial cut below the branch to prevent possible bark tearing when the top cut is made and the branch falls. There is no harm in doing this also on the final cut if the peg is large or heavy.

Not so long ago, it was regarded as obligatory to treat all pruning wounds with a propriety "tree paint" or wound dressing. Recent research, however, has proved this to be mainly of cosmetic value, although some preparations do encourage callous formation.

As for **when to prune trees**, it is probably better to prune in late winter or early spring to give the wound several growing months in which to form a callous before the next winter sets in. The most important exceptions are ornamental cherries, plums and damsons (*Prunus*) which should be pruned (only if necessary) in midsummer, before late July when there is less risk of infection by silverleaf disease, whilst maples (*Acer*) and birch (*Betula*) should be pruned in summer as they tend to "bleed" profusely in the winter/spring period. Evergreens are best pruned in late spring (May ideally).

To sum up!
1. Prune only when necessary
2. The smaller the wound the better
3. Use only sharp tools
4. Do not "flush prune"
5. Do not leave "pegs" or stubs
6. Consider safety at all times
7. If in doubt consult a professional tree surgeon, avoid "cowboys"

top: Storm damaged lower branch of young Tulip Tree (Liriodendron)

centre: Reducing the branch to below breakage

bottom: Undercutting peg of damaged branch

top: final cut back to collar

centre: Correct finish with collar intact

bottom: A well healed pruning cut with excellent callousing

Feeding

Most young trees benefit from an occasional feeding especially when the native soil is not particularly fertile. Mulching with a 5cm layer of an organic material such as weathered manure or well-rotted compost is also beneficial (essential on heavy clay or thin sandy or chalk soils), whilst an application of a general fertilizer is a useful booster or alternative. Such fertilizers should be equally strong in N.P.K. – Nitrogen for growth and healthy foliage, Phosphorous for root growth and seed and fruit ripening, and Potassium for fruit formation.

These fertilizers are best applied in late spring or early summer when growth is at a peak, whilst evergreens also benefit from an early autumn application. The fertilizer, be it in dried or liquid form, should ideally be applied to bare soil around the base of the tree up to the "drip line" or furthest spread of the branches. If the soil circle has been neglected and is covered with weed or grass, this should be cleared or only a proportion of the fertilizer will reach the tree's feeder roots.

Even old or long established trees appreciate feeding especially if they grow on a difficult site. In this instance, a mulch can be given to the root area or fertilizer applied via holes drilled in the ground. The latter method in particular is commonly used for trees growing in grassed areas. Scattering the fertilizer over the root area is a quicker method of application, but obviously less satisfactory in grassed areas as a proportion will be used up by the grass.

Avoid applying fertilizers in dry weather or, in the case of deciduous trees, later than June. Remember, too much fertilizer too regularly applied isn't necessarily beneficial in the long term, and may even cause a dependence on feeding which may not be possible to maintain.

MULCHES

The benefit of organic mulching especially to poor soils cannot be overestimated. According to Alex Shigo, internationally respected aborticulturalist, such mulches are a home for mycorrhizae which help improve a tree's capacity to absorb plant nutrients and water.

How Trees are Named

Trees, like other plants, are given names so that we may refer to them more easily and accurately. Obviously it is much more convenient when ordering a tree to give its name rather than have to describe it, and many a wrong tree has been sold because a salesman misinterpreted a rather vague or inaccurate description.

Most people accept that trees should have names; but why, we often ask, must they be given botanical names, which are difficult to pronounce, complicated and hard to remember? Why can't they be referred to simply by English names?

To understand why, we must first remember that trees are grown all over the world: and when you consider the number of different languages involved, it is obvious that a tree known only by an English name might cause a problem to a Russian or a Chinese or to any non-English-speaking gardener. Botanical names, therefore, are designed as an international system of reference and all who are seriously interested in trees understand that, however many common names a tree may have, it has only one correct botanical name. Mention English holly to an Italian gardener and he probably won't know what you are talking about. Mention its botanical name – *Ilex aquifolium* – and, as likely as not, he will understand.

Pronouncing botanical names correctly does not come easily; it takes practice but it is better to pronounce a name as it reads rather than ignore it. Long names can be broken down, e.g. Liquid-ambar sty-ra-ciflua – *Liquidambar styraciflua*, and Koel-reut-eria panic-ulata – *Koelreuteria paniculata*.

Although botanical names are offputting to many gardeners, especially the beginner, they are well worth learning, telling us, as they do, something about the tree: its county of origin, e.g. *chinensis* – from China; its habitat in the wild, e.g. *sylvatica* – of woods; its habit, e.g. *pendula* – weeping; its leaves, e.g. *latifolia* – broad leaves; its flowers, e.g. *paniculata* – flowers in branched heads; or even the person who first introduced it from the wild, e.g. *Magnolia wilsonii* – after EH Wilson. In fact, the usage and meanings of botanical names is a fascinating study in itself and I can do no

better than recommend that excellent beginners' guide *The Collingridge Dictionary of Plant Names* (the pronounciation and meaning of botanical names, and their common name equivalents) by Allen J Coombes. Whilst equally useful is *Stearn's Dictionary of Plant Names for Gardeners* by WT Stearn. For the names of trees and their families described in this book I am mainly indebted to the following authorities: *Trees and Shrubs Hardy in the British Isles* by W J Bean, 8th edition, revised 4 volumes plus a supplement by D E Clarke, *The Plant Book* by D J Mabberley and *The Hillier Manual of Trees and Shrubs*, 6th edition.

WHY NAMES SOMETIMES CHANGE

Occasionally, just when we have become used to a botanical name, we hear that it has been changed and that some other name is now the correct one. Even to professional gardeners and those well versed in botanical names, such changes are irritating no matter that the reason for the change is understandable. There are two main reasons why a well established name is subject to change –

    a. Botanical
    b. Nomenclatural.

A name changed on botanical grounds occurs when a botanist making a detailed study of a genus decides that a particular species or a group of species can no longer be regarded as belonging to that genus, and is sufficiently distinct botanically to be placed in another or even a new genus: the well known *Cedrella sinensis* for example is now regarded by some authorities as belonging to the genus *Toona* as *Toona sinensis*.

Names changed on nomenclatural grounds are much more frequent and are usually the result of some strict application of the International Code of Botanical Nomenclature or the Code of Nomenclature for Cultivated Plants. A rule common to both codes concerns priority, which states that the correct name for a plant is the first one to be validly published. Researchers delving into archives sometimes find such a name which has been forgotten or overlooked and which in persuance of the code must replace the currently established name. On this basis *Cotinus americanus* became *Cotinus obovatus*.

Sometimes a name change occurs due to a

variety or cultivar having been assigned to the wrong species. Thus, the beautiful golden full moon maple of Japan which we have long known as *Acer japonicum* 'Aureum' becomes *Acer shirasawanum* 'Aureum'. Who should we follow? I can do no better than to recommend the use of modern references on the subject such as *The Plant Finder*, whilst in Holland and Germany, the *Naamlijst van Houtige Gewassen* is excellent, although none of course is infallible.

How Trees are Classified

This is yet another fascinating study and basically is again a question of convenience. As far as the gardener needs be concerned, plant classification starts at family level.

FAMILIES

These are usually large groups of plants, often including many different-looking members but collectively having several important basic features in common. Family names are always written with a capital initial, ending with *eae* or *ae*, e.g. *Rosaceae*, *Leguminosae*. In this book they follow the name of each genus.

GENERA

Most families are made up of smaller groups which, while possessing a common bond (shared characteristics), are sufficiently distinct to be separated from one another. The generic name is the first name of any plant and is always written with a capital initial, e.g. *Crataegus, Malus, Prunus*, etc. It may be likened to one's surname, e.g. Courtney, Thompson, Brock, etc.

SPECIES

Each genus is made up of from one to many individuals (species), each different in its own way from the next but related to one another by a common bond. (Although, in truth a species is still itself a population of individuals it serves our present purpose to regard it as one). The species name consists of two words, the first of which is the genus name and the second the specific epithet. The species may be likened to the individual members of a human family e.g. Christopher, Elizabeth and Lucy Brock are all members of the Brock family just as *Sorbus aria, Sorbus aucuparia* and *Sorbus scalaris* are all species of *Sorbus*. Specific epithets are normally written with a small initial.

VARIETIES

Just as individual people are changeable and have different moods, so plant species in the wild are often variable, reacting to different growing conditions. These variations (varieties), if permanent, are also given names which, like specific epithets, are written with a small initial, e.g. *Platanus orientalis insularis, insularis* being a variety of *Platanus orientalis* differing in its smaller more deeply and more narrowly-lobed leaves.

CULTIVARS

Garden varieties and specially selected forms from the wild which are maintained in cultivation, are referred to as cultivars. Cultivar names are normally written with a capital initial and enclosed in single quotes, e.g. *Acer negundo* 'Elegans'. Since 1959 the International Rules governing cultivar names have required new names to be fancy names in a modern language, e.g. *Acer negundo* 'Flamingo'. New Latin cultivar names are no longer permissible, though those given before are retained.

CLONES

The term clone refers to a plant of which all the individuals are identical, having originated from a common source. Clones can only be maintained true by vegetative means (cuttings, grafting, etc.). Most cultivars of trees are clonal in origin, e.g. *Acer rubrum* 'October Glory', *Robinia pseudoacacia* 'Frisia' etc.

HYBRIDS

Hybrids between two (or more) species are given a botanical name preceded by a multiplication sign e.g. *Arbutus x andrachnoides* or a cultivar name e.g. *Prunus* 'Pandora'.

Pests and Diseases

If I was to list and describe all the pests and diseases which are known to attack trees, the result would read like a "Who's Who" to the Chamber of Tree Horrors. Fortunately, although few trees escape the attentions of certain pests and diseases at some time in their lives, the awful scourges such as the Dutch Elm Disease, which threaten to wipe a tree from the landscape, are mercifully few and far between.

PESTS

Aphids (greenfly and blackfly) of which there are numerous species, may effect most trees at some stage in their development, though they are commonly found on the succulent young growths of spring and summer. The main damage, which is caused by their feeding, is most often seen after their handiwork is completed – growth is stunted and the leaves curl unnaturally or become puckered or discoloured.

Similar symptoms occur with scale insects which suck sap from leaf or bark from beneath a protective brownish scale or shell. Leaves finely peppered with pale spots, or yellowed and falling prematurely, is often the result of an attack by Red Spider Mites which despite their name, are variable in colour. They are particularly active in prolonged dry summers. During the summers of 1989 and 1990 for instance they thrived and affected a wide range of trees.

Whiteflies, which look like tiny white moths also feed on sap and characteristically rise up in clouds when disturbed. More often than not, the above pests, when feeding on leaves, congregate on the undersides and are therefore hidden.

There are also a range of leaf eating pests, many of them the caterpillars of moths and sawflies, as well as weevils – the most notorious of which, the Vine Weevil, is especially fond of evergreens while its larvae feed on roots.

Young trees and seedlings, particularly in spring, are sometimes liable to slug damage especially in damp conditions, and their feeding is not necessarily restricted to the leaves as they will gnaw tender young bark and even roots. Bullfinches can also be a nuisance in some areas, nipping out the flower buds of a wide range of trees such as *Malus* and *Prunus* in late winter or spring.

A more obvious source of injury to young trees is that caused by mammals, especially by deer, hares and rodents. This mostly takes the form of young shoots eaten, bark gnawed or rubbed away and, in the case of cats, bark of clear stems scratched or lacerated.

DISEASES

A good number of plant diseases are specific to a given group or family, e.g. fire-blight, a bacterial disease which attacks members of the Rose family (*Rosaceae*), entering through the flower clusters and causing the spur or shoot to die back leaving it in a shrivelled state as if blasted by a flame gun. Trees which can be affected this way include *Prunus*, *Photinia* and *Sorbus*. Affected branches should be removed and burned. If the disease persists and the tree deteriorates, then the whole tree must be dug up and burned. The disease, however, seems to be prevalent in some areas of Britain and absent or less common in others. It is not inevitable and fear of its appearance should not prevent you from growing these popular trees in your garden.

Verticillium Wilt is a fungus disease parasitic on the roots of a range of young trees causing foliage wilt and shoot die-back. It is especially prevalent on *Cotinus* and *Rhus*. Normally, only odd branches are affected and these should be cut back to living wood and burned. Less commonly the tree is killed outright, in which case it should be removed and burned. The soil around infected trees may be drenched with benomyl.

Honey Fungus or Root Rot (*Armillaria*) of which there are several species, is the most widespread fungus disease affecting ornamental trees (and other plants too), and is particularly prevalent in areas of former woodland, orchards or hedgerows and in the vicinity of old stumps and neglected domestic hedges, especially privet. The characteristic honey-brown toadstools, appear usually in clumps in autumn beneath a dead or dying tree, or on the site of a buried stump. The black root-like rhizomorphs of the fungus attack the roots of its victim, change into fan-like belts of white mycelium and travel progressively in towards the stem collar eventually causing its death. A wide range of trees is susceptible to this disease and its effects on a garden can be heartbreaking. Too often, when you realize a tree is suffering from an attack by this disease it is too late to save it. Infected plants should be dug out and burned and the soil changed before replanting. There are various chemicals on the market which are claimed to offer some control if used early enough, these include Bray's Emulsion, while mixing a portion of copper carbonate in the compost or soil at planting time is claimed by some gardeners to give protection to newly planted trees in infected areas.

Another widespread disease of trees is powdery mildew which, like Red Spider Mite, is especially prevalent during prolonged, warm, dry periods. It shows itself as a fine grey deposit on the leaf surface.

Other causes, such as deficiencies in the soil, lime-induced chlorosis, frost damage, sun scorch etc, can have the appearance of a disease and therefore, before one can decide on the most suitable treatment, the exact nature of the trouble must first be diagnosed. Of the many books dealing with tree troubles, Collins *Guide to the Pests, Diseases and Disorders of Garden Plants* by Buczacki and Harris is thoroughly recommended. Whilst two less forbidding but equally useful guides for amateurs are Dr DG Hessayon's *The Tree and Shrub Expert* and *The Bio Friendly Gardening Guide*.

Most reputable nurserymen have a member or members of staff whose training or experience has taught them to recognise at least the most commonly met with pests and diseases and general ills. Then there are the various County Agricultural and Horticultural Institutes and Colleges whose staffs can be very helpful in sorting out problems of this nature. Although it should be remembered that they have a full-time job to do and are not "on call" to deal with any and all requests from the public.

At the end of the day, trees under stress are the ones most likely to attract serious problems. Lack of water or conversely a waterlogged site are two of the commonest reasons for stress. Both conditions can be compounded, if not actually caused, by compaction of the soil around the tree. This is frequently the case with gardens on new housing sites where heavy machinery has been used or building materials stacked. Attention to the soil, in particular the drainage, will usually bring out an improvement in tree growth.

Stress can also be caused by bark damage. This is particularly common with young trees, resulting from the careless use of machinery especially mowers and strimmers, or from the activities of squirrels, deer, hares, rabbits or even cats. All young trees should be given protection to discourage or prevent damage by animals (see Tree Guards and Shelters under Planting a Tree), whilst the utmost care should be taken when grass cutting in the vicinity of trees.

USE OF SPRAYS

Today's gardener is more aware of the importance of conservation and a clean and safe environment as well as the need for care and consideration for others than at any previous time. The harmful effects of chemicals used "willy nilly" in the garden have been well publicised and I can sympathise with those who refuse to have anything to do with them.

Of course there are non-chemical methods of dealing with some garden pests, such as soapy water for aphids, whilst the possibilities of biological control are becoming increasingly encouraging. On the weed front, too, hard work and persistence can achieve by hand in long term what herbicides do in the short term. But for most working people, time and convenience are still of the essence; and, until that happy day when chemicals are no longer necessary, they will continue to play a role in the control of these unwanted garden visitors. This being so, it behoves me to stress to those intent on using chemicals the importance of their use and storage. Always seek the advice of an expert before choosing anything poisonous to control living organisms. Used without thought, care, or consideration for possible effect and consequence, they are an evil in themselves.

Always follow the maker's instructions, particularly with regard to strength and dosage. It is far better to err on the weak side than risk untold damage by increasing the strength. Sprays of any kind should be applied on a mild, overcast and windless day, preferably in summer between 8 and 10am, and in late afternoon between 6 and 8pm when fewer insects are on the wing and bees are not active. Never allow others, especially children and pets, into the area while spraying; and take the necessary precautions to protect them from accidental contamination after the operation (especially leaf chewing, etc.)

In order to prevent the unnecessary destruction of bees and other harmless insects, avoid spraying a tree when it is in flower. Use the correct equipment, including recommended protective clothing for spraying; and keep separate the equipment used for insecticides and fungicides, and that used for herbicides. Help protect the ozone layer by not using aerosol sprays.

One final point, or rather plea. Be sure to safely dispose of any surplus spray, thoroughly washing out spray equipment after use. This should take place on a patch of waste ground in the garden or on a gravel or unsurfaced path. Never dispose of surplus chemicals down drains or in areas close to ponds, ditches and water courses generally. Be sure to store all chemicals, whatever their use, in their original containers, clearly labelled, sealed and locked in a secure place, away from the house and out of sight and reach of children and pets. Exhausted chemicals containers should be disposed of safely and not left lying around, nor should they be re-used for other purposes.

After each spraying operation – indeed, after using any form of chemical control, be it in liquid, solid or smoke form – be sure to wash any exposed areas of the body. A useful guide to the characteristics and use of chemicals in the garden, *Garden Chemicals* is published annually by British Agrochemicals Association Ltd of 4, Lincoln Road, Peterborough PE1 2RP. I again recommend Dr DG Hessayon's invaluable *The Bio Friendly Gardening Guide*.

A Tree for Every Garden

Such is the diversity of size, shape and effect, that somewhere there exists a tree to suit most, if not all, tastes and situations. There are trees suitable for even the smallest gadens and it should not be necessary to deform a tree by drastic pruning or lopping to make it conform.

Planting a tree which, when mature, will be too large for its position, is all too common these days, nor is it a recent problem. A tour of small gardens on almost any established housing estate will reveal examples of trees planted without any thought for the future.

Foundations weakened or damaged, windows heavily shaded or completely hidden, pavements obstructed: these are just a few of the troubles caused through ignorance of a tree's probable growth and development. Nursery salesmen and garden advisers, consulted for their opinions on the choice of a suitable tree, are sometimes assailed with the remark: "I know it will get too big eventually but then it will be someone else's problem." Particularly is this true of many elderly people whose understandable desire for an immediately effective or an impressive tree blinds them to their own common sense and the experts' better judgement.

Trouble often arises from planting forest-type trees in relatively confined spaces, horse-chestnuts, oak, beech, limes, cedars, and weeping willows are fine in parks and large gardens, but when planted in the garden of the average housing estate they constitute a future headache if not a danger.

SOILS

It never fails to surprise me, the number of people who, because they garden on a chalk soil, believe that the choice of trees they may successfully grow is drastically reduced. With few exceptions, trees are adaptable to most soils so long as they are not waterlogged. Though certain trees are short-lived or do not give of their best on chalk soils, there are few which actively dislike these conditions. These latter include such trees as: *Embothrium*; *Halesia*; many magnolias, *Nothofagus*; *Nyssa*; *Quercus coccinea*, *Q. palustris* and *Q. rubra*; *Sassafrus*; *Stuartia* and *Styrax*. Trees which are short-lived or otherwise disappointing on chalk soils include *Acer rubrum*; *Amelanchier lamarckii*; *Castanea sativa*; *Eucalyptus* (excepting *E. parvifolia*); *Eucryphia* and *Liquidambar*.

On the other hand, there are some trees which appear to thrive better on chalk soils than on most others. Trees such as *Cercis siliquastrum*, many of the ornamental crabs and many *Prunus*, especially the "Japanese Cherries", appear to flower earlier and with more abandon than their counterparts on, say, clay soils; partly due to the fact that chalk soils are basically warmer than clay soils.

ASPECT

The majority of trees described in the following pages prefer an open position, one where their leaves receive the maximum amount of light. There are, however, a number of trees which are adaptable, within reason, to shade. These include many of the hollies (*Ilex*); *Gleditsia triacanthos*; *Prunus lusitanica*; *Stuartia* and *Styrax*. The occurrence of shade should not be confused with the provision of shelter which is quite another matter. Several "delicate" trees enjoy some form of shelter, usually in the young stage, whilst some which are happy without shelter, in the comparatively milder areas of the south and west, may appreciate the provision of it when grown in the north and east and in cold inland areas. Trees which naturally occur in woodland are not normally happy when planted on cold exposed sites. In this category are found *Cercidiphyllum*; *Cornus nuttallii*; *Davidia*; *Eucryphia*; *Nyssa*; *Sassafras*; *Stuartia*, *Styrax*, etc. These trees are happiest when associated with others, though this does not mean they shouldn't be planted as lone specimens in lawns, with sufficient shelter.

TREES FOR EFFECT

I have already mentioned how trees come in many shapes and sizes and are capable of added attractions in the form of flowers, fruits and autumn colour. Some trees also have striped or peeling bark, or coloured twigs which are appealing in winter. One important aspect of a tree, often overlooked, is its foliage value. Many people believe an ornamental tree to be one which flowers. It is well to remember when choosing a tree, that flowers, no matter how colourful, are a temporary feature, and for the rest of the year you are left with leaves and, in the case of deciduous trees, bark and branches in winter. I am not advising *against* buying trees merely for their floral beauty of course. I feel that it is sometimes worth tolerating a year of monotony for the sake of one brief but unforgettable display of flower or, in the case of *Azara microphylla*, a memorable fragrance. But those with small gardens, where there is room for only one tree, quite rightly expect one which will give value for money in the form of several features. Many of these "all-round" trees may be found within *Acer*, *Eucalyptus*, *Malus*, and *Prunus*.

Trees in this Book

The trees described in this book, whilst obviously a personal choice, have been selected with gardens of all sizes and situations in mind. Owners of small gardens will find included a wide choice of suitable and easily available trees, whilst those with large gardens (now a minority) or estates have not been forgotten, and a variety of ultimately large trees are also described. The selection includes a number of trees best suited to the milder areas of Britain and Ireland as well as similarly favoured areas of Europe, e.g. the Mediterranean region and southern Europe in general. The names of these trees are preceded by a dagger, Finally, in an effort to avoid the stereotyped selections of trees described or recommended for planting in many gardening publications, I have included a number of less well known (to the amateur) trees, many of which match or excel the common sorts in hardiness and ornamental effect. For this I make no apologies, and though the problem of availability inevitably arises, I firmly believe that the extra trouble sometimes experienced in obtaining or establishing these trees is amply rewarded by the challenge and satisfaction of growing something different and new. No conifers are described here but Adrian Bloom's *Conifers for Everyone* can be recommended as well as Allen Coombe's *Eyewitness Handbook on Trees*. An excellent guide to the current availability of trees in Britain is *The Plant Finder*, published annually by the Hardy Plant Society which I can thoroughly recommend, especially to those searching for the less common kinds.

KEY TO ABBREVIATIONS

† Trees only suited to mild and Mediterranean areas (see Trees in this Book, page 25).

Size

How fast will it grow? and how big will it be eventually? are two of the first things people want to know about a tree they are considering buying. However, trees are living, growing organisms and cannot be made to measure nor can they be programmed to grow the exact size or shape desired. For a number of reasons, such as soil type, aspect, rainfall, seedling variation etc., individual trees, of the same species even, do not always behave in the same way or grow at the same rate.

The following simplifed key, therefore, should be taken as indicating the expected eventual size of a tree under average conditions in cultivation.

Key to Ultimate Size

VERY SMALL (VS) under 3m (10ft) e.g. *Cotoneaster* 'Hybridus Pendulus'.

SMALL (S) 3–6m (10–20ft) e.g. *Cornus florida rubra* and *Malus transitoria*.

MEDIUM (M) 6–15m (20–50ft) e.g. *Acer platanoides* 'Lacinatum', *Koelrueteria paniculata*.

LARGE (L) over 15m (50ft) e.g. *Aesculus hippocastanum, Platanus acerifolia*.

Award of Garden Merit AGM

Since 1921 the Royal Horticultural Society has shown its regard for excellence in a garden plant by the bestowal of the Award of Garden Merit. Many trees have received this accolade, a seal of approval and a recognition of a tree's merit and suitability for general cultivation. Recently (1993) the list of AGM recipients has been thoroughly revised and updated. The AGM's indicated in this book are based on this revision.

Habit or Shape

Given the brief of this book, it has been impossible to indicate the exact habit or crown shape (branch pattern) of every tree described. The following examples, therefore, have been selected to represent the eight most common most important. They are not meant to be exact, merely a rough guide as many trees change their shape as they mature, for example, many *Sorbus* have a vase-shaped crown when young, becoming rounded or spreading in maturity.
The main crown shapes are;

SPREADING – the most common form with branches growing both outwards and upwards. As they mature they produce a crown which, depending on species and growing conditions, may be irregular or regular. If the latter, the outline is normally **rounded** or dome-shaped e.g. *Acer pseudoplatanus* and *Aesculus hippocastanum*.

WIDE-SPREADING – branches long, in proportion to height, sometimes almost horizontal, crown much broader than high e.g. *Albizia julibrissin*.

WEEPING – branches pendulous e.g. *Pyrus salicifolia* 'Pendula'.

CONICAL – branches spreading or ascending at base, shorter and ascending above, crown noticeably broader in lower half e.g. *Ilex aquifolium* 'Pyramidalis'.

VASE-SHAPED – branches ascending sometimes steeply so, usually arching outwards forming a crown broader in the upper half e.g. *Acer lobelii, Sorbus* 'Joseph Rock'.

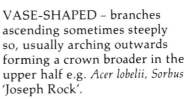

COLUMNAR – branches steeply ascending, forming a relatively narrow, compact crown many times taller than broad e.g. *Keolreuteria paniculata* 'Fastigiata'.

BROADLY COLUMNAR – branches ascending or shortly spreading forming a broader generally looser crown (than a columnar tree) 3–4 times taller than broad e.g. *Catalpa fargesii duclouxii*.

†ACACIA
Leguminosae

A huge genus of evergeen trees and shrubs mainly distributed in the wild in Africa, India and Australia. Only a relative handful, mainly from south-east Australia and Tasmania, are just about suitable out of doors in the milder areas of Britain and Ireland. They are among the most colourful and popular of all trees in Mediterranean gardens. Several species are so commonly planted there, especially in the south of France, that they have escaped and now grow wild in many areas. All have small rounded clusters or racemes of tiny yellow flowers (mainly stamens) which collectively form often spectacular "wands" or "plumes" of colour. The majority prefer well-drained lime-free soils and all flower best in full sun. In cooler areas they are best planted against a south or west-facing wall, but even here they may be badly damaged or killed outright in a severe winter. They make superb, if rather large, conservatory subjects.

Acacia baileyana
S Spreading to Dome-Shaped AGM 1993
The "Cootamundra Wattle" from New South Wales, one of the most widely planted of the hardier kinds in the Mediterranean region. It is grown as much for its silvery-grey fern-like leaves which crowd the branches as for its rich yellow flowers borne in dense racemes. The latter are borne towards the ends of the branches during winter and early spring. It may be hard pruned if necessary immediately after flowering. Less satisactory out of doors in Britain and Ireland than the next. A striking form with leaves purplish when young is known as var. *purpurea*.

Acacia dealbata
S-M Spreading AGM 1993
The "Silver Wattle" from south-east Australia and Tasmania is probably the best-known species in Europe, especially in the south where it is grown commercially for cut flowers (the Mimosa of florists). It is an extremely fast-growing tree with smooth pale green or grey-green young bark and large feathery silver-tinted leaves. The fragrant flowers are produced in great billowy masses in winter. Although shade tolerant in warm countries, it flowers best in full sun. It suckers readily if the roots are damaged. Occasionally, large specimens are seen in southern and western Britain and in Ireland.

Acacia decurrens
S-M Spreading
Similar in characteristics to *A. dealbata* but leaves dark green hence the name "Green Wattle". It is equal to the former in flower power.

Acacia longifolia
S Spreading
A fast-growing wattle of willowy growth with long narrow glossy green leathery leaves and dense cylindrical racemes of bright yellow flowers in late winter – early spring. One of the less hardy species in British conditions but a fine subject for a large conservatory.

Acacia rhetinodes
S Spreading
A fast-growing wattle with slender arching branches and narrow willow-like, bluish-green leaves. The globular flower heads are borne in short racemes along the branches in spring. Not particularly long lived but one of the hardiest and most satisfactory in Britain. It is also reasonably tolerant of alkaline soils.

Acacia baileyana (flower)

ACER
Aceraceae

This large genus of deciduous and evergreen trees contains many of the finest for autumn colour, while the "snakebark" maples are excellent for small gardens and winter effect. Several of the large species are useful for screening and are tolerant even of industrial situations. All the following are deciduous, hardy and unless otherwise indicated, unfussy as to soil, though generally thriving on moist but well-drained soils rather than dry ones. Leaves are generally palmately lobed and are arranged oppositely on the twigs. The generally inconspicuous flowers are carried in clusters followed by winged fruits – "spinning jennies".

Acer buergerianum

S-M Spreading
The "Trident Maple" from China and Japan is an elegant, densely leafy tree with peeling bark and arching branches. The small characteristically three-lobed leaves are a glossy dark green above, bluish-grey beneath, often colouring richly (crimson and dark reds) in late autumn. Tolerant of drought and wind and an excellent tree for town and city gardens, especially in regions offering warm summers. Young plants may require help in forming a strong leader. In China this tree is often planted in the vicinity of temples and on some city streets.

Acer campestre

M-L Spreading AGM 1993
The "Field Maple" is the only maple native in Britain where it is particularly common in chalk areas especially as a hedgerow tree. It is also commonly planted on motorway embankments. Its leaves are five-lobed and turn a characteristic rich gold, sometimes red before falling. It is a reliable tree, adaptable to most soils and situations including exposure, and is one of the last trees to colour in autumn. It is sometimes inclined to produce sucker growths from the base, which are best removed when young unless a bush is required.

Acer campestre 'Elsrijk'

M-L Conical to Spreading
A Dutch selection of dense, broadly conical habit with rich dark green leaves.

Acer campestre 'Postelense'

S-M Spreading
Leaves golden yellow, at their brightest in spring and early summer. One of the most satisfactory golden-leaved trees in its season.

Acer campestre 'Royal Ruby'

S-M Spreading
An improved version of 'Schwerinii' with young leaves purplish-red darkening with age. Of Dutch origin.

Acer campestre 'Schwerinii'

S-M Spreading
Young leaves purple becoming green later. A striking contrast with 'Postelense' in spring and early summer.

Acer capillipes

S-M Vase-shaped to Spreading
AGM 1993
Green and silvery-grey striped bark and arching branches bearing three-lobed, glossy green leaves on red stalks. These later turn yellow, orange and red in autumn. It is a native of Japan and is ideal for a special position. The yellow flower tassels and pink and yellow fruits in summer are a bonus. It is not as long lived as other snake-bark maples but one of the most satisfactory otherwise.

Acer cappadocicum

M-L Spreading
A fast-growing tree with five- or seven-lobed leaves turning rich butter-yellow in autumn. In the wild it occurs from the Caucasus eastwards to the Himalaya.

Acer cappadocicum 'Aureum'

M-L Spreading AGM 1993
One of the best coloured-foliage trees. The leaves are red on emerging, rapidly turning to yellow. Only shows signs of scorch in a long hot summer, otherwise

superb and quite happy in an open position. It may be hard pruned (in late summer) if desired, to form a large but striking bush.

Acer cappadocicum 'Rubrum'

M-L Spreading AGM 1993
Young leaves blood red, a superior form of the type.

Acer cappadocicum sinicum

M-L Speading
Native to south-west China, this splendid tree differs in its smaller five-lobed leaves which are reddish-copper in spring whilst its fruits in autumn have red wings. A tree of class.

Acer carpinifolium

S-M Vase-shaped to Spreading
A distinct and easily recognized Japanese maple on account of its unlobed many-veined leaves which resemble those of a hornbeam (*Carpinus betulus*), often colouring yellow in autumn. A choice species which deserves a place in any collection of fine and unusual trees. It is slow growing and commonly bushy in habit and may develop several main stems from low down.

Acer davidii

S-M Vase-shaped to Spreading
Perhaps the best snake-bark maple for general planting. The green and white striped bark and the vigorously arching branches are best admired in winter. During summer the generally unlobed, rich green, slender pointed leaves are borne on green or red-tinted stalks, becoming yellow in autumn. Native to central and western China where it was originally found by a French missionary – the Abbé David. An excellent form with large lush green leaves on rhubarb-red stalks is known as 'George Forrest', after the plant hunter who introduced it. It received an AGM in 1993.

top: *Acer cappadocicum* 'Aureum'
bottom: *Acer carpinifolium*

29

Acer davidii 'Serpentine'

S Spreading AGM 1993
A fine selection of Dutch origin with leaves smaller than normal. It is worth growing, however, for its striking bark and branches which are purplish in colour with narrow stripes of silvery bloom. Especially effective in winter.

Acer ginnala

S Spreading AGM 1993
Sometimes seen as a large bush, this vigorous species from north China and Japan develops wide-spreading branches bearing neatly three-lobed and toothed leaves, glossy dark green above. These often turn to brilliant orange and crimson in autumn. The yellow flower clusters are borne above the foliage followed by pink-tinted fruits in summer. It is a tough hardy little tree naturally multi-stemmed but easily trained to a single stem if so desired.

Acer griseum

S-M Spreading AGM 1993
Few ornamental trees arouse as much interest as the lovely Chinese "Paper-bark Maple". The orange-brown old bark on the trunk and main branches peels prettily to reveal the cinnamon-coloured new bark. In autumn the leaves, composed of three separate leaflets, turn vivid scarlet and flame when the whole tree glows like a bonfire. Rare in the wild this is one of the most desirable of all garden trees.

Acer hersii

S-M Vase-shaped to Spreading AGM 1993
Vigorous as a young tree, this popular Chinese snake-bark maple, with olive-green bark striated white, develops a wine glass form, the upswept branches arching widely at the tips. The olive-green leaves have two small lateral lobes and colour yellow and orange or occasionally red in autumn. A shapely tree, it is one of the best "snake-barks" for general planting. Named after Joseph Hers, a Belgian railway official in China earlier this century.

top: Acer davidii
bottom: Acer griseum

Acer japonicum

S Spreading

This "Japanese Maple" is often seen as a large multi-stemmed bush, although it may be carefully pruned to form a single-stemmed tree if required. It is one of the finest maples for autumn colour when the rounded, shallowly-lobed leaves turn from soft green to orange and fiery red. The drooping clusters of small red flowers in spring are also attractive. In common with others of the Japanese Maple group, it dislikes strong winds, draughts and exposure and is best situated in a sheltered or woodland garden, preferably on a moist but well-drained acid soil.

Acer japonicum 'Aconitifolium'

S-M Spreading AGM 1993

When happy, this beautiful maple forms a large mound of deeply- and sharply-lobed leaves which are ruby-red or crimson in autumn.

Acer japonicum 'Vitifolium'

S-M Spreading AGM 1993

One of the richest colouring of all Japanese Maples. The large fan-shaped leaves turn a brilliant red in autumn.

Acer lobelii

M-L Broadly columnar to Vase-shaped

The distinct habit of this Italian tree makes it an excellent species for planting in broad avenues and boulevards. It is equally effective, of course, as a single specimen in the medium-sized to large garden. The upswept branches bear twigs which are covered with a white bloom when young and are clothed with rich green, five-lobed leaves which turn yellow in autumn. The crowns of older trees develop a wine glass shape with long upswept branches.

Acer macrophyllum

L Vase-shaped to Spreading

A strong-growing tree, the "Oregon Maple" from western North America bears the largest leaves, flowers and fruits of any maple species. It is an

top: *Acer japonicum* 'Aconitifolium'
bottom: *Acer japonicum* 'Vitifolium'

imposing tree with upswept branches arching and broadening at the top in maturity. The deeply and boldly five- to seven-lobed leaves turn yellow and brown in autumn. It is not best suited for an exposed situation due to its branches being subject to windblow.

Acer micranthum
S Vase-shaped to Spreading AGM 1993
An elegant Japanese maple with small neatly five-lobed leaves which change to a rich red in autumn. An ideal subject for a lawn in the smaller garden.

Acer miyabei
M Spreading
An uncommon maple from Japan with handsome boldly five-lobed softly downy leaves, which turn pale yellow in late autumn. The clusters of greenish-yellow flowers with the leaves in spring are quite decorative.

Acer negundo
M-L Spreading
One of the commonest species in cultivation, the North American "Box Elder", as its common name suggests, looks nothing like the general run of maples, at least not in leaf. These are pinnate, composed of normally three to five separate leaflets. After the willow, poplar and eucalypt, this is one of the fastest-growing trees and is excellent for screening purposes and rapid effect. In America, sugar is made from the sap. All forms of this tree respond favourably to hard pruning every other year, the resultant strong green shoots bearing large attractive leaves.

Acer negundo 'Auratum'
M Spreading
Leaves yellow throughout the season on green shoots which are bloomy white when young. One of the best golden-foliaged trees.

Acer negundo 'Elegans'
M Spreading
The leaves of this effective tree are brightly and irregularly margined with yellow whilst the young green shoots are

covered with a conspicuous white bloom. Unfortunately, both this form and 'Variegatum' are apt to revert and need to be closely watched.

Acer negundo 'Flamingo'
M Spreading
Leaves strongly margined white, flushed pink, especially noticeable when young. A most attractive form, especially when hard pruned to encourage larger, more richly coloured foliage. Reverted green leaved shoots should be removed as soon as they appear.

Acer negundo 'Variegatum'
M Spreading
This tree is similar to 'Elegans' except that the leaves are margined white rather than yellow. It originated in France as a sport on a green-leaved tree and was once very popular as a pot plant for foliage effect. One often sees neglected trees which have almost entirely reverted to the green type.

Acer negundo violaceum
M Spreading AGM 1993
A vigorous form from the wild with violet-coloured young shoots covered with a white bloom. A striking feature in spring are the drooping clusters of reddish-pink flower tassels.

Acer nikoense
S-M Spreading
An uncommon slow-growing Japanese tree distinctive in its leaves which comprise three bold, hairy leaflets turning to red or yellow in autumn. Habit is vase-shaped when young becoming rounded in maturity. Best on a moist well-drained soil sheltered from cold winds. Reasonably lime tolerant. According to some authorities the correct name for this maple is *A. maximowiczianum* but this name is rejected here on account of its possible confusion with another species *A. maximowiczii*.

Acer palmatum
S-M Spreading
Like *A. japonicum*, this tree is commonly referred to as the Japanese maple and is

equally attractive in autumn when its prettily lobed leaves turn to shades of yellow and red. Although quite tolerant of lime in the soil it is undoubtedly better on moist but well-drained acid soils. It prefers a position sheltered from cold winds, otherwise it is quite hardy and easy to grow. Those forms with red or purple leaves in summer colour best in an open rather than shady situation, though exposure to hot direct sunlight in summer should be avoided. Trees purchased under this name are normally seed raised but there are numerous named forms available vegetatively propagated. Many of these are more naturally shrubs than trees.

Acer palmatum 'Atropurpureum'
S Spreading
Leaves rounded, with five- to seven-lobed leaves of a rich reddish colour throughout, colouring richly in autumn. Although 'Atropurpureum' does exist as a specially selected clone, the varietal name *atropurpureum* is also used for any red or purplish leaved seedlings.

Acer palmatum 'Bloodgood'
S Vase-shaped to Spreading AGM 1993
A splendid form, among the best of its kind, with comparatively large leaves of a rich deep red or blackish-red turning crimson in autumn.

Acer palmatum 'Burgundy Lace'
VS-S Vase-shaped to Spreading
AGM 1993
A striking maple with deeply divided, prettily toothed leaves which are a deep red the colour of Burgundy wine at first, paling to bronze or green in summer.

Acer palmatum 'Chitoseyama'
VS-S Weeping AGM 1993
A lovely maple, in time forming a dense mound of arching and drooping branches. The leaves are deeply and attractively divided and of a rich purple-red, paling in summer but colouring richly in autumn.

top: Acer platanoides 'Drummondii'
bottom: Acer negundo 'Flamingo'

Acer palmatum 'Elegans'

VS-S Spreading
A commonly planted maple with deeply-lobed leaves which are yellowish-green at first, changing to green and colouring richly in autumn. A reliable and well proven maple.

Acer palmatum 'Higasayama'

VS-S Vase-shaped to Spreading
Commonly found in old collections under the name 'Roseo-marginatum', this attractive maple has an upright habit when young becoming spreading or rounded in maturity. The small deeply-lobed leaves are pale cream on emerging from the crimson bracts, becoming green with creamy-white margins and rose tinting.

Acer palmatum koreanum

S-M Spreading AGM 1993
A geographical form from Korea with green deeply-lobed leaves giving brilliant tints in autumn. Strong-growing and reliable. The form commonly sold is a vegetatively propagated clone.

Acer palmatum 'Lutescens'

S-M Spreading
A choice strong-growing maple with comparatively large seven-lobed leaves of a delicate yellow-green in spring maturing to rich green. A lovely spring contrast to green or red leaved Japanese maples.

Acer palmatum 'Omurayama'

VS-S Weeping
Vigorous and upright when young, this excellent maple later develops a pendulous nature like a small weeping willow. The brilliant green leaves are deeply divided and hang down along the slender branches colouring richly in autumn.

Acer palmatum 'Osakazuki'

S Spreading to Rounded AGM 1993
One of the best known and most reliable Japanese maples. Deservedly popular for its comparatively large leaves which turn an intense scarlet in autumn. Easy, reliable and strongly recommended.

Acer palmatum 'Sango Kaku'

S-M Vase-shaped AGM 1993
A deservedly popular maple better known as 'Senkaki'. The habit, like many other Japanese maples, is vase-shaped for many years, becoming rounded in maturity. Although the light green leaves turn a characteristic soft yellowish-orange in autumn, it is for its brilliant coral-red young shoots that this maple is usually grown.

Acer palmatum 'Seiryu'

VS-S Vase-shaped to Spreading
AGM 1993
A vigorous maple of the Dissectum group, upright when young, spreading later, the bright green leaves finely dissected giving a charming filigree effect. In autumn they turn yellow, sometimes with red tints.

Acer palmatum 'Shishigashira'

S Broadly columnar to Vase-shaped
Also known as 'Ribesifolium', this distintive maple has an upright habit with close-packed branches and clusters of deeply-lobed and toothed green leaves colouring rich yellow in autumn.

Acer palmatum 'Trompenburg'

S Vase-shaped to Spreading
An upright tree when young broadening later. The leaves are divided into five to seven finger-like lobes which curve downwards along the margins. In colour they are an outstanding rich deep purple-red changing to crimson in autumn.

Acer penslyvanicum

S-M Vase-shaped to Spreading
AGM 1993
The "Moosewood" or "Striped maple" of eastern North America. One of the best trees for the small garden, having rather

upswept branches with superb snake-bark. This is coloured a beautiful pale jade-green with silvery-white striations. The comparatively large three-lobed leaves turn bright yellow in autumn. It is not one of the best maples for chalk soils.

Acer pensylvanicum 'Erythrocladum'

S-M Vase-shaped to Spreading
AGM 1993
An unusual form in which the young shoots in winter turn a rich lobster red with silver striations, quite striking. Best as a young tree. It may be hard pruned occasionally and maintained as a shrub.

Acer platanoides

L Spreading AGM 1993
A native of Europe (but not the British Isles), the "Norway Maple" is one of the toughest, fastest-growing and most popular of the larger species. It is also one of the few maples with attractive flowers. These are yellow and are made more conspicuous in that they appear in bunches from the twigs before the leaves emerge in April. A large tree in full flower really stands out on a cold bleak day. The sharply five-lobed leaves present an equally colourful display in autumn when they turn to yellow or red.

Acer platonoides 'Columnare'

M-L Broadly columnar
A distinct form of columnar habit with densely packed branches, becoming a broad pillar of gold in autumn.

Acer platanoides 'Crimson King'

L Spreading AGM 1993
This is one of the easiest and most effective trees of its colour with leaves which are crimson-purple in summer.

Acer platanoides 'Drummondii'

M-L Spreading AGM 1993
A strikingly variegated tree in which the leaves possess a broad creamy-white margin. Unfortunately, it is apt to revert and green-leaved shoots must be removed as soon as they appear.

Acer platanoides 'Globosum'

S Rounded
In contrast to the tall spires of *A. p.* 'Columnare', this form develops a broad, dense, globular crown. The branches are rather brittle and easily damaged by clumsily placed ladders or climbing children. It presents a ball of yellow in autumn.

Acer platanoides 'Laciniatum'

M Spreading
Known as the "Eagle's-claw maple" because of the curved claw-like points to the leaf lobes. Ultimately, a smaller tree than the type and of denser more upright habit.

Acer pensylvanicum 'Erythrocladum'

Acer platanoides
'Schwedleri'

M-L Spreading AGM 1993
Although it will develop into a large tree,
this popular maple is perhaps most
effective when established specimens are
hard pruned every other year in late
summer to encourage the young growths
with their rich crimson-purple leaves.

Acer pseudoplatanus

L Spreading to Dome-shaped
Given time and space, the "Sycamore" is
one of the noblest of all hardy deciduous
trees. It is also without doubt one of the
toughest of all trees, tolerating conditions
which would defeat most others. It was
the tree most commonly planted by
Pennine and Highland farmers to shelter
their bleak windswept homesteads. It was
also one of the few trees which tolerated
the smoke of towns and cities when
industrial pollution was at its worst.
Although apparently wild in the British
Isles it is native only to continental
Europe and Western Asia. People with
gardens in the country or near parks and
woodlands should be beware of the grey
squirrel, which is partial to sycamore bark
and will ruin a tree, if not cause its death.
Seedlings, which appear often in great
numbers, are best removed the first
season, before they become established.

Acer pseudoplatanus
'Atropurpureum'

L Spreading to Dome-shaped AGM 1993
A selected form of the "Purple Sycamore"
with dark purple undersides to the leaves.
It is very effective when the leaves are
blown and ruffled by a strong breeze.

Acer pseudoplatanus
'Brilliantissimum'

S Rounded to Dome-shaped AGM 1993
Perhaps the most popular, certainly most
spectacular sycamore, with its glorious
shrimp-pink young foliage in spring.
Later this changes to yellow-green and
finally greenish. 'Prinz Handjery' is very
similar, differing only in the purple
suffusion of the leaf undersurface in
summer.

Acer pseudoplatanus
'Erectum'

L Broadly columnar to Vase-shaped
A useful sycamore with strongly
ascending branches.

Acer pseudoplatanus
'Leopoldii'

L Spreading to Dome-shaped AGM 1993
One of several sycamores with variegated
leaves. In this form they are speckled and
splashed with yellow and a shade of pink.

Acer pseudoplatanus
'Worleei'

M Spreading to Dome-shaped AGM 1993
The beautiful "Golden Sycamore" has
leaves which are dark orange in spring
becoming yellow in summer. A very
attractive tree, particularly when seen
from a distance.

Acer rubrum

L Spreading
In its native eastern North America, the
"Red Maple" is considered one of the
most spectacular trees in autumn leaf.
The dark green three- to five-lobed
leaves, bluish-green beneath, become rich
red or yellow above before falling. In
early spring the naked branches are
bespattered with bright red flower
clusters. In Britain and Europe it
generally colours best on moist but well
drained soils.

Acer rubrum
'October Glory'

L Spreading AGM 1993
An excellent American raised selection
reliable in its brilliant orange and red
autumn colour.

Acer rubrum 'Scanlon'

M-L Broadly columnar to Dome-shaped
AGM 1993
A tall, broadly columnar to dome-shaped
tree with leaves in autumn changing from
green to yellow then pink-tinted and
finally red. The best form of the Red
Maple for restricted spaces.

Acer rubrum
'Schlesingeri'

L Spreading
The most reliable "Red Maple" for autumn colour. It is also generally the first to turn, and creates a rich splash of deep red when most other trees are still quite green.

Acer rufinerve

S-M Vase-shaped to Spreading
AGM 1993
A Japanese snake-bark maple with ascending branches, developing a vase-shaped habit when young, becoming rounded in maturity. The bluish-white bloomy shoots and buds are distinctive, while the bark of the older stems is prettily striated as in *A. penslyvanicum*. The broad, three-lobed leaves are deep green turning a rich orange and red in autumn.

Acer rufinerve
'Albolimbatum'

S-M Vase-shaped to Spreading
A commonly cultivated form in which the leaves are margined, streaked and mottled white.

Acer saccharinum

L Spreading AGM 1990
A hardy, fast-growing North American tree, the "Silver Maple" is well named as the deeply five-lobed leaves are silvery white beneath. These turn to butter-yellow or sometimes red in autumn. A large tree is a breathtaking sight when its leaves are ruffled by the wind and the long branches move about. It is one of the most vigorous and attractive of all large maples and ought to be more widely planted in suitable sites. It is commonly planted as a street tree in continental countries. Although it will take normal wind conditions, it is not suitable for exposed windswept sites nor indeed for those town or city situations where sudden squalls or turbulence are wont to damage branches. Not to be confused with *A. saccharum*, the Sugar Maple.

top: *Acer pseudoplatanus*, the Sycamore
bottom: *Acer rubrum* 'Schlesingeri'

37

Acer saccharinum
'Laciniatum'

M-L Spreading
One of the most graceful large trees in cultivation. Its long slender branches are gently drooping, often sweeping the ground and are thickly clothed with leaves which are more deeply lobed and finely cut than in the type. 'Wierei' is a specially selected form of even more graceful attributes.

Acer shirasawanum
'Aureum'

VS to S Spreading AGM 1993
Previously known (though incorrectly) as *A. japonicum* 'Aureum'. A most attractive tree, rather slow-growing but worthy of patience. The scalloped, rounded leaves are pale yellow-green in spring darkening to a rich yellow later colouring red, orange or even purplish in autumn. It is best grown in a sheltered, moist but well-drained situation and is not satisfactory in a soil which dries out in summer nor in a hot sunny situation. Known in Japan as the "Golden Full-moon Maple".

Acer triflorum

S-M Spreading
Native of north-east China and Korea, this lovely and distinctive maple is worth growing both for its bark and its autumn foliage. The former, on older trees certainly, is vertically fissured and peeling in cinnamon-red, brown and grey tones. The leaves which are composed of three leaflets, glaucous beneath, colour brilliantly, usually orange and crimson before falling. The name *triflorum* refers to the flowers borne in clusters of three.

Acer truncatum

S-M Spreading
A tough hardy tree from northern China, with greenish-yellow flower clusters in May and glossy green leaves bearing five slender pointed lobes. Reddish-purple at first they colour richly in autumn. It is one of the best maples for general cultivation on most soils and particularly good in town and city. Commonly planted on the streets of Beijing (Peking) and around the Great Wall of China.

top: *Acer shirasawanum* 'Aureum'
bottom: *Acer truncatum*

AESCULUS
Hippocastanaceae

The Horse Chestnuts and Buckeyes are among the easiest of deciduous trees to grow, preferring no particular soils or situations. They are an interesting and ornamental genus, the majority growing too big for the small garden, and are therefore seen at their best in large gardens, parks and estates. The leaves are generally large and divided into many finger-like leaflets. The flowers are borne in dense terminal panicles to be replaced by hard brown nuts enclosed in a green, often spiky shell. Autumn colours are normally yellow and can be quite impressive.

Aesculus x carnea

M-L Spreading
After the "Common Horse Chestnut", the "Red Horse Chestnut" is the most frequently planted member of the genus, either as a single specimen or as an avenue. The rose-pink flowers in May are followed by usually smooth-shelled fruits. It is a hybrid between *A. hippocastanum* and *A. pavia*, the "Red Buckeye", although nothing is known of its origin.

Aesculus x carnea 'Briotii'

M-L Spreading to Dome-Shaped
AGM 1993
This popular cultivar differs from the type in its generally more compact head of branches and richer-coloured flowers.

Aesculus flava

M-L Conical to Spreading to Dome-shaped AGM 1993
The "Yellow Buckeye", sometimes found catalogued as *A. octandra* is one of the most satisfactory trees of its kind. The handsome glossy green leaves turn pale yellow then orange and red in autumn, while the conical flower heads in May are yellow with just a hint of green. They are followed by smooth rounded or ovoid fruits. Fairly adaptable as to soils, it thrives best in a moist but well-drained loam and will take some shade. Seedling trees are preferable to those grafted on the common horse chestnut.

top: *Aesculus neglecta* 'Erythroblastos'
bottom: *Aesculus hippocastanum*

Aesculus hippocastanum

L Spreading AGM 1993

The "Common Horse Chestnut" is one of the most familiar and commonly planted trees, being particularly popular with children who gather its "sticky-buds" in winter and its fruits – "conkers" – in autumn. Unfortunately, trees in public places are often damaged by sticks and other debris thrown by children in their efforts to dislodge these fruits. The stout, erect "candles" of white, yellow changing to red-eyed flowers in May make this one of the most impressive of all large ornamental trees and, as a consequence, it has long been a favourite as an avenue, village and commemorative tree. Though for so long a part of the English scene, it is native only to the wild borderlands between Albania and Greece.

Aesculus hippocastanum 'Baumannii'

L Spreading AGM 1993

Differing from the type in its double flowers which are longer lasting and do not produce fruit. This may be preferred to the type for planting where the public have access.

Aesculus indica

L Spreading AGM 1993

Flowering from June into July generally four to six weeks later than *A. hippocastanum*, the "Indian Horse Chestnut" is, to some eyes, a more refined tree, with cleaner-cut and therefore more elegant foliage, and longer, more slender panicles of white, pink-flushed flowers. This handsome tree is a native of the north-west Himalayas and is a magnificent tree for large gardens and parks, preferring moist rather than dry soils. A selected form flowering more freely with more richly coloured flowers is known as 'Sidney Pearce' after the raiser.

Aesculus neglecta 'Erythroblastos'

M Spreading AGM 1993

This slow-growing, uncommon tree reminds one of *Acer pseudoplatanus* 'Brilliantissimum' in that the young foliage in spring is coloured a beautiful shrimp-pink. Later it becomes pale yellow-green, turning to orange and yellow in autumn. It is best planted in semi-shade, sheltered from early morning sun.

Aesculus turbinata

L Spreading

The "Japanese Horse Chestnut" is a large tree of robust habit with leaves similar in form to those of *A. hippocastanum*, but larger especially on young trees which are stout and rather stiff in appearance. The flowers too, though similar in colour, are produced in June, two or three weeks later than those of the common tree and are carried in dense erect cylindrical heads followed by spineless pear-shaped fruits.

AILANTHUS
Simaroubaceae

Consisting of only a few species, these tall deciduous trees are mainly natives of China. They are very fast-growing, hardy and tolerant of most soils and situations, especially industrial areas.

Ailanthus altissima

L Spreading AGM 1993

Known as the "Tree of Heaven", this handsome species quickly makes a shapely tree, even sending up stout suckers if allowed. The leaves are large and pinnate, composed of numerous leaflets. Male and female flowers, which are not very ornamental, are normally borne on separate trees. The bunches of reddish key-like fruits are very handsome on female trees in a good year. This is undoubtedly one of the best trees for planting in cities and towns, as many people living in London and New York will have observed. When hard-pruned to ground level, young trees produce strong shoots bearing huge ornamental leaves, similarly when an established tree is felled or blown down.

ALBIZIA
Leguminosae

A large genus of deciduous trees and shrubs related to the "Mimosa" and resembling it in leaf. Only two species are in general cultivation, of which the following is the more satisfactory and the one most commonly planted.

Albizia julibrissin

S Wide-spreading

Known as the "Silk Tree" or "Pink Siris", this is a small tree with wide-spreading branches, usually becoming flat-topped or umbrella-shaped with age and two to three times as broad as high. The large, deeply divided leaves create a pleasing fern-like effect over which, during summer, hover delightful fluffy clusters of pink-stamened flowers. These are sometimes followed by curious flattened pods. This is one of the best trees for creating a subtropical effect in the garden and is very popular as a foliage plant in exotic summer bedding displays. Although hardy and able to withstand cold winters, it requires long hot summers to ripen its wood. In the British Isles, it is seen at its best in the south and south-east of England, particularly near the sea, where it is often grown against a sunny sheltered wall. Superb specimens are to be seen on the Continent, particularly in southern and eastern Europe. It is a native of Iran, eastwards to China.

Albizia julibrissin 'Rosea'

S Wide-spreading

Similar to the type in habit, this beautiful form differs in the colour of the flower stamens, which are deep rose, very effective against the fronded foliage. It is hard to imagine anything more satisfying and pleasing than this tree when in full flower.

top: Ailanthus altissima
bottom: Albizia julibrissin 'Rosea'

ALNUS
Betulaceae

Hardy deciduous trees, the "Alders" are generally grown because of their tolerance of wet conditions, although several have handsome leaves and others long catkins in early spring or in a few species, in autumn. They are mainly of vigorous growth.

Alnus cordata

M-L Conical to Broadly columnar
AGM 1993
One of the handsomest species, the "Italian Alder" rapidly makes a tall specimen, its branches clothed with glistening dark green, heart-shaped leaves, accompanied from summer onwards by attractive green cone-shaped fruiting heads. The yellow catkins 7cm. long drape the branches in early spring. This splendid tree is quite at home on dry as well as wet soils.

Alnus firma

S-M Spreading
A little known but handsome alder from Japan which deserves wider planting. It develops a graceful crown of long slender arching branches clothed with leaves, which in their parallel venation bear more than a passing resemblance to the hornbeam *Carpinus betulus*. The short but rich yellow male catkins drape the branches in March and April. The tree normally offered in British cultivation is the hardier and downier-leaved variety *hirtella*. The bark of older trees is grey and brown, flaking attractively.

Alnus glutinosa

L Conical to Spreading
The "Common Alder" is a familiar native tree of riversides and lakesides, its naked branches strung with yellow male catkins in March. The sticky, stalked buds produce characteristic pear-shaped shining green leaves. It has a wide distribution in the wild from Europe to western Asia and North Africa.

top: Alnus cordata
bottom: Alnus glutinosa 'Imperialis'

Alnus glutinosa 'Aurea'

S-M Conical to Dome-shaped
The leaves of this attractive form are
bright yellow in spring and early summer,
gradually fading to green later. It is more
vigorous than *A. incana* 'Aurea'.

Alnus glutinosa 'Imperialis'

M Conical AGM 1993
One of the loveliest of all alders. The
leaves of this tree are deeply cut into
slender lobes giving the tree a delicate
and graceful appearance.

Alnus incana

M-L Conical to Spreading
One of the hardiest and most adaptable of
trees, the "Grey Alder" produces hanging
male catkins in February and later boldly-
toothed leaves which are grey and hairy
beneath. It is specially useful in cold
exposed areas and hails from Europe and
the Caucasus.

Alnus incana 'Aurea'

S-M Conical to Dome-shaped
The young shoots of this alder are
reddish yellow, a colour which is
maintained throughout winter. The
catkins in late winter are orange, while
the emerging leaves are bright yellow
fading gradually to green in late summer.

Alnus incana 'Pendula'

S Weeping
One of the best small weeping trees, the
branches forming a dense mound clothed
with greyish-green leaves.

Alnus rubra

M Conical
Fast-growing, handsome and hardy, the
"Red Alder" or "Oregon Alder" from
north-west America is an ideal tree for
those in a hurry, but only if theirs is a
medium-sized to large garden. Older
trees have drooping branches while the
comparatively large leaves are boldly
toothed and parallel veined. The long,
yellow male catkins drape the branches in
March at which time it is quite
spectacular. In the wild the pale bark of

mature trees give this tree the aspect of
an aspen.

Alnus x spaethii

M Conical to Spreading AGM 1993
A vigorous tree, a hybrid (*A. japonica* x *A.
subordata*) notable both for its large leaves,
purplish when young, and its outstanding
catkins in late winter.

Alnus firma

AMELANCHIER
Rosaceae

A small genus of deciduous trees and shrubs notable for their white flowers in spring and their often rich autumn colours. The following species perform best on lime-free soils. They are often shrubby in habit with many stems from the base, but are easily trained to a single stem by removing all competitors when young. Pruning back the long extension shoots by two thirds in summer will encourage freer flowering and a more compact habit. This is certainly recommended for smaller gardens. The species are mostly native to North America with one in Asia and another in Europe.

Amelanchier 'Ballerina'

S Vase-shaped to Spreading AGM 1993
A fine selection of upright habit but spreading later. It differs from *A. lamarckii* in its larger flowers, in a more or less pendant truss and in its more reliable fruiting. The fruits, by the way, are sweet and edible and make a most acceptable jam or pie filling if you can pick them before the birds do.

Amelanchier laevis

S Vase-shaped to Spreading
The "Allegheny Serviceberry" is less often seen in cultivation than the next species but it is equally attractive in flower and autumn foliage. It differs mainly in the unfolding leaves in spring, which are generally hairless and a distinctive yellow-green colour.

Amelanchier lamarckii

S Rounded to Spreading AGM 1993
Sometimes referred to as "Snowy Mespilus" or "Juneberry" because of its white flowers in spring and its summer ripening fruits. Commonly grown by nurserymen and gardeners wrongly as *A. canadensis* (a suckering shrub) this is one of the best small ornamental trees for general cultivation except on shallow, chalk soils. Quite hardy. The white flowers appear before or with the bronze coloured young leaves in April, creating an effect like a cloud of snow from a distance, whilst the leaves in autumn give a reliable display of fiery tints. It occurs as an apparently wild tree in southern and eastern England as well as in parts of western Europe.

ARALIA
Araliaceae

Only a few species of this useful genus of deciduous trees, shrubs and herbaceous plants are in cultivation, where they are mainly grown for their large, handsomely divided leaves. Though hardy, they are best given a site sheltered from strong, cold winds to protect their leaves. They are generally unfussy as to soil.

Aralia elata

S Spreading to Wide-spreading AGM 1993
The Japanese "Angelica Tree" is perhaps one of the best trees for the small garden in spite of its suckering habit. It is easily trained to form a tree and the prickly suckers should then be removed. These make excellent gifts to gardening friends but must be lifted when quite small. The huge Angelica-like leaves, sometimes 1m long, form ruffs at the ends of the branches, and in late summer and early autumn are topped by the large branched heads of white flowers. It makes a bold feature wherever it is planted.

Aralia elata 'Variegata'

S Spreading to Wide-spreading
AGM 1993
An outstanding form though slow-growing, the leaflets irregularly margined and shaded creamy-white.
'Aureovariegata' is similar except that the leaflets are variegated yellow at first fading to creamy-white later. Both forms are normally grafted onto the green leaved type or else on A. spinosa and a wary eye should be kept for green-leaved suckers which need to be removed.

ARBUTUS
Ericaceae

A small group of handsome evergreen trees, all but A. menziesii tolerant of lime in the soil. All the following possess shining dark green leathery, toothed leaves and clusters of white pitcher-shaped

top: Aralia elata
bottom: Arbutus menziesii
opposite: Amelanchier lamarckii

45

flowers. *They resent disturbance and so are best planted small from containers. They prefer warm districts and are subject to frost damage in cold inland areas.*

Arbutus x andrachnoides

S-M Spreading AGM 1993
The superb cinnamon-red peeling bark of this eventually wide-spreading tree is its chief attraction. The white flowers are produced during late autumn or late winter and are replaced by small red fruits. It is a hybrid between *A. unedo* and *A. andrachne*.

Arbutus menziesii

M-L Spreading AGM 1993
The "Madrone" is a noble tree from the Pacific coast of North America, strong growing when once established and at all times impressive with its bold foliage and rich cinnamon-red bark, later peeling to reveal the pea-green young bark. The flowers are borne in large loose terminal heads in May followed, in a good year, by pea-sized orange-red fruits. Given shelter and a lime-free soil, it is a tree worth planting to mark a special occasion.

Arbutus unedo

S-M Spreading
The "Strawberry Tree" is usually seen as a rugged picturesque tree with shreddy brown bark. The white flowers are produced during late autumn when the small strawberry-like fruits of the previous year are turning to red. The fruits are edible but insipid. This is an excellent tree for windswept coastal gardens but prefers more shelter in cold and inland districts. It is native to the Mediterranean region and south-west Ireland. 'Rubra' is a more compact form with pink-tinged flowers. AGM 1993

AZARA
Flacourtiaceae

A small group of evergreen trees and shrubs native of South America. The following species is the only tree normally satisfactory in cool climates.

Azara microphylla

S-M Broadly columnar to Spreading AGM 1993
One of the hardiest of its kind, it is still best given a sheltered position such as a wall, screen or among other trees. The tiny dark green leaves are borne in large arching sprays, beneath which crowd the tiny mustard-yellow flowers in February or March when they impart to the air around a delicious fragrance of vanilla.

BETULA
Betulaceae

The main attributes of this popular group of hardy, deciduous trees are the rich yellow of their leaves in autumn and their ornamental bark. This varies from white or blackish to red or amber depending on species. Many have conspicuous and attractive drooping yellow male catkins in early spring. The birches are mostly elegant trees adaptable to most soils and situations, though growing more slowly on those of a dry shallow chalky nature.

Betula albosinensis

M Conical to Spreading
The "Red Birch" of China, a most beautiful and desirable (eventually tall) tree of graceful habit. The leaves are thin and tapering, creating a light airy canopy; but by far its most admired characteristic is the peeling smooth orange-red bark which when young is coated with a glaucous white bloom. A variety with longer leaves but equally ornamental is *septentrionalis*, AGM 1993, while 'Fascination' is a selected form named in Holland.

Betula alleghaniensis

M Spreading
Better known as *B. lutea*, the "Yellow Birch" of eastern North America is distinct on account of its amber coloured young bark which darkens and peels with age. The inner bark smells of oil of wintergreen when bruised, a characteristic shared with *B. lenta*. It is a handsome, reliable birch well worth planting for its bark and autumn foliage.

Betula ermanii

M-L Spreading
A handsome species with creamy-white bark tinted pink, becoming orange-brown and peeling on the branches. It is a native of north-east Asia and is sometimes represented in gardens by the variety *subcordata*. One of the best selections of this birch in British cultivation is known as 'Grayswood Hill' AGM 1993, not to be confused with *B. utilis jacquementii* 'Grayswood Ghost'.

Betula lenta

M Spreading
The "Cherry Birch" of eastern North America, so-called on account of its dark almost blackish non-peeling bark, smooth and shining when young. The inner bark of the stem and branches smells of oil of wintergreen when bruised.

Betula maximowicziana

M Spreading
The "Monarch Birch", a handsome Japanese tree easily recognised by its robust habit, its large leaves and long catkins in spring. The bark is orange-brown at first, becoming grey or whitish eventually, while the heart-shaped leaves may be as much as 15cm long. A most satisfactory tree suitable for the larger garden.

Betula nigra

M Spreading AGM 1993
Unlike the normal run of birches, the "River Birch" from eastern USA is notable for its dark shaggy bark which, with its characteristic diamond-shaped leaves, makes it one of the most easily recognised species. It is often seen as a picturesque multi-stemmed tree and, as its name suggests, is particularly useful in wet areas, though it will not tolerate permanently waterlogged ground.

Betula nigra 'Heritage'

M Spreading
A chance seedling found in the USA in 1968, regarded by some authorities as among the top ten trees for American landscapes and gardens. Its richly peeling bark is creamy-white and tan, more

top: Betula ermanii 'Grayswood Hill'
bottom: Betula albosinensis septentrionalis

47

resembling that of *B. utilis* than typical "River birch". It is a robust grower resistant to bronze birch borer, a serious pest in North America. Dark glossy green leaves, pale beneath, turning yellow in autumn.

Betula papyrifera

L Spreading
The "Canoe Birch" or "Paper Birch" of North America is famous for its striking white outer bark, peeling, often in large sheets, from the trunk. The bark was used for many purposes by the North American Indians including cladding for their birch-framed canoes.

Betula pendula

M-L Conical to Spreading AGM 1993
"Lady of the Woods" is just one of the names given to our native "Silver Birch" and aptly describes the grace and beauty of this fast-growing tree. Its white bark and often drooping branchlets make it an ideal subject for lawns, etc., especially when planted in groups.

Betula pendula 'Crispa'

M-L Weeping AGM 1993
A most graceful form which develops into a tall slender tree with gracefully drooping branches and deeply cut long pointed leaves. It is slender enough to be included in the small garden. Commonly sold under the name 'Dalecarlica' which correctly belongs to another, less ornamental tree.

Betula pendula 'Fastigiata'

M-L Broadly columnar
A tall birch with closely erect branches. A useful form but lacking the elegance of the type. A selection of better habit is 'Obelisk'.

Betula pendula 'Tristis'

M Weeping AGM 1993
An elegant spire-like tree with gracefully drooping branches. Similar in habit to 'Crispa' but leaves neither deeply cut nor slender pointed.

top: Betula utilis jacquemontii 'Jermyns'
bottom: Betula pendula

48

Betula pendula 'Youngii'

S Spreading and Weeping AGM 1993
"Young's Weeping Birch" develops a
characteristic broad mushroom-headed
habit with branches reaching to the
ground. It is an ideal shade tree and a
super hideaway for children.

Betula utilis

M-L Spreading
The "Himalayan Birch" is one of the most
variable of all birches, not surprising
considering its range in the wild from
Afghanistan in the west to China in the
east. Typically, the bark is white or cream
coloured but there are some forms mainly
from the eastern Himalaya and China
with bark of a dark copper or orange-
brown colour. Most forms are
satisfactory and ornamental, and this
remains one of the most satisfactory of all
birches for general cultivation. The birch
previously known as *B. jacquemontii* is
included here as *B. utilis* var. *jacquemontii*. It
is mainly represented in cultivation by
several named selections such as
'Doorenbos', 'Grayswood Ghost'
'Jermyns' and 'Silver Shadow', all of which
have superb white or creamy-white bark.

Betula utilis jacquemontii 'Doorenbos'

M. Spreading AGM 1993
A lovely birch of Dutch origin similar in
most respects to Silver Shadow, the bark
is outstanding.

Betula utilis jacquemontii 'Grayswood Ghost'

M Spreading
A handsome tree from a famous Surrey
garden. One of the best white barked
birches.

Betula utilis jacquemontii 'Jermyns'

M Spreading AGM 1993
Arguably the best all-round birch for
general cultivation, with excellent
creamy-white, peeling bark, orange-
coloured on young branches, especially
effective in winter. It has rich yellow leaf
tints in autumn and is equally impressive

in early spring when the branchlets are
draped with the long yellow male catkins.

Betula utilis jacquemontii 'Silver Shadow'

M. Spreading AGM 1993
Previously distributed by the Hillier
Nurseries as *B. jacquemontii*. A vigorous
white-stemmed birch of easy cultivation
and a joy to behold.

BUXUS
Buxaceae

*The booxwoods are mainly represented in
cultivation by shrubby cultivars of B.
microphylla and B. sempervirens. Whilst
some cultivars of the last named will reach a small
tree size after many years, the following is the only
box that can reasonably be expected to reach such
proportions.*

Buxus balearica

S Broadly Columnar
A handsome if uncommon evergreen
from the Balearic Islands and south-west
Spain, notable for its erect habit and large
firm glossy green leaves.

CARPINUS
Betulaceae

*A small but distinguished group of hardy,
deciduous trees suitable for most soils and
situations. Their leaves turn yellow or gold in
autumn, whilst the hop-like clusters of pale green
fruits stud the older branches in summer.*

Carpinus betulus

M-L Spreading AGM 1993
Although most often seen as a hedge, the
"Hornbeam" is a splendid tree for
planting alone or in groups. Older trees
develop a characteristic and attractive
grey fluted trunk. The strongly ribbed
and toothed leaves turn yellow in autumn
while the clusters of peculiar three-lobed
seed bracts hang from the branches. It is

a very hardy and adaptable tree of great individual beauty and occurs as a native in east and south-east England (especially Epping Forest) as well as in Europe and western Asia, where in the latter region I have seen large forests in the mountains above the Caspian Sea in northern Iran.

Carpinus betulus 'Fastigiata'

M Conical to Rounded AGM 1993
A much-planted form which is quite narrow, almost columnar as a young tree but broadening with age until it is first conical then rounded. Not suitable for the small garden.

Carpinus betulus 'Frans Fontaine'

M Columnar to Broadly columnar
A Dutch selection narrower in habit than 'Fastigiata' and therefore more suited to restricted areas.

Carpinus betulus 'Incisa'

S Spreading
A curious but attractive form of neat habit, the leaves smaller and deeply cut and toothed. Sometimes called the "Oak-leaved Hornbeam".

Carpinus caroliniana

S-M Spreading
An uncommon tree in British and European cultivation, the "American Hornbeam" is well worth considering where the common Hornbeam (*C. betulus*) would be too large. It is shade tolerant and adaptable to a wide range of soils and situations, even damp conditions. The finely toothed, parallel veined leaves turn to gold in autumn.

Carpinus cordata

S-M Rounded to Spreading
Native to Japan, Korea and China, this handsome tree is characteristically oval and compact when young, broadening later. The comparatively large, heart-shaped leaves turn a rich gold in autumn.

Carpinus japonica

S-M Conical to Spreading
An impressive, though slow-growing Japanese tree with its wide-spreading branches, its boldly ribbed slender pointed leaves and pendulous fruit clusters. Bushy in habit when young.

Carpinus turczaninowii

S-M Spreading
A rather dense-headed tree with slender, arching branches lined with small, neatly pointed leaves which often give rich autumn colour. Quite suitable for the smaller garden.

Carya ovata

CARYA
Juglandaceae

The hickories are a small group of hardy, deciduous, generally tall-crowned trees related to the walnuts (Juglans) and resembling them in their large striking pinnate leaves and hard-shelled fruits. They differ, however, in the branchlets which possess a solid, not chambered pith. They are mostly stately trees for the larger garden, woodland or park, sometimes excelling in autumn when their leaves turn a rich yellow. They enjoy best a rich, loamy, moist but well-drained lime-free soil but are fairly adaptable so long as extremes are avoided. They are best grown in situ from freshly gathered nuts or planted quite small (one-year seedlings) from containers, taking care not to damage the fragile tap root. In the wild they are mainly found in eastern North America with a few in China. Due to their often fragile branches, they are not suitable for exposed sites nor for planting near buildings or public rights of way.

Carya cordiformis

M-L Spreading AGM 1993
The "Bitternut Hickory" is one of the most satisfactory species for general cultivation, its slender branches creating a vase-shaped crown in maturity. The greyish-brown bark is shallowy ridged whilst the large leaves are composed of from five to nine leaflets. The buds are a characteristic bright yellow especially noticeable in winter. The nuts are thin shelled and the kernel is bitter to the taste.

Carya ovata

M-L Spreading AGM 1993
Well named the "Shagbark Hickory", the loose grey bark of the main stem comes away in large flakes, each flake attached by its middle. The leaves are 30cm or more long, larger on young trees or vigorous shoots, and comprise five leaflets. Although valuable for its edible nuts in the United States, it does not receive sufficient summer heat to be of similar importance in Britain.

Carya tomentosa

M-L Conical to Spreading
Less common in cultivation than the previous species, the "Mockernut Hickory" is well worth growing for its autumn colour and handsome appearance. The large leaves, normally composed of seven leaflets, are fragrant, especially when bruised. The buds too are comparatively large, the terminal ones 2cm long, occasionally more, whilst the bark is smooth and dark grey becoming shallowly ridged in maturity.

CASTANEA
Fagaceae

A handsome genus of hardy deciduous trees growing happily in most types of soil except shallow chalk soils.

Castanea mollissima

M Spreading
The "Chinese Chestnut", whilst not as commonly planted as the next species, is quite as ornamental, differing mainly in its smaller size, slower growth and its downy shoots and fruit capsules. Its fruits are of good quality and it is widely cultivated for them in China, as well as in parts of the United States where it has replaced the native chestnut both as an ornamental and a nut tree. It thrives best in warmer, drier climates than are normal in Britain but is nevertheless quite hardy.

Castanea sativa

L Spreading AGM 1993
The "Sweet" or "Spanish Chestnut" is one of the fastest-growing of all trees and as such makes an excellent screen. The boldly toothed oblong leaves are accompanied in July by long catkins of pale yellow flowers which, though individually small, look effective *en masse*. These are followed by the familiar rich brown edible nuts enclosed in their prickly shells. Trees are variable in their quality of nut and even then require long hot summers to produce worthwhile crops. Old trees develop a gorgeous, deeply grooved, spiralling bark. Although common and apparently wild in parts of the British Isles, it is a native only of southern Europe, North Africa and western Asia.

CATALPA
Bignoniaceae

A small genus of deciduous trees with unusually bold foliage and loose terminal heads of foxglove-like flowers in late summer. They are hardy trees, happy in most soils, but should not be planted in exposed gardens where their leaves will suffer.

Catalpa bignonioides
M Rounded to Spreading AGM 1993
Because of its normally spreading habit the "Indian Bean Tree" is only suitable for the medium-sized to large garden and is a favourite park tree. The large heart-shaped leaves, which are late in appearing, are an admirable foil for the white, yellow and purple-marked flowers in July and August. These are replaced after a hot summer by long slender pods. It is native to the eastern USA and is seen at its best in the southern and south-eastern areas of the British Isles.

Catalpa bignonioides 'Aurea'
S-M Rounded to Spreading AGM 1993
A striking form with yellow leaves, one of the best trees of its colour. Worth growing for this reason alone.

Catalpa x erubescens 'Purpurea'
S Spreading AGM 1993
A hybrid between *C. bignonioides* and the Chinese *C. ovata*, this tree has the wide-spreading habit of the former. Its flowers, which appear during the same period, are also similar in colour to *C. bignonioides* but smaller and more numerous. The young shoots and leaves are dark, almost black-purple, maturing to dark green.

Catalpa fargesii duclouxii
M Broadly columnar
A free-growing, eventually tall Chinese tree with heart-shaped, slender pointed leaves and terminal trusses of lavender-pink, two-lipped flowers in June, spotted and stained brownish-red and yellow in the throat. An uncommon tree in cultivation, it is one well worth growing

top: Catalpa bignonioides
bottom: Celtis australis

in the larger garden.

Catalpa speciosa

M. Broadly columnar to Spreading
The "Western Catalpa" from the United
States, a handsome tree differing from
the more commonly planted "Indian Bean
Tree" in its taller crown, spirally ridged
bark, slender pointed scentless leaves
(those of the other disagreeably scented
when bruised) and its larger flowers
appearing earlier often by two to three
weeks.

CELTIS
Ulmaceae

*The Hackberries or Nettle trees are a relatively
small genus of deciduous trees in the same family
as the elms, differing principally in their
pendulous berry-like fruits. They are much like an
elm in leaf and aspect and make most acceptable
substitutes where elms have been lost from Dutch
elm disease. They are suitable for a wide range of
soils especially those of a dry or chalky nature and
are reasonably tolerant of pollution and salt spray.*

Celtis australis

S-M Spreading to Rounded
Rarely seen outside specialist collections,
this handsome tree develops a smooth
grey bark while its leaves, rough to the
touch, have a characteristic long drawn-
out point. Native of south-east Europe
and south-west Asia; it is particularly
suited to warm dry sites especially in
cities and towns. Known as the Southern
Hackberry.

Celtis occidentalis

M-L Spreading to Dome-shaped
An uncommon tree in British cultivation,
native to eastern North America. It grows
quite tall eventually with a dome-shaped
crown of long, arching branches. Bark
rough and flakey, pinkish-grey. Leaves
unequally broad-based, pointed, dark
shiny green above. A tough adaptable
tree.

Catalpa x erubescens 'Purpurea'

CERCIDIPHYLLUM
Cercidiphyllaceae

One of the loveliest of deciduous trees, mainly known for its autumn colour, the flowers being insignificant. It thrives best on a moist but well-drained soil, being slow and less satisfactory on dry chalk soils. Cold exposed sites should be avoided as its young growths are subject to frost injury in spring.

Cercidiphyllum japonicum

M Broadly columnar to Spreading
AGM 1993
A graceful tree with single or several main stems and long, slightly pendulous branches. The small heart-shaped bright green leaves, reddish-purple when young, are carried oppositely on the twigs: and as autumn treads its colourful path these assume smoky-pink, red or butter-yellow tints when, at the same time, they emit a characteristic aroma of burnt sugar, noticeable for a considerable distance. It is native to Japan and China.

Cercidiphyllum japonicum

Cercidiphyllum japonicum magnificum

M Broadly columnar to Spreading
AGM 1993
A rare variety from Japan with larger leaves and smoother bark.

Cercidiphyllum japonicum magnificum 'Pendulum'

VS-S Weeping
An unusual form developing a dome of long weeping branches. It is well worth training the leader on a young tree to as great a height as practical. Large specimens are said to be spectacular, especially in autumn. It was originally introduced to the West wrongly as a form of *C. japonicum*.

Cercidiphyllum japonicum 'Rotfuchs'

M Broadly columnar to Spreading
A German-raised selection in which the leaves are tinted reddish-purple through summer. The name means 'Red Fox'. Recently introduced to Britain and worth searching specialist nurseries for.

CERCIS
Leguminosae

A small genus of deciduous trees, easily recognised by their rounded leaves arranged alternately on the shoots and for their small pea-flowers which are borne in bunches from the naked branches. Their main requirement is a sunny, well-drained position. They resent disturbance so should be planted as small as possible.

Cercis canadensis 'Forest Pansy'

S Spreading AGM 1993
In British cultivation the "Redbud", *Cercis canadensis* is less satisfactory as a flowering tree than in its native eastern America, and certainly inferior in this respect to the "Judas Tree". In 'Forest Pansy' however, the flowers are secondary to the wine-purple leaves which become

more subdued in tone as the summer advances. One of the best coloured-leaved small trees for the garden. Like the next species it thrives best in warm dry areas.

Cercis siliquastrum

S-M Rounded to Wide-spreading
AGM 1993

The "Judas Tree", so legend has it, is the tree on which Judas Iscariot hanged himself in the garden; however, it is prized for its rose-lilac flowers which inundate the branches in May before the blue-green leaves emerge. There is also a white-flowered form *alba* and a form with deeper coloured flowers known as 'Bodnant'. In a good (hot) year these are followed by flattened red pods which persist on the boughs into winter. It is native to the eastern Mediterranean region and thrives in full sun. It is excellent on shallow chalk soils and is one of the best trees for continental climates.

†CITRUS
Rutaceae

Few flowers bring back memories of the subtropical regions more clearly than those of citrus. Their delicious scent instantly conjures up scenes of sun and heat: and these conditions are essential to their successful cultivation, which is why they can only be grown out of doors on a permanent basis in the warmest areas of Europe, especially the Mediterranean region. One of the finest selections of Citrus fruits once flourished in the famous gardens at La Mortola on the Italian Riviera. I once knew a fine specimen of Meyer's Lemon grown against a warm south-facing wall in the south of England. It was however, given protection each winter. In less favoured areas these trees can be grown in large containers and given a place outside on a sunny patio or courtyard in summer, as long as they are kept in frost free conditions in a conservatory or greenhouse for the winter. They grow best in a light fertile loam and respond favourably to feeding. All the following are small evergreen trees or shrubs and are mainly grown for their decorative fruits which contain citric acid and are rich in vitamin C. Their white flowers are normally produced in spring and are deliciously fragrant.

Citrus aurantiifolia

Although similar in many respects to the "Lemon", the "Lime" has smaller flowers and smaller greenish-yellow fruits, the greenish pulp containing less citric acid. The juice is acid to the taste and was drunk to prevent scurvy on long sea voyages.

Citrus aurantium

The "Seville Orange" from northern India is one of the hardiest of the commonly grown citrus fruits, though 'hardy' in this instance is relative. It is a small tree with thorny branches and winged leafstalks. The deep orange globular fruits have a thick roughened peel and a bitter pulp. The peel is often candied, whilst the pulp, when chopped and grated provides a basis for orange marmalade.

Citrus grandis

The "Shaddock" or "Pomelo" from south-east Asia is well known for its strikingly large globular to pear-shaped fruits which can be 25cm across. The yellow peel is thick and spongy while the pulp is relatively acid to the taste and fragile.

Citrus limon

A tree of ancient lineage, the "Lemon" is an easily recognised thorny-stemmed tree, free flowering over a long period. In ideal conditions, flowers and fruits are produced throughout the year. The characteristic yellow ellipsoid fruit with a distinct "nipple" at one end contains a pale acid pulp, very rich in vitamin C.

Citrus limon 'Meyer'

More familiarly known as Meyer's Lemon, this is perhaps the hardiest of true citrus and is often grown as a conservatory or house plant in the colder areas of western Europe. It was introduced from near Peking by the American plant collector Frank Meyer early this century, the orange coloured peel of its lemon-shaped fruits suggesting to some authorities a hybrid with the "Sweet Orange" *C. sinensis*. In the United States this plant is being replaced by 'Improved Meyer' which is claimed to be more resistant there to infection and virus diseases.

Citrus paradisi

The large fruits with thin yellow peel of the "Grapefruit" are well enough known, as is the pale or pinkish pulp with its pleasant, slightly bitter taste. They are often produced in heavy clusters at the ends of the branches, which may have given rise to the name 'grapefruit'.

Citrus reticulata

The "Tangerine", "Mandarin", "Clementine" and "Satsumi" are all covered by the above name though they are of different origins. Their fruits are characterised by their small size, orange loose peel, and their sweet, juicy, sometimes seedless pulp.

Citrus sinensis

The "Sweet Orange". Another tree of ancient lineage ideally suited to Mediterranean climates. It is more resistant to cold than most other fruits but will not tolerate persistent frosts even where summers are hot. The normally thin-peeled rounded fruits with their sweet juicy orange pulp are easily recognisable even by the very young.

CLADRASTIS
Leguminosae

A small genus of hardy deciduous trees with pinnate leaves. The leaf stalks are swollen at the base enclosing the buds, whilst the roots support nitrogen-fixing bacteria which help improve soil fertility.

Cladrastis lutea

M Spreading
The "American Yellow-wood", a handsome tree from the south-east United States with a smooth grey beech-like bark and large bright green pinnate leaves with broad leaflets which turn a clear yellow in autumn. The fragrant white pea-flowers are borne in large loose drooping heads in late May or June. It is tolerant of dry but not wet situations, preferably on a lime-free soil. This most desirable but little-planted ornamental

tree is attractive in summer and in winter when the grey sinuous branches of an old tree are particularly striking. It flowers more reliably in warmer, drier climates.

Cladrastis sinensis

S-M Spreading
Quite different in aspect to *C. lutea*, this Chinese tree has smaller darker green leaves with more numerous smaller leaflets. It is, however, more spectacular and reliable in its flowering in Britain, the fragrant bluish-white pea-flowers borne in large erect conical heads in July. It is one of the last trees to break leaf in early summer, and is adaptable as to soil in a sunny, well-drained position.

CLETHRA
Clethraceae

A small genus of mainly deciduous shrubs suitable for lime-free soils. The following is the only species attaining tree size.

†Clethra arborea

S-M Broadly columnar to Spreading
A distinguished, fast-growing evergreen tree from Madeira with bold foliage and loose terminal heads of pure white fragrant flowers like those of lily-of-the-valley. These are remarakable in appearing from late summer into autumn (August-October). This beautiful and desirable, but decidedly frost-tender tree is suitable only for the warmer sheltered (especially woodland) gardens of south-west Britain and Ireland and gardens in similar climates in Europe. In the wild in Madeira it is commonly found as a shrubby bush in laurel thickets and forests in the mountains.

†CORDYLINE
Agavaceae

A small genus of trees and shrubs with long narrow evergreen leaves borne in crowded heads or tufts. The small flowers are produced in large branched heads. The following is the species most often cultivated in Britain and Europe.

Cordyline australis
S-M Spreading AGM 1993
The so-called "Cabbage Palm" or "Cabbage Tree" of New Zealand, a familiar sight in gardens in coastal areas of southern and western Britain and Europe as well as in warm sheltered areas further inland. It is normally available as a bold leafy tuft in a container, gradually developing an erect stem which later branches, each ascending branch sporting a large dense brush of narrow leathery, flexible leaves. Tiny white fragrant flowers are densely borne in huge branched heads in summer followed by whitish berries.

A striking dusky purple-leaved cultivar 'Atropurpurea' and the creamy-striped 'Albertii' are less hardy although very desirable. All forms when young are commonly used as spot plants in bedding displays and as impressive summer pot plants on the terrace or patio. Established plants damaged during severe winters usually break anew from the base the following year, in which case the old stem should be removed.

CORNUS
Cornaceae

A large genus of deciduous and evergreen trees and shrubs containing a wide selection of ornamental species grown for flower, fruit, foliage or colourful stems. Those tree species having colourful bracts around the flower-head are commonly referred to as "flowering dogwoods"; but as all species produce flowers this is something of a misnomer. Unless otherwise indicated, they are hardy and tolerant of most soils in sun or half shade.

Cornus controversa
S-M Conical to Spreading
A magnificent tree, its branches produced almost in whorls, spreading horizontally to form a distinct tiered arrangement. Its leaves are distinct in being borne alternately on the branches (only one

other species of Cornus, *C. alternifolius* has this arrangement) and turn yellow or purplish-red in autumn. The flattened heads of creamy-white flowers crowd the upper sides of the branches in June and July and are followed by blue-black berries. It is a native of China and Japan.

Cornus controversa 'Variegata'
S-M Conical to Spreading AGM 1993
This is perhaps the most beautiful and effective of all hardy variegated trees. Its wide-spreading branches are produced in tiers and bear comparatively narrow creamy-white variegated leaves. It is slow-growing but beautiful at any age, whilst a mature tree is a guaranteed show-stopper.

Cornus 'Eddie's White Wonder'
S Spreading AGM 1993
A first-class flowering tree, a hybrid between *C. florida* and *C. nuttallii*, raised by H.M. Eddie, a nurseryman in British Columbia. In May the branches are plastered with large white bracted flower-heads, whilst the leaves colour richly in autumn. It flourishes best on a rich well-drained loamy soil.

Cornus controversa 'Variegata'

Cornus florida

S Spreading

Although rarely as spectacular in British cultivation as it is in its native eastern United States, this "Flowering Dogwood" is still a desirable tree given a warm sunny position. It thrives best in the drier south-east of Britain than the wetter west, while in Europe it appreciates the continental climate and is especially good in the Mediterranean region. The flower-heads are formed in autumn but the four bracts do not expand and colour until the following May and are then white and spectacular. The leaves often colour rich red or reddish-purple in autumn. In America it has been threatened by a wilt disease which can cause the death of the tree, but to the best of my knowledge this disease is not present in Britain. It is not at its best on shallow chalk soils.

Cornus florida 'Rainbow'

VS-S Spreading

A lovely variegated form of slow growth. The leaves are variegated deep yellow and green, becoming suffused carmine-red in autumn. Flower bracts are white.

Cornus florida 'Cherokee Chief'

S Spreading AGM 1993

An American selection with bracts of a deep rose.

Cornus florida rubra

S Spreading

A lovely form in which the bracts are pink or reddish tinted, otherwise it is similar to the type.

Cornus florida 'Welchii'

VS-S Spreading

A handsome but slow-growing form with leaves variegated green, creamy-white and pink, spectacular in autumn when they turn to rose-red or reddish-purple.

Cornus florida 'White Cloud'

S Spreading

In optimum conditions, one of the most reliable and free flowering white forms.

Cornus kousa

S Spreading

One of the most interesting and attractive trees for the small garden, particularly when its spreading branches are covered by the conspicuous white-bracted flowerheads which are star-like when viewed from above. These appear in late May and June, often followed by strawberry-like fruits which are edible but seedy and insipid. In some gardens the leaves turn to a rich bronze and crimson in autumn. It is native to China, Korea and Japan and relishes a moist but well drained soil in sun or semi-shade. It cannot be recommended for dry shallow chalk soils.

Cornus kousa chinensis

S Spreading AGM 1993

The Chinese variety which, as generally grown, is a superior form with larger bracts. 'China Girl' and 'Milky Way' are two of several selections notable for their free-flowering habit.

Cornus kousa 'Satomi'

S Spreading AGM 1993

A lovely form in which the bracts are broad and rosy-red fading to pink in hot weather, deepening with age.

Cornus macrophylla

S-M Spreading

A most attractive but rarely planted tree, in some respects resembling C. controversa, having a similar tiered habit of branching but leaves opposite not alternate. The cream-coloured flowers, although individually small, are carried in dense domed heads along the upper sides of the spreading branches in June. In a good year these are followed by dark blue berries. A native of the Himalayas, China and Japan, this is a tree well worth considering for the larger garden where it makes an impressive lawn specimen.

Cornus nuttallii

S-M Spreading

In its native western North America, this is regarded as one of the most beautiful flowering trees. In the British Isles, however, it is comparatively short-lived and rarely reaches the size of wild trees. It does, however, flower relatively young; and given a sheltered, moist, well-drained position with its head in the sun, it will flourish for 15 to 20 years or more. It dislikes dry shallow chalk soils and is not satisfactory in colder areas of the British Isles. As in *C. kousa*, the large bracts are the conspicuous part of the flowerhead; these are creamy-white, becoming pink-tinged, and appear quite spectacular in May. Fruits are red as in *C. kousa* and the leaves turn to yellow, occasionally red, in autumn. Several selections have been made and named, of which 'Ascona' and 'Monarch' are two of the best for flower display.

Cornus 'Porlock'

S Spreading AGM 1993
A hybrid between *C. capitata* and *C. kousa* showing the influence of the former in its leaves which are semi-evergreen. The creamy-white bracted flowerheads are pink-tinted with age; and on older specimens certainly, they spangle the spreading branches in June or early July to be followed in a good year by the long stalked pendulous strawberry-like fruits. 'Norman Hadden' is a similar selection. Like *C. kousa*, they flourish best on a rich well-drained loamy soil and in full sun.

CORYLUS
Betulaceae

Deciduous trees and shrubs of which our native "Hazel" is the most familiar species. All are hardy easy-to-grow subjects for almost any soil.

Corylus colurna

L Conical AGM 1993
The "Turkish Hazel" is normally encountered only in large gardens and parks, and then only rarely. Its stately appearance and pale flaking bark make it of interest even in winter, and again in spring when the branches are hung with countless yellow catkins. It is found wild in south-eastern Europe and western Asia.

COTINUS
Anacardiaceae

A genus of only two species of hardy deciduous trees or shrubs, the most popular of which is the "Venetian Sumach" C. coggygria. This is typically shrubby but can be trained to a single stem if desired when it will form a small broad crowned tree. Both species have a poisonous sap which can cause blistering on sensitive skins. Care must be taken, therefore, when pruning, although this operation is rarely necessary.

Cotinus coggygria

VS-S Rounded AGM 1993
The "Venetian Sumach" or "Smoke Tree", native over a wide area from southern Europe north-east through the Himalaya into China. A variety is very common in the mountains above the Great Wall! Normally seen as a large dense bush, it often matures to form a low broadly dome-shaped or rounded tree. The rounded green leaves turn rich

Cornus 'Porlock'

orange-purple or red in autumn, whilst the fluffy grey or pink-tinged flower-heads in summer turn pale grey in fruit. There are several named selections available with wine-purple foliage of which 'Notcutt's Purple' and 'Royal Purple' AGM 1993 are the most well known, in Britain certainly. They contrast effectively with grey or silver leaved plants.

Cotinus 'Flame'

S Dome-shaped to Spreading AGM 1993
A free-growing small tree or large shrub of bushy growth with bold foliage, green in summer turning to orange and red in autumn. One of the most reliable for the brilliance of its autumn display. It was raised by the French nursery firm of Chenault under the name Chenault's Variety and is probably a hybrid between *C. coggygria* and *C. obovatus*.

Cotinus 'Grace'

Continus 'Grace'

S Dome-shaped to Spreading AGM 1993
A deliberate hybrid between *C. obovatus* and *C. coggygria* 'Velvet Cloak' raised by Peter Dummer of the Hillier Nurseries in 1978. Its bold foliage, purple-tinted in summer turns to firecracker colours of orange and scarlet in autumn. The flowerheads are also large and pink-tinted. This plant has received an Award of Merit and a First Class Certificate from the RHS. It is likely to make a small tree especially if trained when young to a single main stem.

Cotinus obovatus

S Dome-shaped to Spreading AGM 1993
The "American Smoke Tree" differs from its Eurasian counterpart *C. coggygria* in its larger size and larger leaves and flower-heads. Indeed, when trained to a single stem it makes a most handsome small tree with grey to greyish-brown bark which is attractively scaly on mature trees. The blue-green, bold leaves, bronze-pink when young, give reliable and rich autumn colours of yellow, orange, red and smoky purple. The pale pink flowerheads are large and billowy. It is excellent on dry especially limy or chalk soils. Avoid giving it too rich a diet.

COTONEASTER
Rosaceae

A large genus of mainly shrubs but containing several tree-like species which, when young, may easily be trained to a single stem if required. The cotoneasters are hardy easy-to-grow subjects for any soil. All have white flowers normally in May and June.

Cotoneaster frigidus

S Spreading
One of the most satisfactory deciduous trees for small gardens, particularly those in towns and cities, forming a rounded head of branches with comparatively large oval leaves. The heavy bunches of crimson berries weigh down the branches

in autumn and remain throughout winter. It is native to the Himalayas. Several hybrids of *C. frigidus* with *C. salicifolius* are grown as large shrubs but can be trained as small, wide-spreading trees. They are spectacular in flower and fruit and include 'Cornubia' (red berries) 'John Waterer' AGM 1993 (red berries) 'Rothschildianus' AGM 1993 (yellow berries) and 'St. Monica' (red berries).

Cotoneaster frigidus
'Fructu-luteo'
S Spreading
A striking form in which the fruits are creamy-yellow at first, deepening with age.

Cotoneaster
'Hybridus Pendulus'
VS Weeping
When grafted on an erect stem, this normally evergreen Cotoneaster, a hybrid of *C. frigidus*, makes a delightful if stiffly weeping tree. The hanging branches are crowded with small sealing-wax-red berries from autumn onwards. No garden is too small to contain this tree.

CRATAEGUS
Rosaceae

The "Thorns" are a large, often unwieldy, genus of deciduous, generally small trees. Being tough, easy to grow and hardy, they have often in the past been ignored or relegated to utility jobs such as hedging or for growing where few other trees would survive. Obviously their adaptability makes them of great value in difficult sites, but it should not be forgotten that several species in particular are of great ornamental merit and worth growing for this alone.

Crataegus crus-galli
S Spreading to Rounded
It is possible that the true "Cockspur Thorn" is no longer in cultivation outside America. However, the tree generally grown as such is a useful subject with thorny branches and glossy, toothed leaves which colour orange and red in autumn. The white flowers in May and June are replaced by red fruits which last well into winter.

Crataegus laevigata
'Paul's Scarlet'
S Spreading AGM 1993
This popular double red-flowered thorn has been much planted and deservedly so. It originated as a sport of a double pink thorn in a garden in Hertfordshire over a hundred years ago. 'Punicea' is a single flowered version whilst 'Rosea Flore Pleno' has double pink flowers. AGM 1993. *C. laevigata* is now the correct name for *C. oxyacantha*.

Crataegus x lavallei 'Aurora'
S Vase-shaped to Spreading
The original hybrid (*C. stipulacea* x *C. crus-galli*), raised in the Segrez Aboretum in France and the tree commonly grown in Holland and elsewhere on the Continent. It mainly differs from 'Carrierei' in its bronzed instead of green young foliage.

Crataegus x lavallei 'Carrierei'
S Vase-Shaped to Spreading AGM 1993
This splendid hybrid between *C. stipulacea* and *C. crus-galli* develops a dense head of

Crataegus tanacetifolia

branches, thickly clothed with dark glossy green leaves which are often retained until December. The comparatively large white flowers are replaced by large long-persistent, orange-red fruits. It is commonly planted as a street tree, usually as *C. x lavallei*.

Crataegus monogyna
S-M Spreading
Our native "May", "Hawthorn" or "Quick" needs no introduction. It still forms mile after mile of countryside hedge, in spite of short-sighted attempts by many farmers to eradicate it from the English scene. The display of sweet-smelling white flowers in May rivals that of any exotic or foreign tree. It is one of the few trees to withstand both highly alkaline and strongly acid soils, dry or wet, and to withstand both industrial pollution and exposure.

Crataegus monogyna 'Pendula'
S Weeping
An attractive form with weeping branches and white flowers. A form with pink flowers is 'Pendula Rosea'.

Crataegus monogyna 'Stricta'
S Broadly columnar to Vase-shaped
A useful form of erect habit ideal for windswept areas and confined places. The flowers are white.

Crataegus orientalis
S Spreading to Rounded
The deeply-cut greyish-green hairy leaves of this attractive, slow-growing Oriental Thorn are a suitable foil for the white flowers in early June, and later for the large downy red or orange-red fruits. It is an excellent round-headed tree for the small garden, with almost thornless branches. Sometimes offered as *C. laciniata* which is a synonym. Unfortunately, because of its slow growth this splendid tree is rarely offered by the nursery trade.

Crataegus persimilis 'Prunifolia'
S Spreading to Rounded AGM 1993
One of the most commonly planted and

most attractive of the thorns. In fact this is a real all-rounder, with a neat rounded crown, healthy glossy green leaves and white flowers in June. In autumn the leaves ignite in a blaze of orange and red accompanied by bunches of rich red fruits. Commonly sold as *C. prunifolia*.

Crataegus phaenopyrum
S Spreading
The "Washington Thorn", a densely branched tree with sharp thorns and sharply toothed three- to five-lobed leaves, glossy dark green above. The white sweet-scented flowers are carried in dense heads in July (one of last thorns to flower) and are followed in autumn by bright glossy red fruits often hanging from the branches throughout winter. The leaves often provide rich autumn tints. It is an excellent tree of its kind, though comparatively neglected in Britain and Europe.

Crataegus pinnatifida 'Major'
S Spreading
In every respect a bold handsome thorn, too little planted in Britain although hardy and adaptable to most soils and situations. The leaves are leathery and large, deeply cleft and a rich glossy dark green above. The large white flowers are produced at the end of May into June, followed in autumn by large, fleshy red edible fruits. One of the most ornamental trees of its kind, it originates from North China where its fruits are commonly eaten as sweetmeats.

Crataegus tanacetifolia
S Spreading
The "Tansy-leaved Thorn". This unusual and little known tree is one of the most distinct and ornamental of all thorns. The greyish, hairy, deeply-cut and toothed leaves are crowded on the normally thornless branches. In June they are accompanied by the comparatively large fragrant white flowers with contrasting red anthers borne in rounded clusters. These are replaced by conspicuous yellow fruits like small crab apples. It is a first-rate tree, but like *C. orientalis*, maddeningly slow in growth, and likewise rarely offered by the nursery trade.

DAVIDIA
Nyssaceae

The single species which represents this genus is one of the most talked-about and spectacular of all hardy trees. It will grow in most soils, though thriving best in a moist but well-drained soil.

Davidia involucrata

M-L Spreading AGM 1993
A vigorous tree with heart-shaped leaves, white-felted beneath, similar in shape to those of a lime tree but more conspicuously veined. In May the fragrant young leaves emerge from the buds accompanied by small baubles of purple-anthered flowers, each suspended on a slender stalk. These in themselves are of little beauty but are subtended by two large conspicuous white bracts which flutter and shine all along the branches. These bracts have earned for this tree several appropriate common names including "Dove Tree", "Ghost Tree" and "Pocket Handkerchief Tree". The flower baubles are replaced by hard, green ripening to brown, plum-sized fruits which remain on the branches after the leaves have fallen. This wonderful tree was first discovered by the French missionary, Père David, in China in 1869. Although fast-growing it does not usually produce flowers until ten years old or more. In cultivation *D. involucrata* is most often represented by its variety *vilmoriniana*, AGM 1993 which, apart from its greater hardiness, mainly differs from the typical tree in its leaves which are smooth or almost so beneath.

DIOSPYROS
Ebenaceae

A large, mainly tropical, genus of evergreen and deciduous trees. Male and female flowers are found on separate trees but they are of limited ornamental merit, and the following hardy species are principally grown for their leaf, fruit and bark characteristics. They are best suited to a moist but well-drained loamy soil.

Diospyros kaki

S Spreading
The "Kaki-fruit" or "Chinese Persimmon" flourishes best in a continental climate of warm summers and cold winters, where it fruits reliably and regularly. It is fairly satisfactory, however, in the warmer areas of Britain, where its large glossy-topped dark green leaves render it easily recognisable. The bright orange-yellow edible fruits are similar to large tomatoes at a glance differing in their large calyx, leathery skin and sweet pulp. They are very colourful on the normally leafless branches in late autumn and early winter.

Diospyros lotus

S-M Spreading
Known as the "Date Plum", this vigorous tree is perfectly hardy though little grown in Britain and Europe. The leaves, although smaller than those of *D. kaki*, have a similar lustrous appearance above; whilst the small rounded fruits up to 2cm across ripen to purplish or dull yellow, studding the naked branches in autumn. They are sharp to taste and not worth eating. The bark of a mature tree is attractive in a rugged way.

Davidia involucrata vilmoriniana

Diospyros virginiana
S Spreading
The Persimmon of America also has glossy-topped leaves and a rugged dark grey-black bark. The leaves sometimes colour well before falling in autumn, whilst the small fruit is yellowish to pale orange. In parts of the United States this tree is orcharded for its edible fruits.

DRIMYS
Winteraceae

A small genus of evergreen trees and shrubs from the southern hemisphere. They are best suited to the milder, wetter areas of Britain and Ireland and they abhor dry shallow chalk soils. The following species thrives best in a sheltered situation and is often grown against a house wall. In the woodland gardens of south-west England and Ireland, it is sometimes seen as a tall multi-stemmed tree.

†Drimys winteri
S-M Conical
The main feature of this species is its bold leaves, which measure up to 20cm long, pale or dark green above and blue-green beneath. The sweetly-scented ivory-white flowers are carried in loose clusters in May, but not on very young trees. Its bark is strongly aromatic and was once used by sailors as a spice to "sweeten" bad meat and as a treatment against scurvy. It is native over a wide area of South America. 'Latifolia' is a larger leaved more vigorous form commonly found in old Cornish woodland gardens and often available in the trade.

EMBOTHRIUM
Proteaceae

Few trees are as striking as the Embothrium in flower. It is a fast-growing tree and requires a moist but well-drained position in full sun to succeed, disliking lime of any kind in the soil. When given shelter of other trees, particularly in woodlands, it tends to become drawn and lanky and may eventually fall over. It also resents disturbance and is therefore best planted small from a container.

Embothrium coccineum
S-M Spreading
In May and early June an established specimen of the "Chilean Fire Tree" may be seen from some distance, its branches thickly covered with slender-tubed flowers of an intense orange-scarlet or crimson. Hailing from South America, it is variable in leaf and also in hardiness. In cultivation those plants generally sold under the names *lanceolatum* or 'Norquinco Valley' AGM 1993 are the hardiest, and even then are usually satisfactory only in the south and west of the British Isles. Not always easy to establish, this spectacular tree is worth persevering with.

Drimys winteri

†ERIOBOTRYA
Rosaceae

A small genus of evergreen trees mostly with bold foliage. They require a warm sunny sheltered position to thrive and are adaptable to most well-drained soils.

Eriobotrya japonica

S Spreading to Rounded AGM 1993
The "Loquat", a native of China long cultivated in Japan, is most frequently seen in the warmer areas of Europe, especially the Mediterranean region where its small pear-shaped, edible, yellow fruits can be found on sale in shops and markets in spring. It is, however, hardy in the milder areas of Britain and Ireland and although fruits are rarely developed here, this tree is well worth growing for its bold, dark green, parallel-veined leaves, grey or brown woolly beneath. In autumn after a warm summer the loose terminal heads of white flowers fill the air with the sweet scent of hawthorn. The fruits or seeds of the Loquat are frequently brought home from the Mediterranean as souvenirs by returning holidaymakers.

EUCALYPTUS
Myrtaceae

The "Eucalypts" or "Gum" trees comprise a large genus of several hundred species found in the wild almost entirely in Australia, where they are as much a part of the landscape as elms used to be in England. They are fast-growing evergreens with distinctive foliage and often flaky bark and bring a touch of the sub-tropical to our gardens. Only a comparative few, however, are hardy enough for general cultivation in Britain. These are tolerant of most soils, but, with the exception of E. parvifolia and possibly E. dalrympleana, are rarely long-lived on dry shallow chalk soils. They resent disturbance and are normally grown and sold by nurserymen in containers. To be successful, they should be planted as small as is practicable (30 cm is ideal) in summer. Resist the temptation to buy tall seemingly ready-made trees in containers. The leaves of juvenile and adult trees are often very different in shape and size, both being excellent for cutting. The tendency to develop a single tall slender stem may be curbed, if so desired, by pruning the main stem back to near ground level one or two years after planting. This will normally produce a sheaf of attractive sucker growths and a more bushy reduced habit. Tall leaders may also be pruned when young and slender to encourage a stronger root system and a more robust basal stem. Unless otherwise stated, the flowers of the following species are white and appear in summer. In the absence of petals their attraction consists of dense bunches of conspicuous stamens. In the wild, some eucalypt species have a wide altitudinal range in the mountains. In practice this often means that seed collected from specimens growing at the higher altitudes provide hardier trees more suitable for British conditions. It does no harm, therefore, to enquire of suppliers the source of their seed.

Eucalyptus camphora

S-M Broadly columnar to Spreading
A fast-growing species with dark bark which, when old, is shed in long ribbons. The leaves are lance-shaped glossy green and up to 12.5cm long. It is fairly hardy and makes a nice contrast when planted near the blue or silvery-leaved species such as E. gunnii and E. glaucescens.

Embothrium coccineum

†*Eucalyptus citriodora*

M-L Conical to Spreading
The "Lemon-scented Gum", is a decidedly tender species only suitable for the mildest areas and even there subject to winter damage. It is most successful in southern Europe, though long popular elsewhere as a conservatory subject. The narrowly lance-shaped green and downy leaves are strongly lemon-scented when bruised. Bark of older trees is smooth, grey or pink-tinted.

Eucalyptus coccifera

S-L Spreading AGM 1993
The "Tasmanian Snow Gum" possesses a striking marbled silvery-grey and cream bark. The young branches are often covered in a bluish-white bloom, whilst the mature leaves are lance-shaped and bluish-green or grey, smelling of peppermint when bruised. The hardiest, smaller forms of this species are from seed collected at the tree line in the mountains of Tasmania, whilst those grown from seed collected at lower elevations make larger trees suitable only for the milder areas. Damaged or felled trees commonly produce vigorous sprouts from the rootstock or lower stem.

Eucalyptus dalrympleana

L Speading AGM 1993
A most elegant tree, tall and conical as a single-stemmed specimen. The beautiful cream, brown and grey patchwork bark is only marginally more effective than the long scimitar-shaped grey-green adult leaves which are bronze-coloured when young. It is proving very hardy, certainly in the south and west of the British Isles and is reasonably lime-tolerant.

†*Eucalyptus ficifolia*

S Spreading to Rounded
Known as the "Red-flowered Gum" in Australia, this is one of the most spectacular of all gums for its bold dense clusters of red or scarlet flowers (there are also forms with white, cream or pink flowers). Its leaves are smooth and leathery, lance-shaped and shiny green to 14cm long. In warm, regions, including Tresco on the Isles of Scilly and the

Mediterranean region, it is a real eye-catcher in flower. If only it were hardy!

†Eucalyptus globulus

L Spreading AGM 1993

Frequently planted in the milder parts of Britain and Ireland, the "Tasmanian Blue Gum" makes a noble tree in maturity often with a massive bole and smooth white or greyish bark, shed when old in long thin ribbons. Juvenile plants are silvery-white all over with large opposite leaves, whilst the adult leaves are curved or sickle-shaped, glossy green and pendant up to 30cm long. Seedlings were once commonly used as spot plants in subtropical bedding displays.

Eucalyptus gregsoniana

S Spreading

Known as the "Wolgan Snow Gum", this eucalypt is similar in merit to *E. pauciflora niphophila*, differing mainly in its narrower almost willow-like grey-green drooping leaves. It is not common in cultivation but worth searching for.

Eucalyptus gunnii

L Spreading AGM 1993

The most popular and well known gum tree in cultivation and hardy in all but the coldest areas of the British Isles. The silvery-blue juvenile foliage of the "Cider Gum" gives way to sage-green, sickle-shaped adult foliage, whilst the flaking bark exhibits shades of grey, cream, green and brown. It is commonly seen in gardens in warmer areas as a multi-stemmed specimen and as such is more likely to cope with strong winds.

Eucalyptus mitchelliana

M Weeping

Known in Australia as "Weeping Sally", this most attractive gum is proving encouragingly hardy in the few places it has been planted in Britain. The pale adult bark and the arching habit of the branches, with long, weeping, slender red branchlets, is most appealing; whilst the slender, pale, greyish-green leaves to 15cm long are a decided bonus.

Eucalyptus parvifolia

S-M Spreading AGM 1993

A popular and useful gum on account of it being hardy and tolerant of shallow chalk soils. The small narrow adult leaves are grey-green and the bark an attractive piebald cream and grey.

Eucalyptus pauciflora

S-M Spreading

When collected from its highest altitudes in south-east Australia the "Cabbage Gum" is easily one of the hardiest eucalypts. It is also one of the most attractive in its silvery-grey, cream and pale green marbled bark and large sickle-shaped glossy green leaves on shining dark red shoots.

Eucalyptus pauciflora debeuzevillei

S-M Conical to Spreading

A little known eucalypt from New South Wales where it is found only in a few mountains. It mainly differs from *E. pauciflora* in its broader leaves; and it is just as hardy, if not more so. A young tree in my garden is growing strongly and promises to be every bit as impressive as the Snow Gum (*E. pauciflora niphophila*).

Eucalyptus pauciflora niphophila

S-M Spreading AGM 1993

The "Snow Gum" is without doubt one of the hardiest of all eucalypts, and spectacular in its smooth bark marbled like a python's skin. The large sickle-shaped grey-green leaves are borne on shoots which are attractively coated with a blue-white bloom. It is perhaps the best eucalypt for small gardens.

Eucalyptus perriniana

M-L Conical to Spreading

"Spinning Gum", a handsome tree with smooth brownish and grey bark, peeling when old in long strips from the upper stem. The juvenile leaves are rounded, the adult leaves lance-shaped or sickle-shaped, in both cases blue-grey or glaucous. A relatively hardy gum, it is attractive at all stages.

Eucalyptus urnigera

M-L Conical to Spreading
A relatively hardy, erect-stemmed tree of
strong growth with white to reddish-
brown bark peeling with age. Adult leaves
are broad lance-shaped, green or greyish
and leathery. It is known as the "Urn
Gum" from the shape of its seed capsules.

EUCOMMIA
Eucommiaceae

*A monotypic genus from China. Male and female
flowers are borne on separate trees; but as neither
flowers nor fruit are of ornamental merit, it
matters not which sex is planted.*

Eucommia ulmoides

S-M Spreading
A small hardy deciduous tree with
attractive grey-brown, ridged or
furrowed bark and elm-like slender
pointed shining green leaves. An
uncommon tree in British gardens, it has
long been cultivated in China for its
medicinal bark. The leaves contain a
rubber substance known as gutta-percha
which can be demonstrated by gently
tearing a leaf in half. Suitable for most
soils, it makes an ideal if unusual lawn
specimen.

EUCRYPHIA
Eucryphiaceae

*A small genus of beautiful late summer and
autumn-flowering trees, thriving best in a moist
but well-drained soil sheltered from wind and
draughts but open to partial sun. They resent
dryness at the roots and should never be planted
where the soil is exposed to the sun. With the
exception of* E. glutinosa *they are evergreen and
tolerant of chalk soils but are rarely seen at their
best in these conditions.*

Eucryphia glutinosa

S Spreading AGM 1993
Often seen as a large multi-stemmed
shrub, this deciduous Chilean species is
perhaps the most satisfactory of the
genus. Its glossy, dark green leaves are
divided into three to five leaflets which
turn to orange and red in autumn. The
white flowers, with yellow stamens
resembling small single roses, appear in
July and August. It is not lime-tolerant.
Sometimes grown as *E. pinnatifolia*, a
synonym.

Eucryphia x intermedia

S-M Broadly columnar
A fast-growing hybrid between *E. glutinosa*
and *E. lucida*. The slender branches are
densely clothed with evergreen leaves
varying from simple to trifoliolate in
form. These are joined by myriad small,
white, yellow-stamened flowers in
August and September. There are several
cultivars of more-or-less equal merit of
which 'Rostrevor' AGM 1993 is the best
known.

Eucryphia lucida

S-M Broadly columnar
The "Leatherwood" of Tasmania, a lovely
free-growing species with small oblong
leathery leaves, dark glossy green above,
pale or blue-green beneath. The fragrant
white flowers with red-tipped stamens
crowd the branchlets in June and July. An
important source of nectar for honeybees
in Tasmania.

Eucryphia milliganii

S Columnar
A delightful species of narrow, erect habit
when young, with small neat evergreen
leaves and equally miniature white, cup-
shaped flowers in late June and July. It is
native to Tasmania and is an excellent
miniature tree for the small sheltered
garden.

Eucryphia x nymansensis 'Nymansay'

M Broadly columnar AGM 1993
One of the most spectacular trees when
in flower: a broad column of dark,
evergreen, simple and divided leaves
crowded in August and September with
pure white, yellow-stamened flowers. It is
a hybrid of *E. glutinosa* with the tender *E.
cordifolia* and is a feature of many gardens

in the south and west of the British Isles. There are several similar cultivars, of which 'Nymansay' is easily the best known and most commonly planted.

EUPTELEA
Eupteleaceae

A genus of two species of hardy deciduous trees more notable for their foliage than their flowers. They are suitable for most soils even growing on shallow soils over chalk. The following is the species most usually seen though it is rarely available in the trade.

Euptelea polyandra
S-M Spreading
A relatively fast-growing Japanese tree with a slender stem, occasionally multi-stemmed if allowed. The tiny flowers are without petals: the males crowded into dense clusters of red-anthered stamens, the females less obvious and followed by winged seeds. It is for its leaves that this tree is worth growing. These are rounded, jaggedly toothed and with a tail-like point. They are borne on long slender stalks and are reddish-bronze when young changing to a glossy green. In autumn they often give attractive yellow and red tints.

FAGUS
Fagaceae

Although only a small genus, this contains several of the most impressive hardy, large, deciduous trees in the northern hemisphere. They are of no beauty in flower nor are their fruits of ornamental merit.

Fagus engleriana
M Conical to Rounded
An uncommon Chinese beech with a characteristic multi-stemmed habit, conical when young broadening later. The leaves are a light green, handsomely veined and tapered at both ends, turning gold in autumn. Although this tree does not compete for overall effect with our native species it is, none the less, distinct and ornamental in its own right. It is quite hardy and suitable to most soils.

Fagus orientalis
L Spreading
The "Oriental Beech" from south-east Europe and south-west Asia is equal in merit to our native beech, differing most notably in its fluted stem and larger leaves up to 12cm long turning a rich orange-brown in autumn. It is a handsome free-growing tree enjoying the same conditions as its more familiar relative. I have seen this tree forming extensive forests in Turkey and the Caucasus.

Eucryphia x nymansensis 'Nymansay'

Fagus sylvatica

L Spreading AGM 1993
No praise is too great for our native "Beech". Both in its dappled-green, spring attire and its magnificent autumn gold, it rivals, if not excels, any foreign tree. Even in winter the huge grey columns of a beech wood demand our attention and admiration. A single, well shaped, large specimen represents all one could wish for in a parkland or large garden tree. It is tolerant of most soils, reaching perhaps its finest proportions on the chalk hills of southern England. Elsewhere in the British Isles it has been planted and become naturalised. Because of its shallow roots and heavy shade, the beech is one of the most difficult trees to underplant. It is distributed in the wild throughout Europe and has given rise to many forms and cultivars.

Fagus sylvatica 'Asplenifolia'

L Spreading AGM 1993
The "Fern-leaved Beech" presents a graceful appearance when well grown, its leaves varying in shape from long and narrow to short, and deeply lobed. One of the finest hardy deciduous trees for large gardens and parks, it is magnificent in maturity. Sometimes catalogued under the name *heterophylla*.

Fagus sylvatica 'Aurea Pendula'

S-M Weeping
A slow-growing but desirable tree, usually of slender habit, with steeply weeping branches and leaves clear yellow when young, becoming green later. It does best when grown out of direct sun to prevent scorch, and should be trained to a tall stake or cane to encourage a high crown.

Fagus sylvatica 'Dawyck'

L Conical to Broadly columnar AGM 1993
Slender as a young tree, the "Dawyck Beech" gradually broadens to maturity when it forms an imposing column of green, becoming coppery-gold in autumn. It originated in the gardens at Dawyck, Peebleshire.

Fagus sylvatica 'Dawyck Gold'

M-L Conical to Broadly columnar AGM 1993
Less tight in habit than 'Dawyck', the leaves are suffused yellow when young becoming green later, then golden in autumn. Raised at the Aboretum Trompenburg in Rotterdam.

Fagus sylvatica 'Dawyck Purple'

M-L Columnar to Broadly columnar AGM 1993
Leaves purple, darker when young: a striking purple-leaved columnar tree. Raised at the Aboretum Trompenburg in Rotterdam.

Fagus sylvatica 'Pendula'

M-L Pendulous
There are in cultivation several weeping forms of the beech, but the one most commonly sold in Britain is a magnificent tree with high arching and spreading branches and long pendulous branchlets.

Fagus sylvatica 'Purpurea Pendula'

Fagus sylvatica 'Purple Fountain'

VS-S Pendulous AGM 1993
Raised by the Dutch nurseryman Herman Grootendorst in 1975, this selection is described as a very slender, narrow-crowned tree with a self-supporting leader and drooping branches and branchlets. It is a seedling of 'Purpurea Pendula' with similarly purple but paler leaves.

Fagus sylvatica purpurea

L Spreading
"Purple Beech". Purple-leaved seedlings often arise in the wild and in cultivation. Several have been given clonal names such as 'Riversii' AGM 1993 and 'Swat Magret', with deep purple foliage, and 'Cuprea' the "Copper Beech" with paler foliage. All are popular and impressive in spite of their "unnatural" colour.

Fagus sylvatica 'Purpurea Pendula'

VS-S Weeping
A mushroom-headed tree with strongly weeping branches and dark purple leaves. It is suitable for the small garden and makes a good lawn specimen. Young trees should be trained to a tall stake or cane.

Fagus sylvatica 'Purpurea Tricolor'

L Spreading
An unusual free-growing cultivar in which the purple leaves have a rose-flushed, creamy-pink margin, especially attractive and most noticeable on their emergence in spring. It is most commonly sold as 'Roseomarginata'.

Fagus sylvatica 'Rohanii'

M Columar to Spreading
A curious form, erect-branched when young, leaves narrower than those of the type with boldly toothed and wavy almost crisped margins. In colour they are brownish-purple fading to greenish in time.

Fagus sylvatica 'Zlatia'

M Spreading
Sometimes called the "Golden Beech", the leaves in spring are suffused yellow, a colour which reappears in late summer and autumn.

FIRMIANA
Sterculiaceae

A small genus of deciduous trees and shrubs suitable for most well-drained soils.

Firmiana simplex

M Spreading
A noble foliaged tree, the tall straight stem having a smooth greenish bark and whorled branches. The boldy three- to five-lobed leaves are very large and carried on long stalks alternately towards the ends of the branches. Small yellow flowers are borne in large branched heads in summer, followed by curious fruits with leaf-like lobes upon which are borne two to three pea-sized seeds. One of the most striking trees of its kind, it thrives and flowers best in a continental climate (warm summers and cold dry winters). Unripened young growths are subject to frost damage in a severe winter. Commonly planted on the streets of Beijing (Peking) in China.

FRANKLINIA
Theaceae

A monotypic genus native to Georgia in the United States where it is now considered extinct. Fortunately, it is becoming more available in cultivation. It requires a moist but well-drained preferably lime-free soil and a warm position sheltered from cold winds.

Franklinia alatamaha

S Spreading
A choice deciduous tree often multi-stemmed with bright green glossy-topped leaves which often give rich autumn tints. Flowers are fragrant, similar to those of a

Stuartia, cup-shaped, 7.5cm across with five white petals and a central boss of yellow stamens; they are produced in late summer and autumn. Although hardy, this gree grows and flowers best where warm summers are a regular feature.

FRAXINUS
Oleaceae

A large genus of tough fast-growing trees with oppositely arranged pinnate leaves and small flowers of little beauty except in the Ornus group. They are tolerant of most soils and conditions, including smoke-polluted atmosphere and windswept or coastal areas.

Fraxinus americana

M-L Conical to Spreading
The "White Ash" of eastern North America, a handsome fast-growing tall-domed tree with grey furrowed bark and dark green foliage. The leaves are composed of seven broad leaflets which are pale or greenish-white beneath, sometimes colouring richly in autumn. It is suitable only for medium-sized-to-large gardens and parks.

Fraxinus americana 'Autumn Purple'

M-L Spreading
A fine selection with deep green leaves turning reddish-purple in a good autumn. The autumn colour is more reliable in a continental climate like that of the United States and Europe.

Fraxinus augustifolia

L Spreading
Although native of the west Mediterranean region and North Africa, the "Narrow-leaved Ash" is nearly as hardy and adaptable as our native species, from which it differs in its brown winter buds and narrower leaflets which are entirely without hairs. It is most suited for the southern warmer parts of Britain.

Fraxinus augustifolia 'Raywood'

L Spreading AGM 1993
Although relatively narrow and compact as a young tree, the "Claret Ash" opens out in maturity and therefore is not entirely suitable for planting in confined areas. Its leaves are usually borne in threes and the narrow leaflets turn a glorious plum-purple in autumn. Its best colour performances are in full sun on dry or well-drained soils and is one of the few trees which are seen at their best in eastern England. Commonly grown and sold under the name F. *oxycarpa* 'Raywood'.

Fraxinus chinensis rhyncophylla

M Spreading
An uncommon Chinese ash of the Ornus group producing terminal branched heads of greenish-white flowers in June. It is mainly noted, however, for its lush dark green foliage. A tree worth searching for.

Fraxinus excelsior

L Spreading AGM 1993
The "Common Ash" is a familiar native tree, easily recognized by its rugged furrowed bark and pinnate leaves in summer and its grey twigs and black buds in winter. The fruits – "keys" – hang in bunches throughout summer and autumn. A valuable timber tree, it is vigorous in both stem and root, being a gross feeder, and therefore not suitable for small or densely planted gardens. It is tolerant of most soils and conditions, including polluted atmosphere and windswept or coastal areas.

Fraxinus excelsior 'Allgold'

M-L Spreading
A Dutch selection claimed to be an improvement on 'Jaspidea'. The younger branches are golden-yellow while the leaves, green on emerging, are yellowish in summer and strikingly so in autumn. Fruits few or none.

Fraxinus excelsior 'Altena'

L Conical to Spreading
Vigorous non-fruiting selection with a straight stem and dense, broadly conical crown. Leaves late emerging.

Fraxinus excelsior 'Atlas'

M-L Conical to Spreading
Less vigorous than 'Altena' with straight
stem and a dense ovoid crown. Late
leafing with glossy dark green leaves.
Non-fruiting.

Fraxinus excelsior diversifolia

L Spreading
The "One-leaved Ash", sometimes grown
as 'Monophylla', a curious form in which
the leaves are composed of a single large
leaflet, occasionally two or three. In other
respects it compares with the typical tree
except that it tends to be more conical in
habit when young and is non-fruiting.

Fraxinus excelsior 'Jaspidea'

L Spreading AGM 1993
Known as the "Golden Ash", the golden
twigs of this large vigorous tree are most
obvious in winter, whilst in autumn the
leaves turn to clear yellow.

Fraxinus excelsior 'Pendula'

M Pendulous AGM 1993
The "Weeping Ash" is one of the most
commonly encountered weeping trees, its
mound-like form being found in many
parks and large gardens where it was
once commonly planted, especially by the
Victorians, to form arbours. Young
specimens should be trained to a tall stake
or cane to obtain a high crown.

Fraxinus excelsior 'Westhof's Glorie'

L Conical to Spreading AGM 1993
A popular selection of Dutch origin much
planted along roadsides in Holland and
elsewhere. It is vigorous with a straight
stem and a dense rather ovoid crown
broadening later. The late emerging
leaves are a glossy dark green while fruits
are few.

Fraxinus latifolia

L Spreading
A strong-growing tree, the "Oregon Ash"
has large dark green leaves with five to
nine leaflets which, like the shoot, are
covered in a pale brown. It is rare in
cultivation in Britain where it is quite
hardy and ornamental.

top: *Fraxinus ornus*
bottom: *Fraxinus velutina*

73

Fraxinus ornus

M Rounded to Spreading AGM 1993
Native to southern Europe and western
Asia, the "Manna Ash" or "Flowering
Ash" has all the good qualities of the
common sort with, in addition, attractive
panicles of whitish flowers in May. The
resultant "keys" are warm brown in
autumn. It makes a neat tree with a
dense, rounded head. A form of sugar is
obtained from the sap of the stems.

Fraxinus pensylvanica 'Zundert'

L Spreading
A non-fruiting Dutch selection of the
North American Green Ash. Vigorous in
growth with a straight stem and large,
glossy green leaves, greyish-green
beneath turning rich yellow in a good
autumn. Very adaptable especially on
"difficult" sites.

Fraxinus sieboldiana

S Spreading
An attractive slow-growing Japanese tree
of the Ornus group suitable for small
gardens. Both branchlets and buds are
greyish and downy, whilst the leaves are
composed of five dull green abruptly
pointed leaflets. The creamy-white
flowers are borne in crowded heads in
June followed by deep-purple shining
fruits in dense bunches. It is an
ornamental and unusual tree for the
connoisseur's lawn. Trees grown under
the name F. mariesii also belong here.

Fraxinus velutina

S-M Spreading
The "Arizona Ash" is one of the best
trees for tolerating hot and cold extremes
of temperature, as instanced by its
success in northern Iran as well as in its
native country. In drier climates than
ours, the bark is a striking silvery grey. In
the British Isles it is a tree perhaps best
suited to the eastern half of England. The
young shoots and leaves are covered with
a greyish down and the leaves colour
butter-yellow in autumn. It is native to
south-western USA and Mexico.

GENISTA
Leguminosae

A large genus principally of shrubs but the following species can be encouraged to form a superb small weeping tree.

Genista aetensis

S. Weeping AGM 1993
The "Mount Etna Broom", a hardy, easy
to grow broom with arching and weeping
rush-like branchlets "dripping" with small
fragrant yellow pea-flowers in late
summer. Grown by nurserymen in
containers as it does not like disturbing
once planted. It grows best in a well-
drained sunny position. Plants should be
trained early if a single or multi-stemmed
tree is required.

GLEDITSIA
Leguminosae

The most notable feature about this small genus of deciduous trees is the usually formidable armour of the trunk and branches. This takes the form of vicious large, often branched spines. The leaves are much divided into leaflets, giving them a frond-like appearance, whilst the insignificant greenish flowers are succeeded by flattened pods which drape the branches in autumn. They are fast-growing trees tolerant of most soils (except water-logged) and situations, preferring dry sunny regions.

Gleditsia triacanthos

L Spreading
The "Honey Locust" is one of the best
trees for large gardens and parks in cities,
especially where atmospheric pollution is
a problem. Its fiercely armed stems,
feathery leaves turning yellow in autumn,
and large pods, often 40cm or more long,
make this a most interesting and desirable
tree, particularly in the east of England
and in the south of France. It is also
shade-tolerant, in which situations the
stems are less thorny. It is a native of
North America. Two excellent selections
with ascending branches are
'Shademaster' and 'Skyline'.

Gleditsia triacanthos 'Bujotii'

VS Pendulous
An elegant weeping tree with slender branches and leaves with narrow leaflets often mottled white, suitable for the smallest gardens.

Gleditsia triacanthos inermis

M Spreading
A distinct form with thornless stems and branches and an open spreading crown casting light dappled shade.

Gleditsia triancanthos 'Ruby Lace'

M Spreading
Similar in growth and habit to 'Sunburst' but instead of being yellow the young foliage is purplish-bronze.

Gleditsia triacanthos 'Sunburst'

M Spreading AGM 1993
A beautiful form with spineless stems and bright-yellow young foliage throughout the year. Where it flourishes, it is one of the most effective golden trees. Quite unlike *Robinia pseudoacacia* 'Frisia' in effect.

GRISELINIA
Cornaceae

A small genus of evergreen trees and shrubs native of New Zealand and South America. Male and female flowers are borne on separate plants but are of limited ornamental merit.

Griselinia littoralis

S-M Dome-shaped to Spreading
AGM 1993
A handsome evergreen tree of dense bushy habit when young, thickly clothed with bold leathery leaves of pale apple-green or yellow-green colour, most suited to the milder areas of Britain and Ireland, where it is capable of making a substantial tree in time. It is commonly multi-stemmed from the base but can be trained to a single stem initially if required. Tolerant of sea winds and salt spray in the south and west, it is adaptable to most soils including shallow soils over chalk; and once established, it will tolerate shade or drought.

†*Griselinia littoralis* 'Variegata'

S Dome-shaped to Spreading
Less hardy than the green-leaved type, this cultivar is none the less well worth growing in warmer areas of Britain and Ireland. The leaves are grey-green and dark green, irregularly margined creamy white. Young leaves are dark green with a golden margin. There are also forms in which the leaves have a central variegation, but some of these are unstable and have a tendency to revert.

Gleditsia triacanthos 'Sunburst'

GYMNOCLADUS
Leguminosae

A small genus of deciduous trees with large, handsome much divided leaves.

Gymnocladus dioica
L Spreading
A hardy, late-leafing tree with a deeply fissured grey, reddish-tinged bark. The stout younger shoots are covered with a blue-white bloom, whilst the bold, twice-divided leaves may grow to as much as 90cm long and 60cm across. A tough and adaptable, easily recognised eastern American tree, it is slow-growing in Britain where it lacks the long hot summers of its native country. The small greenish-white male and female flowers are borne on separate trees in branched heads in late May to early June (those of the female scented). They are followed in October (on female trees) by long, drooping, leathery reddish-brown pods containing a few large hard-shelled seeds embedded in a sweet sticky pulp. The seeds crushed were used as coffee substitute by the early American settlers, hence the common name for this tree "Kentucky Coffee Tree".

HALESIA
Styracaceae

A small genus of hardy deciduous trees mostly native to the south-east United States and best suited to moist soils in sun or half-shade. The pendant white bell-shaped flowers in spring have earned for them the name 'snowdrop' or 'silverbell' trees. The green pear-shaped normally four-winged fruits which follow hang on the branches into winter.

Halesia carolina
S Spreading
The "Carolina Silverbell", a charming hardy flowering tree of shrubby habit when young, later developing a wide spreading habit often with several main stems from low down. It can, however, be trained to a single stem if desired. The leaves often provide pale yellow autumn colour but it is the flowers which most please: these are carried in clusters along the shoots of the previous year in May. Also known as *H. tetraptera*, a synonym.

Halesia diptera magniflora
S Spreading
Similar to the last in habit and leaf but with larger flowers and fruits with only two wings. Like *H. carolina*, it is shrubby when young and requires careful pruning to encourage a tree-like habit. It is worth the effort, however, as the larger flowers of a purer white are exceptional in May. It performs best in drier areas of Britain and grows to perfection in some continental gardens.

Halesia monticola
S-M Conical to Spreading
The "Mountain Silverbell" is perhaps the one most suited to British conditions. It makes a larger tree than *H. carolina* and differs also in its larger flowers and fruits. It is usually represented in British cultivation by the variety *vestita* AGM 1993, a vigorous tree with leaves felted beneath when young remaining downy into maturity.

Halesia monticola 'Rosea'
S-M Conical to Spreading
Similar in habit to the last but with pink-flushed flowers.

HOHERIA
Malvaceae

A small genus of both deciduous and evergreen trees and shrubs from New Zealand. They are best suited to the warmer and milder areas of the British Isles, where they are beautiful summer-flowering subjects.

Hoheria sexstylosa
S-M Broadly columnar AGM 1993
Although requiring a sheltering wall in all but the mildest areas of the British Isles,

this superb fast-growing evergreen tree is worthy of a place in any garden. Its erect habit, arching or pendant branchlets and narrow, jaggedly-toothed, glossy green leaves offset the clouds of white flowers in July and August.

Hoheria sexstylosa 'Stardust'

S-M Broadly columnar
A new selection which appears hardier than most with neater leaves and showers of starry flowers from an early age.

HOVENIA
Rhamnaceae

A monotypic genus, hardy except in severe winters or in cold inland areas. Suitable for well-drained soils, preferably in a sunny sheltered position.

Hovenia dulcis

S-M Spreading
Reasonably hardy in Britain, the "Raisin Tree" from China and Japan bears three-veined shining green leaves up to 15cm long. The common name refers to the red fleshy flower stalks which become swollen, sweet and edible after flowering. The flowers themselves are small and of little ornamental merit. A handsome small tree for the large courtyard or sheltered lawn, it fruits most satisfactorily in warmer climates.

IDESIA
Flacourtiaceae

An interesting monotypic genus native to China and Japan.

Idesia polycarpa

M Spreading
The main consistent feature of this tree is its large handsome heart-shaped leaves, which are blue-green beneath and carried on long red-flushed stalks. The fragrant though insignificant greenish-yellow flowers are followed (in a good year) by

top: Hoheria sexstylosa 'Stardust'
bottom: Idesia polycarpa

large clusters of pea-shaped green turning to deep red berries, but only on female trees. Trees of both sexes are required and even then a long hot summer is normally essential to berry formation. It prefers a moist but well-drained soil.

Often represented in British cultivation by the variety *vestita* with leaves downy beneath, both trees perform best in a continental climate of warm summers and cold dry winters. It is commonly planted in north-east American cities such as New York where the colourful fruits can be seen on female trees even in winter.

ILEX
Aquifoliaceae

The "Hollies" are a large and varied genus, containing both evergreen and deciduous species, many of which in general appearance appear quite unrelated to the familiar "English Holly". Male and female flowers are generally borne on separate trees and this means that trees of both sexes must be present before berries are produced. In districts where hollies are common there is generally no problem. The hollies here described are popular both as ornamental and utility trees. They are tolerant of a great range of soils and conditions, including atmospheric pollution and coastal blasts. The majority develop into tall conical or columnar trees but may be pruned in July or August if growth proves too vigorous. If a formal habit is desired, trees may be clipped (using secateurs) at the same time. Hollies are tolerant of shade, but then growth is usually more open and less compact and (on female trees) fruiting less abundant.

Ilex x altaclerensis

M-L Broadly columnar
Commonly referred to as the "Highclere Holly", these hybrids between forms of the "English Holly" and the tender *I. perado* from Madeira are comparatively fast-growing evergreens. They are, however, less hardy than cultivars of the "English Holly" in cold northern areas of Europe. Even in Holland these hybrids are subject to frost damage, whereas in Britain they are generally considered hardy.

Ilex x altaclerensis 'Belgica Aurea'

S-M Conical to Broadly columnar
AGM 1993
A strong-growing, erect holly of fine proportions clothed with long smooth or few-spined leaves which are green, marbled paler green and grey and boldly margined cream. Berries are produced on older trees freely in a good year. The variegation on young plants, particularly in winter, is more yellow than silver. Also grown, though wrongly, under the name 'Silver Sentinel'. One of the hardiest of this group, even in Holland.

Ilex x altaclerensis 'Camelliifolia'

S-M Conical to Broadly columnar
AGM 1993
A superb holly when well grown, its purple shoots and long, dark glossy green, almost spineless leaves being enough in themselves to make it a must for the large garden. The large red berries therefore come as a pleasant bonus.

Ilex x altaclerensis 'Golden King'

M Conical to Broadly columnar
AGM 1993
One of the most effective and reliable variegated hollies. Of strong growth, its smooth or few spined leaves are green with a bold yellow margin and are effective both alone and when accompanied by the comparatively large red berries.

Ilex x altaclerensis 'Hodginsii'

M-L Conical to Broadly columnar
AGM 1993
This is perhaps the most commonly planted of the hybrids, especially in the north of England where it was and still is favoured for city as well as seaside planting. It is a male cultivar, and though no berries are produced, its boldly spined blackish-green glossy topped leaves are handsomely borne on purple shoots. As the tree matures, the leaves lose much of their armature.

Ilex x altaclerensis 'Lawsoniana'

M Conical to Broadly columnar
AGM 1993
A bright and attractive holly, the dark green leaves marked with a large splash of golden yellow. Unfortunately, it tends to throw out green-leaved reversions and these must be pruned out as soon as they appear.

Ilex x altaclerensis 'Ripley Gold'

S-M Conical to Broadly columnar
A female cultivar with conspicuous gold-blotched leaves and large red berries, it is a sport of 'Golden King' originating in a garden in Ripley, Hampshire.

Ilex x altaclerensis 'Wilsonii'

S-M Conical to Broadly columnar
AGM 1993
A bold foliaged female holly, the leaves broad, attractively veined and spine toothed. The relatively large red fruits are usually freely borne. Leaves on older especially fruiting branches are generally less spiny.

Ilex aquifolium

M Broadly columnar to Spreading
The "English Holly" is one of the most popular and familiar of all evergreens. As a utility plant it is exceptional, tolerating almost any soil and situation it is possible to find in the British Isles. The red berries borne on female trees during autumn and winter are perhaps the best known of all ornamental fruits, being especially associated with Christmas. It is a native of Europe and North Africa and is commonly orcharded for cutting in parts of North America. There are innumerable cultivars, varying in sex, habit, colour and shape of leaf and colour and freedom of berry.

Ilex aquifolium 'Amber'

M Conical to Broadly columnar
A dense bushy holly with dark green prickly leaves and bold amber or orange berries. Occured as a seedling in a Hampshire nursery hedge.

top: Ilex aquifolium 'Argentea Pendula'
bottom: Ilex x altaclerensis 'Lawsoniana'

Ilex aquifolium
'Argentea Marginata'

M Conical to Broadly columnar AGM 1993
The common silver-margined holly,
normally represented in cultivation by a
female clone with attractive berries.

Ilex aquifolium
'Argentea Pendula'

S Weeping
Known as "Perry's Weeping", this
splendid holly forms a broad mound of
close-packed weeping branches with
silver-margined leaves and abundant
berries. Young specimens need to be
trained to a tall stake or cane to
encourage a high crown.

Ilex aquifolium
'Aurea Marginata'

M Conical to Broadly columnar
This attractive holly is represented by
several clones in cultivation, male and
female. All have golden-yellow margined
leaves, the female with red berries.

Ilex aquifolium 'Bacciflava'

M Conical to Broadly columnar
"Yellow-berried Holly". A handsome holly
with dark green spiny leaves and bright
yellow berries usually freely born.

Ilex aquifolium
'Golden Milkmaid'

S Conical to Broadly columnar
A striking holly in which the green leaves
bear a central splash of gold. Both male
and female clones are in cultivation and
are sometimes found under the name
'Aurea Medio-picta'.

Ilex aquifolium
'Golden Queen'

M Conical to Broadly columnar
AGM 1993
Perhaps the finest of the golden-
variegated hollies, with large boldly
spined leaves of deep green, marbled and
shaded pale green and grey and strongly
margined yellow. In spite of its name it
produces no berries, being a male clone.

top: Ilex aquifolium 'Pendula'
bottom: Ilex aquifolium 'Ovata Aurea'

Ilex aquifolium 'Green Pillar'

S-M Columar AGM 1993
A distinct female holly of narrowly
columnar growth – at least while young.
Green prickly leaves and red berries
together with its strict habit make this
suitable for smaller gardens.

Ilex aquifolium 'Handsworth New Silver'

S-M Conical to Broadly columnar
AGM 1993
This is a splendid silver-variegated holly
of good habit, with purple shoots,
comparatively narrow, silver-margined
leaves and heavy crops of berries. One of
the best variegated hollies for general
cultivation.

Ilex aquifolium 'J.C. van Tol'

M Conical to Broadly columnar
AGM 1993
This outstanding clone of Dutch origin is,
without doubt, one of the best berrying
hollies for general cultivation. The leaves
are almost spineless and dark glossy
green in appearance.

Ilex aquifolium 'Madame Briot'

S-M Concial to Broadly columar
AGM 1993
A lovely holly with purple shoots, and
strongly spined leaves which are dark
green, mottled and shaded yellow and
grey with a golden-yellow margin. In
addition it produces large crops of berries.

Ilex aquifolium 'Ovata Aurea'

S Conical to Broadly columnar
An uncommon but highly desirable holly
for the small garden. Of slow growth, it
develops a neat compact habit with
purple-black twigs and prettily scalloped,
spineless, deep green, gold-margined
leaves. It is a male clone and does not
produce berries.

Ilex aquifolium 'Pendula'

S Weeping
This holly forms a broad mound of

top: Ilex aquifolium 'Madame Briot'
centre: Ilex aquifolium 'Bacciflava'
bottom: Ilex aquifolium 'Handsworth New Silver'

weeping close-packed stems clothed with dark green spiny leaves and inundated with red berries. A splendid holly for a large lawn. Young specimens should be trained up a tall stake or cane to produce high crown.

Ilex aquifolium 'Pyramidalis'

S Conical AGM 1993
Next to 'J.C. van Tol', this is probably the most reliable holly for berries. These are produced in large quantities, even when other female hollies are having an off-year. The leaves are variable in shape and are often spineless. 'Pyramidalis' alone or planted with 'Pyramidalis Fructuluteo' makes an impressive informal screen.

Ilex aquifolium 'Pyramidalis Fructuluteo'

M Conical AGM 1993
Similar in every respect to the last but berries bright yellow. A strong upright holly worth planting in isolation with red berried hollies for contrast.

Ilex aquifolium 'Silver Milkmaid'

S Conical to Broadly columnar
AGM 1993
A striking female holly whose boldly spined dark green leaves have a creamy-white central splash. It is free fruiting in a good year. Sometimes catalogued under the name 'Argentea Medio-picta'.

Ilex aquifolium 'Silver Queen'

S-M Conical to Broadly columnar
AGM 1993
A distinctive male form with broad, deep green, silver-margined and regularly spined leaves carried on deep purple shoots. It makes a handsome pollinator for berrying hollies.

Ilex x koehneana

M Conical to Broadly columnar
A strong-growing bold foliaged holly, a hybrid between the English Holly and the Japanese Holly (*Ilex latifolia*). The leaves are large, glossy green and fringed with small spine-tipped teeth, while female plants produce masses of glossy large red berries which last well into winter. It is commonly represented in cultivation by the cultivar 'Chestnut Leaf' AGM 1993, while female plants produce glossy large berries which last well into winter.

Ilex pedunculosa

S Conical to Rounded
A most distinctive and attractive holly with slender pointed non-spiny leaves of a shining bright green above. Bright red berries are borne on slender pendulous stalks on female trees in autumn. It is hardy and elegant, preferring a moist but well-drained lime-free soil sheltered from strong winds.

JUGLANS
Juglandaceae

A small genus of deciduous trees, mostly fast-growing, with often large pinnate leaves borne alternately on the shoots. They are unfussy as to soil and situation but are best planted where late spring frosts cannot damage the emerging foliage.

Juglans ailantifolia

M Spreading to Dome-shaped
The "Japanese Walnut" is easily recognised by its normally broad-spreading habit and large glandular hairy leaves which may reach 60cm long – longer on young trees. It is hardy enough for the British climate but requires plenty of space in which to develop: a bold-foliaged tree with attractive male catkins, too little planted in general cultivation. The edible nuts, are rarely satisfactory in British conditions, lacking no doubt the summer warmth necessary to ripen them.

Juglans nigra

L Spreading to Dome-shaped AGM 1993
The "Black Walnut" is a splendid fast-growing tree of noble proportions, with a characteristic deeply furrowed bark and large handsome leaves. It is a native of the eastern USA and has few rivals for its combination of stately habit and bold foliage. A cut-leaved version 'Laciniata' is even more desirable but rarely available.

Juglans regia

M-L Spreading AGM 1993

A familiar tree in parks and estates, the "Common" or "English Walnut" provides one of the most valuable of all nuts, especially popular at Christmas time. It is a distinctive tree with its grey bark and pinnate leaves which emit an acrid aroma when bruised. When cultivated for its nuts it is worth obtaining one of the later leafing French cultivars of which 'Franquette' and 'Mayette' are two of the best known. 'Purpurea' is an uncommon form of German origin with reddish-purple leaves of a lovely shade.

Juglans regia 'Laciniata'

M Spreading to Dome-shaped

An unusual and attractive form of slow growth in which the leaflets are deeply cut and the branchlets somewhat pendulous.

KALOPANAX
Araliaceae

A monotypic genus from north-east Asia thriving best in a continental climate but hardy enough and quite satisfactory in Britain. It does best in full sun in a moist but well-drained soil.

Kalopanax pictus

M Spreading

A hardy deciduous tree rather gaunt in habit when young but improving with age. The young branches are armed with yellowish prickles replaced by short broad-based spines on the bark of the main stem. The handsome large maple-like five- to seven-lobed leaves are borne alternately on stalks even longer than the blade. In late summer the small white flowers are borne in large flattened heads and, if conditions are suitable, are followed by small black fruits. Not often seen in private gardens, this interesting tree is well worth growing for its bold foliage. Even more exotic in effect is the variety *maximowiczii* in which the leaf stalks are reddish and the larger blades are deeply lobed almost to the base.

top: *Ilex x koehneana*
bottom: *Koelreuteria paniculata*

KOELREUTERIA
Sapindaceae

A small genus of deciduous trees thriving in full sun and a well-drained soil. They are noted for their handsome compound foliage, flower and fruit.

†Koelreuteria bipinnata
S-M Spreading
The "Chinese Flame Tree" is much less hardy than the better known *K. paniculata* and is best seen in warmer countries. It is especially good in Mediterranean gardens. It differs from the next in its larger leaves which are much more divided as well as in its rose-pink fruit capsules. It makes a splendid lawn specimen for exotic effect.

Koelreuteria paniculata
S-M Spreading AGM 1993
Known as "Goldenrain Tree", "China Tree" or "Pride of India", this beautiful hardy, wide-spreading tree is best suited for the medium-to-large-sized garden or park. Its deeply and prettily divided leaves turn bright yellow in autumn, while the large terminal panicles of yellow flowers in July and August are followed by conspicuous green bladder-like fruits. This is a splendid tree, thriving in a well-drained soil and full sun. It is native to North China and Mongolia.

Koelreuteria paniculata 'Fastigiata'
S-M Columnar
Suitable for restricted areas this columnar form has one major drawback: its reluctance to flower – in Britain certainly.

+ LABURNOCYTISUS
Leguminosae

A bigeneric hybrid between a laburnum and a broom (Cytisus). Its requirements and merits are similar to those of the former.

+Laburnocytisus adamii
S Vase-shaped to Spreading

A hardy deciduous tree, a graft hybrid between *Laburnum anagyroides* and the "Dwarf Purple Broom" *Cytisus purpureus*, raised in France in 1825. The ascending crown is a curious mixture, some branches bearing the yellow-tasselled laburnum flowers, others the flesh-pink tassels of the hybrid, while in addition there are scattered "witches broom"-like clusters of cytisus growth with rose-purple flowers. When in flower, and only then, this tree is a colourful sight and a guaranteed talking point among visitors. It is just as poisonous as its Laburnum parent.

LABURNUM
Leguminosae

A small genus of hardy deciduous trees and shrubs with trifoliolate leaves and pendulous tapering "chains" of yellow pea-flowers in late spring or early summer. All parts of these trees are poisonous especially the seeds, and those with small children in the family are best advised not to plant them in their garden. Although comparatively short lived, the laburnums are absolutely reliable in flower and are adaptable to most soils and situations. They flower more freely in an open sunny situation and are particularly good on shallow soils over chalk.

Laburnum alpinum
S Spreading
A native of southern and central Europe and cultivated since the late sixteenth century, this is perhaps the most attractive of the laburnums as a tree, developing a characteristic and picturesque gnarled appearance in maturity. The lush, glossy, deep green leaves are parted in early June by the conspicuous hanging chains of fragrant yellow flowers.

Laburnum alpinum 'Pendulum'
VS Weeping
A distinct form of dome-shaped habit with steeply weeping and richly leafy branches, suitable for the smallest garden.

Laburnum x watereri 'Vossii'

S Spreading AGM 1993
A hybrid between *L. alpinum* and *L. anagyroides*, this "Golden Chain" is certainly the most spectacular in flower, when the long chains of fragrant yellow flowers thickly drape the spreading branches in early June. It produces little seed and therefore is preferable to the species for general cultivation.

†LAGERSTROEMIA
Lythraceae

A large genus of both evergreen and deciduous trees and shrubs, requiring a warm sunny, well-drained position. The following is the only species in general cultivation.

Lagerstroemia indica

S Spreading to Rounded
The "Crape Myrtle" is a small deciduous tree, sometimes seen as a large shrub, the trunk and main stems displaying a most attractive mottled grey, pink and cinnamon bark. The small leaves are rather privet-like in appearance and often colour effectively in late autumn. The beautiful, crinkly-petalled flowers are borne in panicles at the ends of the current year's shoots, and though formed in summer do not open until late summer and autumn. In colour they vary from lilac-pink to red or even white, a well-shaped tree in full flower presenting a magnificent sight. This superb flowering tree is a feature of many continental cities and towns, particularly in southern and eastern Europe. In order to flower well, it requires a long, continuously hot summer and, in the British Isles, is perhaps only worth considering in southern and south-eastern regions of England – even here, against a sunny, sheltered wall. It is a native of China and Korea.

†LAURELIA
Lauraceae

A genus of only three evergreen trees of which the following is only worth considering for milder areas of Britain and Ireland, especially in woodland gardens of the south-west where good sized specimens are not uncommon.

Laurelia serrata

S-M Dome-shaped or Broadly columnar
A distinctive tree with its leathery, glossy green, saw-toothed leaves which are pleasantly aromatic when bruised and borne in pairs on four-angled downy green branchlets. It grows best in a moist but well-drained sheltered position in sun or shade and is particularly suited to woodland cultivation.

Laburnum x watereri 'Vossii'

LAURUS
Lauraceae

This genus comprises two species of evergreen trees of which only the following is at all well known and then mainly for the culinary value of its foliage. Male and female flowers are borne on separate trees. The small creamy-yellow male flowers occur in dense clusters, crowding the second year shoots in April.

Laurus nobilis

S-M Broadly columnar AGM 1993
The "Bay Tree" or "Bay Laurel" is an excellent evergreen, particularly when used in formal surroundings. Its leathery, spicily aromatic leaves are well known to the housewife and cook. Less familiar are the shining black, cherry-like fruits borne on female trees during summer. It was the leafy sprigs of this tree which formed the victor's crown of the Greeks and Romans. It is a native of the Mediterranean region and will grow in most soils but is subject to winter damage in cold inland areas.

Laurus nobilis 'Augustifolia'

S Broadly columnar
The "Willow-leaved Bay", a distinct and unusual form with narrow willow-like leaves.

Laurus nobilis 'Aurea'

S Broadly columnar to Dome-shaped AGM 1993
A striking form with golden-yellow leaves, particularly effective during winter and spring when it gives a welcome splash of bright colour. One of the best golden-foliaged evergreens, though surprisingly little planted.

LIGUSTRUM
Oleaceae

The privets are a small but variable group of trees and shrubs tolerant of most soils and situations. Many people think only of the hedging "Privet"

top: Laurus nobilis
bottom: Laurus nobilis 'Aurea'

(L. ovalifolium) *when the name arises, which is a pity, as there are several first-class species well worth growing for foliage, flowers and fruit, the latter however, with the leaves, are poisonous.*

Ligustrum lucidum

M Rounded to Spreading AGM 1993
The "Tree Privet" is a superb evergreen tree from China, suitable for a special position. The comparatively large, glossy, dark green, leathery leaves are borne in a dense, rounded head which, in late summer and early autumn, is transformed by the panicles of creamy-white flowers which terminate the shoots into a striking display noticeable from a considerable distance. Large specimens develop an attractive grey fluted trunk. Although relatively hardy, it is not suited to consistently cold inland areas or exposed situations. It is seen at its best in warm areas, especially in southern Britain where it should be given a sunny, well-drained position. It is excellent on chalk soils and makes a splendidly impressive specimen on a large lawn.

Ligustrum lucidum 'Excelsum Superbum'

S-M Rounded to Spreading AGM 1993
A striking form in which the leaves are mottled and margined creamy-white and yellow. It is less hardy than the type and is best planted where cold blasts cannot singe the young spring growths.

LIQUIDAMBAR
Hamamelidaceae

A small genus of deciduous trees with usually five-lobed leaves colouring richly in autumn. The flowers are insignificant. They thrive best in a moist but well-drained soil and are not suitable for dry shallow chalk soils. Being native to regions enjoying warm summers, they are not ideally suited to northern Britain except in warmer pockets or microclimates.

Ligustrum lucidum

Liquidambar formosana

M-L Conical to Spreading
The Chinese version of the American "Sweet Gum" is less commonly seen in British cultivation but it can be just as spectacular in autumn. The dark green leaves have three broad triangular lobes and are capable of yellow, orange or red tints before they are shed. Even better is the form occasionally offered by nurserymen as *monticola*.

Liquidambar styraciflua

L Conical to Spreading AGM 1993
One of the finest hardy trees in autumn when the handsomely lobed leaves turn to shades of yellow, orange, crimson or purple. It is occasionally mistaken for a maple (*Acer*) but the alternately arranged leaves easily distinguish it, those of a maple being opposite. It is a native of the eastern USA where it is known as the "Sweet Gum" from the gum-like amber sap.

Liquidambar styraciflua 'Lane Roberts'

L Conical to Spreading AGM 1993
A fine form selected for its reliable autumn colour which is a rich dark crimson-red.

Liquidambar styraciflua 'Silver King'

M Conical to Spreading
An attractive form with leaves margined creamy-white becoming rose and purple flushed in autumn.

Liquidambar styraciflua 'Variegata'

M Conical to Spreading
A spectacular tree in autumn when the yellow striped and mottled leaves exhibit a rose and purple suffusion.

Liquidambar styraciflua 'Worplesdon'

L Conical to Spreading AGM 1993
Another well proven selection displaying rich autumn tints, reliable and free-growing in the right situation.

top: Liquidambar styraciflua (detail)
bottom: Liquidambar styraciflua

LIRIODENDRON
Magnoliaceae

Only two species of deciduous tree represent this interesting genus. Both are hardy and fast-growing, happy in most soils including those on chalk, but thriving best in a deep, moist, well-drained loam. The leaves of these trees are like no others in cultivation.

Liriodendron chinense

M-L Spreading

Less often seen than its American counterpart, the "Chinese Tulip Tree" is similar in most respects except that the leaves are generally larger especially on young trees, more narrowly waisted and blue-green beneath. The flowers are smaller and more green than yellow, lacking the blue-green band of the other. It makes a similarly handsome tree for a lawn or border though it is less commonly available commercially.

Liriodendron tulipifera

L Spreading AGM 1993

The "Tulip Tree" is, without doubt, one of the finest ornamental trees in the temperate regions. It is one of the select band of trees to which the description 'stately' can be applied. Its peculiar four-lobed, saddle-shaped leaves are attractive at all times, especially in autumn when they turn to butter-yellow. The common name for this tree refers to the cup-shaped flowers which are yellowish-green in colour, marked orange and blue-green within. These are produced at the ends of the branches in June and July, but not on very young trees. It is a native of eastern North America.

Liriodendron tulipifera 'Aureomarginatum'

L Spreading AGM 1993

A striking form in which the leaves possess a broad border of yellow, brighter in spring and becoming yellowish-green by late summer.

top: Liriodendron tulipifera (young tree)
bottom: Liriodendron tulipifera (mature tree)

Liriodendron tulipifera 'Fastigiatum'

M Conical to Broadly columnar
AGM 1993
A comparatively fast-growing tree,
narrow when young, broadening with
age. It is particularly suited for medium-
sized gardens and is especially effective in
autumn when it stands like a pillar of
gold. 'Arnold' is a more compact selection
made at the Arnold Arboretum in
Massachussets.

LOMATIA
Proteaceae

A small genus of evergreen trees and shrubs of the
Protea *family from the southern hemisphere with
curious spidery flowers in dense spikes or loosely
branched heads. They flourish best in a moist but
well-drained lime-free loam in a sunny sheltered
situation.*

†Lomatia ferruginea

S Broadly columnar to Spreading
A choice erect-branched tree with rich
reddish-brown velvety shoots clothed
with large, deeply divided fern-like
evergreen leaves. The buff and scarlet
flowers are produced in short dense
spikes during summer. It is a handsome
foliage tree with curious exotic-looking
flowers, only suitable for the mildest
areas of Britain and Ireland, mainly in the
south-west.

†LYONOTHAMNUS
Rosaceae

*A monotypic genus, native to several Pacific
islands off the California coast.*

Lyonothamnus floribundus

S-M Conical to Spreading
This species is usually represented in
cultivation by the variety *aspleniifolius*, an
exotic-looking evergreen tree with
reddish-brown and grey cord-like bark
and curiously divided fern-like leaves

top: Lomatia ferruginea
bottom: Magnolia campbellii

glossy dark green above. The small white flowers are borne in large branched terminal heads in summer but not on young trees. When happy, this tree grows vigorously with lush foliage, but it does demand a warm sunny sheltered position and in Britain certainly is normally grown against a south or south-west facing wall.

MAACKIA
Luguminosae

A small genus of hardy deciduous trees grown principally for their young foliage. They are suitable for most soils, preferably in an open or sunny situation. Leaves are pinnate like those of an ash.

Maackia amurensis
S Spreading
An uncommon tree in cultivation grown more for its young foliage than its flowers which are small, dull white and packed in stiff, erect, spike-like racemes in summer. By contrast, the emerging leaves are striking in their silvery hairy nature, later expanding and turning green.

MACLURA
Moraceae

A monotypic genus from North America related to the Mulberry (Morus). The insignificant male and female flowers are borne on separate trees and both sexes are required to produce fruit.

Maclura pomifera
M Broadly columnar to Spreading
The "Osage Orange", so called because of its large orange-shaped fruits. It is a hardy, tough, deciduous tree with thorny branches and glossy, green, long pointed leaves which often turn an attractive pale yellow in autumn. Female flowers when pollinated produce rounded inedible fruits the size of a cricket ball with a green or yellowish-green pimply rind. Rarely seen in British cultivation, this tree is well worth considering for difficult sites as it is adaptable to most soils.

MAGNOLIA
Magnoliaceae

The magnolias are among the elite of flowering trees and shrubs. In beauty and poise of bloom they have few rivals and yet they are by and large a most amenable and accommodating race. In their ranks are both evergreen and deciduous species and hybrids, most of which enjoy a moist but well-drained, loam and a sunny position. On some magnolias, flowers are borne in late winter or spring before the leaves, while others flower with the leaves during summer. These are often followed by crimson fruit clusters. Most are hardy and unless otherwise mentioned prefer a lime-free soil. *Likewise, those here described are deciduous unless otherwise indicated.*

Magnolia acuminata
M-L Conical to Spreading
Known as the "Cucumber Tree", in reference to the shape of its young fruits, this fast-growing species from the eastern USA is mainly valued for its handsome large foliage. The comparatively small, dull, greenish-yellow flowers are produced with the leaves during May and June.

Magnolia campbellii
M-L Spreading
The Queen of the Himalayan forests, this deciduous tree is the pride and joy of many a famous garden in the milder areas of Britain and Ireland. Although hardy enough in itself, the magnificent bowl-shaped pink flowers (white on trees in the wild), opening in February or March depending on the season, are subject to frost damage and it is, therefore, not a wise choice for gardens in colder areas. Seedling trees can take up to 30 years to flower, and it is best to choose a grafted specimen of a selected form of which several are available from specialist growers.

Magnolia campbellii 'Charles Raffill'
M-L Spreading AGM 1993
A superb and reliable hybrid between *M.*

campbellii and its Chinese subspecies mollicomata. It is vigorous in growth producing (earlier in life then *M. campbellii*), large goblet-shaped flowers which are deep rose-pink in bud expanding to rose-purple outside, white with a pinkish-purple marginal flush on the inside. They are at their best in February or March before the leaves.

Magnolia cylindrica
S Spreading AGM 1993
A hardy deciduous magnolia with handsome foliage and exquisite white goblet-shaped flowers before the leaves April. A rarely planted but fast rising sta for general cultivation, it is now becoming more available through specialist nurserymen. It makes an ideal lawn specimen.

Magnolia dawsoniana
M Conical to Spreading
A magnificent Chinese species of conical habit when young. The large goblet-shaped flowers are pale rose, suffused purple on the outside, opening before the leaves in spring but not on young specimens. It does best in a sheltered (especially woodland) situation, preferabl in full sun. It also shows some tolerance to lime in the soil.

†Magnolia delavayi
S-M Dome-shaped to Spreading
One of the most handsome evergreen foliage trees in British cultivation, but suitable only for a warm sheltered position preferably against a wall or in a woodland garden, even in the south and south-west. The large, rigidly leathery sea-green leaves are ideal backing for the parchment-coloured, creamy-white flowers which appear fleetingly in late summer and early autumn, and even the are only fully open and most powerfully scented at night. It normally develops a bushy multi-stemmed habit and is one of the few magnolias tolerant of lime in the soil, even shallow chalk soils.

top: *Magnolia acuminata*
bottom: *Magnolia grandiflora*

Magnolia denudata
S-M Spreading AGM 1993
The famous "Yulan" of China and Japan, commonly planted there in temple and monastery gardens and courtyards. A much branched often wide-spreading tree suitable for an isolated position open to the sky but sheltered from cold winds. The exquisite fragrant white goblet-shaped flowers are produced before the leaves in early spring.

Magnolia 'Elizabeth'
S-M Conical to Spreading AGM 1993
A hybrid of *M. acuminata* and *M. denudata* raised in the USA. It has a neat habit but is mainly notable for its fragrant primrose-yellow cup-shaped flowers in April-May.

Magnolia grandiflora
S-M Conical to Dome-shaped
Only two evergreen magnolias are grown in general cultivation and this species is the better known and certainly the most satisfactory. In Britain it is usually seen against a warm sheltering wall and requires this in colder areas; however, in warmer localities especially in southern Europe, it makes an imposing free-standing specimen. Old specimens are often gnarled and full of character. The bright, dark green leathery leaves are shining above and densely clothed with rust-coloured hairs beneath – at least when young. The large, fragrant, creamy-white, globular flowers appear at the ends of the shoots during late summer and early autumn. It is fairly tolerant of chalk soils and is a native of the south-eastern USA. There are several selected named clones, which, due to being grown from cuttings, have the advantage of flowering at an earlier age than those grown from seed. 'Exmouth' and 'Goliath' are two of the most reliable and well proven for general cultivation, the latter with broader darker green leaves than the other. Both were awarded the AGM in 1993. 'Ferruginea' is more erect and compact in growth, whilst the leaves when young are a lovely foxy-red colour beneath. 'Charles Dickens' is of more recent origin but well recommended.

Magnolia 'Heaven Scent'
M-L Spreading AGM 1993
One of the most satisfactory deciduous tree magnolias for gardens. This American-raised hybrid is later flowering than most others of its kind and is less likely to suffer from frost damage. It is vigorous and upright when young, flowering freely from an early age. The flowers are goblet-shaped, white flushed pale rose-purple on the outside.

Magnolia hypoleuca
M-L Spreading AGM 1993
A splendid vigorous large-leaved Japanese magnolia worth growing for its foliage alone. The flowers, cup-shaped to saucer-shaped, are large and richly fragrant, creamy-white in colour occasionally pink-tinted on the outside with age, with a contrasting ring of crimson stamens giving a dark "eye" to the flower. They are borne in June at the tips of the branches and look superb above the ruffs of leaves. They are followed by bold scarlet fruit clusters. The species was previously known as *M. obovata*.

Magnolia 'Iolanthe'
S-M Spreading AGM 1993
A beautiful hybrid of New Zealand origin producing in spring large cup-shaped blooms, rose-pink on the outside creamy-white within. These appear from an early age.

Magnolia x loebneri 'Leonard Messel'
S-M Conical to Rounded AGM 1993
A free-flowering hardy magnolia, often bushy when young, with multi-tepalled lilac-pink frost resistant flowers, darker in bud, appearing before the leaves in April. Like *M. x loebneri* 'Merrill' it is tolerant of chalk soils.

Magnolia x loebneri 'Merrill'
S-M Spreading AGM 1993
A free-flowering hardy magnolia, one of the best of its kind for general cultivation, even tolerating lime in the soil. The white multi-petalled flowers appear on the naked branches in April and are fragrant.

Magnolia x loebneri is a hybrid between the tree *Magnolia kobus* and the shrubby *Magnolia stellata*.

Magnolia macrophylla

S Spreading to Rounded
The "Big Leaf Magnolia" from the southeast United States is worth growing for its very large thin-textured leaves, silver-grey beneath, which may measure as much as 60cm or more on young specimens. It forms in time a spreading crown, the leaves, mainly gathered towards the ends of the branches, are an ideal foil for the equally spectacular creamy-white fragrant flowers in June. It requires a warm sheltered position, flourishing best where regular summer sun ripens growth, as in the Mediterranean region. In the cooler summers of Britain and Ireland, insufficient ripening means flowering is less free; and unripened and spring growths are subject to frost damage.

Magnolia x loebneri 'Leonard Messell'

Magnolia 'Maryland'

S-M Conical to Spreading AGM 1993
An American raised hybrid magnolia, a cross between *M. grandiflora* and *M. virginiana*. It is compact in habit, at least when young, with glossy-topped evergreen leaves. Both in leaf and flower this tree resembles a smaller neater version of *M. grandiflora* flowering over roughly the same period. It thrives and certainly flowers best in a warm sunny sheltered position. 'Freeman' is a similar hybrid.

Magnolia salicifolia

S-M Conical to Spreading AGM 1993
A free-growing hardy magnolia of erect habit and often multi-stemmed when young. The narrow leaves and the shoots are pleasantly aniseed scented when bruised, whilst the pure white fragrant flowers are inclined or slightly pendant, decorating the naked shoots in April even on young trees.

Magnolia 'Sayonara'

S-M Spreading AGM 1993
A lovely Californian raised hybrid freely bearing its large white, goblet-shaped blooms before the leaves in spring. The tepals have a pink flush at base.

Magnolia x soulangiana

S-M Spreading AGM 1993
A hybrid between *M. denudata*, the 'Yulan' and *M. liliiflora*, this is probably the most popular and widely planted of all magnolias. It is variable in habit and flower colour and several clones have been given names. Multi-stemmed and eventually wide-spreading (to 10m or more) and flowers before the leaves in April. 'Alba Superba' is one of the first of this group to flower, with white flowers, flushed rose-purple at base and scented; 'Alexandrina' AGM 1993 is erect in growth with white flowers rose-purple flushed on the outside, crowding the branches; 'Brozzonii' AGM 1993 has very large white flowers, shaded light purple at base, is late-flowering and considered the aristocrat of the group; 'Lennei' AGM 1993 is wide-spreading in habit with large globular flowers dark rose-purple outside,

creamy-white stained purple within, late in appearing (May) and often recurring in smaller numbers in late summer and early autumn; 'Rustica Rubra' AGM 1993 has rich rose-red flowers over a long period; 'Picture' is erect in habit and bears huge purple-flushed blooms.

Magnolia tripetala

S Spreading
A hardy American magnolia, often multi-stemmed. It is mainly grown for its magnificent foliage like large papery paddles arranged in an impressive ruff at the ends of the branches, hence the common name 'Umbrella Tree'. The long tepalled cream-coloured flowers in May and June give off a rather unpleasant pungent aroma. It requires a position sheltered from cold winds if the leaves are not to be retarded or damaged.

Magnolia x veitchii

M-L Spreading
A vigorous handsome deciduous tree, the result of a cross between *M. campbellii* and *M. denudata*. It possesses the best attributes of its parents and a large tree is magnificent in early spring when covered in its goblet-shaped flowers. Two selections are most often seen in cultivation: 'Peter Veitch', of more vigorous upright habit and free-flowering with pink goblet-shaped flowers before the leaves in April and 'Isca', which tends to a more spreading habit with smaller, white flowers. Neither produces flowers much before ten years of age.

Magnolia virginiana

S-M Spreading
The "Sweet Bay" was probably the first magnolia to be grown in England, having been introduced from the eastern USA in the late seventeenth century. It is a useful tree of quiet charm, with often long persistent leaves glossy green above and blue-white beneath. The globular creamy-white flowers are rather small, but sweetly scented and produced over a long period from June to September. A hardy tree it is happy on most soils but thrives best where summer sun and warmth are guaranteed.

Magnolia 'Wada's Memory'

S-M Conical to Spreading AGM 1993
A hardy vigorous tree, either a seedling of *M. kobus* or a hybrid with *M. salicifolia*, commonly multi-stemmed from the base. The long slender branches in April are freely decorated with large multi-tepalled fragrant white flowers which are pendant or inclined in posture creating a snow-cloud effect from a distance. It is one of the hardiest and most satisfactory magnolias of its kind.

top: *Magnolia x soulangiana*
bottom: *Magnolia virginiana*

MALUS
Rosaceae

With the possible exception of Prunus, the "Ornamental Crabs" offer more deciduous trees suitable for the small garden than any other genus. Some are grown for flower, some for fruit, whilst others offer coloured foliage or autumn tints. As a group they are amenable to most soils and situations, flowering best in full sun.

Malus 'Adams'

S Spreading to Rounded
Highly thought of in North America and in Holland, this densely branched tree is clothed with glossy green leaves, bronzy-brown when young. These are almost hidden in April-May by bright pinkish-red flowers, crimson in bud, followed by carmine-red fruits. An improvement on 'Hopa', it is equally suitable for cold northerly countries.

Malus baccata 'Gracilis'

S Dome-shaped
A dome-shaped very hardy tree with slender branches pendant at extremeties, small glossy green leaves, and small star-shaped white flowers pink in bud. They are replaced by late ripening small round creamy-yellow fruits with an orange blush. A free-flowering tough adaptable crab, it is scab and mildew resistant.

Malus coronaria 'Charlottae'

S Vase-shaped to Spreading
The branches of this lovely crab are upright at first, becoming spreading with age. The large, lobed leaves often give rich orange-red tints in autumn while the light pink, fading to salmon, semi-double flowers are richly fragrant of violets, opening late (for a crab) in May.

Malus 'Crittenden'

S Spreading
A handsome crab of Japanese origin possibly a seedling or hybrid of M. prunifolia var. rinkii. The pale pink flowers are replaced by glossy red rounded fruits up to 2.5cm across which remain on the branches almost throughout winter.

Malus 'Everest'

S Spreading AGM 1993
An excellent crab for the smaller garden, of conical habit when young. Flowers 5cm across, red in bud fading white followed by orange to orange-yellow fruits.

Malus floribunda

S Spreading to Rounded AGM 1993
A round-headed tree transformed, at the end of April, into a mound of pale blush flowers which crowd the arching branches and are crimson in bud. The small fruits which follow are yellow. It is a familiar tree in many gardens and is utterly reliable. It originated in Japan and is probably a hybrid. It is said to be scab resistant.

Malus 'Golden Hornet'

S Vase-shaped to Spreading AGM 1993
There are several yellow-fruited crabs, but if only one were to be chosen it should be this. The white flowers in April are replaced by rich golden-yellow, globular or conical fruits which thickly cluster the ascending branches, persisting until December then turning brown.

Malus hupehensis

S-M Vase-shaped to Spreading
AGM 1993
This splendid crab has several desirable features to offer, the first of which is its grey and brown flaking older bark. In April, the branches are wreathed in sweetly scented, white flowers, pink in bud, a tree in full flower resembling a snow-cloud from a distance. The fruits which follow are small and yellow, tinged with red. It is a native of both China and Japan. In the former country its leaves were once used for making tea.

Malus 'John Downie'

S Vase-shaped to Spreading AGM 1993
Together with 'Golden Hornet' this is the most popular of the fruiting crabs for small gardens. The pink-budded white flowers in late May are followed by comparatively large, conical, bright orange and red fruits. These are of good flavour and may be used in preserves.

Malus 'Katherine'

S Spreading AGM 1993
A pretty crab for the small garden, developing a dense rounded crown with showers of deep pink buds opening to pink semi-double flowers, followed by bright red crabs with a yellow cheek.

Malus 'Liset'

S Spreading to Rounded
A dense-crowned tree with leaves glossy purple from the outset. The flowers, red in bud, open to a bright purplish-red in May and are followed by small dark purple fruits. It is considered by many an improvement on 'Profusion'.

Malus 'Maypole'

S Columnar
A useful tree for small gardens or where space is restricted. Large pink blossoms in May are followed by purple fruits in autumn.

Malus 'Neville Copeman'

S Spreading AGM 1993
A seedling selection from the old, French 'Eleyi'. The green leaves are shaded purple throughout summer. Light purple flowers are followed by conical orange-red crabs.

Malus 'Professor Sprenger'

S Spreading to Rounded
Conical in habit at first, this crab is notable for its small ovoid, deep amber fruits changing to coral, freely borne and remaining on the branches into early winter. The flowers in May are pink in bud, opening pure white. Scab and mildew resistant, it is a first-rate, reliable ornamental crab of Dutch origin. Regarded by some authorities as one of the best ornamental trees in North American and European cultivation, it is hardly known in Britain.

Malus 'Profusion'

S Spreading
Trees with red or purple foliage are not everyone's cup of tea, but in this tree the colour is mainly restricted to the young

top: Malus floribunda
bottom: Malus 'Profusion'

foliage which is coppery crimson fading to bronze-green. The wine-red, slightly fragrant flowers are 3–4cm across and thickly clothe the branches in spring, to be followed by small, oxblood-red fruits. It is one of the best of the coloured-leaf crabs.

Malus 'Red Jade'

VS-S Weeping
One of the best weeping crabs, forming a dome-shaped crown with slender drooping branches and white pink-tinged flowers in late April or early May. These contrast well against the bright green leaves, and are replaced by small ovoid fruits ripening to a bright red which remain on the branches until late winter: an excellent small tree for the lawn.

Malus 'Red Sentinel'

S Conical to Spreading AGM 1993
In this tree the white pink-budded flowers in early May are succeeded by attractive deep red fruits, 2.5cm across, which are borne along the branches in large clusters and persist long into winter – a most useful asset on a cold dreary December or January day. A larger tree than 'Red Jade', developing an ovoid crown of ascending branches, it is scab resistant and thoroughly reliable in flower and fruit.

Malus x robusta

S Spreading
This is a variable hybrid between *M. baccata* and *M. prunifolia*, with white or pink-flushed flowers in spring followed by red or yellow cherry-like fruits. The crabs known as 'Red Siberian' and 'Yellow Siberian' are red and yellow fruited clones of this hybrid and are fine garden trees. They are also scab resistant. Both received an AGM in 1993.

Malus spectabilis

S Vase-shaped to Spreading
A most beautiful tree commonly planted in temple and palace gardens and courtyards in Beijing (Peking) and elsewhere in North China. The branches are ascending at first, spreading with age. These are decorated with large flowers,

top: *Malus tschonoskii*
bottom: *Malus* 'Van Eseltine'

deep rose-red in bud, opening blush during late April and early May, followed by yellow fruits. 'Riversii' is an equally beautiful clone with rose-pink, double flowers. Both are said to be highly resistant to fire-blight.

Malus toringo
S Spreading to Rounded
A first-class crab with a broad dense crown clothed with bright green three- to five-lobed leaves which turn yellow in autumn. The branches are crowded during April with small white flowers, reddish-pink in bud, whilst in autumn they are replaced by small rounded yellow fruits. It is usually offered by nurserymen under the better known name *M. sieboldii* and is scab resistant.

Malus transitoria
S Spreading to Rounded AGM 1993
If I were to choose just one crab for all-round effect, it would be this beautiful Chinese species. Its slender arching branches produce a broad mushroom of a head clothed with prettily lobed leaves which are bright green in summer, turning butter-yellow in autumn. Added to this are the small but abundantly produced white flowers in May and the equally plentiful golden-yellow currant-like fruits in autumn. It is a tree of great charm.

Malus trilobata
S-M Conical to Vase-shaped
Although rarely seen, this splendid though slow-growing tree is one of the best for restricted spaces, and is thoroughly hardy and easy to grow. Its erect branches are clothed with deeply three-lobed leaves which resemble more those of a maple than those of a crab. These become attractively tinted red and yellow in autumn. The large white flowers appear clustered along the branches in May or early June, followed by green ripening to red and yellow fruits. It is a native of the eastern Mediterranean region and northern Greece, and is scab and mildew resistant.

Malus tschonoskii
S-M Conical AGM 1993
Unquestionably the best crab for the brilliance and reliability of its autumn colour, the bold foliage silvery grey on emerging, passing through green before turning to yellow, orange, purple and scarlet. By contrast, the white flowers in early May are rarely freely borne and are partially hidden by the foliage; whilst the brownish-yellow, purple-flushed fruits, attractive enough individually, are (in Britain certainly) rarely borne in sufficient numbers to capture one's attention. It is native to Japan. A form with an even narrower ovoid, denser crown is known in Holland as 'Select'.

Malus 'Van Eseltine'
S Broadly columnar to Vase-shaped
An ideal crab for the small garden with its columnar, later vase-shaped, habit. The semi-double flowers up to 5cm across are rose-scarlet in bud opening shell-pink and densely crowding the branches in May. They are followed, though not freely, by yellow fruits with a brownish-red tinge.

Malus 'Wintergold'
S Rounded to Spreading
A reliable and free-flowering crab with white flowers, deep carmine in bud, followed by small yellow fruits normally persisting well into winter.

Malus 'Golden Hornet'

MAYTENUS
Celastraceae

A large genus mainly of tropical trees and shrubs but containing one or two suitable for colder climates.

Maytenus boaria
S-M Broadly columnar to Spreading or Weeping

An evergreen tree of dense habit with slender often pendulous branchlets clothed with small, narrow, dark green, finely-toothed leaves. Flowers are green and inconspicuous. Curiously uncommon in cultivation, this is a most attractive South American tree of loose graceful habit, like an evergreen version of a weeping willow but more densely branched. It is adaptable to most soils, acid or alkaline, and enjoys an open preferably sunny position. In Britain it thrives best in the south and west.

Maytenus boaria

†MELIA
Meliaceae

A small genus of trees and shrubs native to the tropical and subtropical regions of the world. The following species is the hardiest but is only suitable outside in the warmer areas of Europe, especially the Mediterranean region.

Melia azedarach
S-M Spreading

A fast-growing, openly branched, exotic-looking tree with large elegant much divided leaves, up to 60cm long, of a shining rich green. These are joined at the ends of the shoots in late spring and summer by the large, loosely branched heads of lavender-lilac fragrant flowers. Almost as ornamental are the small globular yellow fruits which persist on the leafless branches throughout winter. The hard bony seeds have been used by monks and others strung together to make rosaries, hence the English name "Bead Tree".

MELIOSMA
Sabiaceae

A small genus of trees and shrubs from eastern Asia and America, grown for foliage and flowers.

Meliosma veitchiorum
S-M Spreading

A hardy deciduous Chinese tree with stout branches and branchlets bearing large pinnate leaves to 60cm long, even larger on strong growing shoots; these are borne on reddish stalks, adding to their ornamental effect. They are topped in May, on older trees certainly, by large branched heads of small creamy-white, honey-scented flowers followed in a warm summer by small violet fruits. The winter buds are reddish-brown and prominent. A rare tree in cultivation, it is well worth searching for. It prefers a lime-free moist but well-drained loam in sun or half shade. *M. oldhamii* is similar but equally elusive in the trade nursery.

MESPILUS
Rosacceae

A monotypic genus related to Crataegus *but with much larger flowers and fruit. It is hardy and easy to grow on most soils.*

Mespilus germanica
S Spreading
The truly wild "Medlar" is a bushy spiny-branched shrub, interesting in itself but not as ornamental as the several forms selected for their larger edible fruits, such as 'Dutch', 'Nottingham' and 'Stoneless'. In these, the dark green and downy leaves are larger and an ideal foil for the solitary white or pink-flushed flowers 2.5–4cm across in May or early June. These are followed by the curious brown apple-shaped fruits to 5cm across with their five tail-like persistent sepals. They are amenable to cultivation in most soils, thriving best in an open, preferably sunny, situation. Traditionally, the fruits are eaten when "bletted", that is, when decaying. They also make a most acceptable jelly or preserve.

†MICHELIA
Magnoliaceae

A genus of trees related to the magnolia, mainly found in the tropical parts of south-east Asia.

Michelia doltsopa
S-M Conical to Spreading
Semi-evergreen tree from the eastern Himalaya, south-east Tibet and south-west China, often densely branched with handsome leathery leaves, glossy dark green above and 15–30cm long. The multi-petalled magnolia-like flowers are formed in the upper leaf axils in autumn, not opening until the following April when they burst from their rich brown sheaths, cream-coloured or white, with a rich fragrance. This spectacular flowering tree is only suitable for moist, well-drained, lime-free soils in the mildest areas in sun or half shade. There are some fine specimens in Cornish and Irish gardens.

MORUS
Moraceae

A small genus of deciduous trees, the mulberries, while offering no beauty of flower, are, nevertheless, of great interest and attractive in both leaf and autumn colour. Growing best in the warmer southern areas of the British Isles, they are happy in most soils, particularly those of a rich nature, and are admirably suited to city and town gardens and those by the sea. Their roots are rather brittle, therefore great care should be taken when planting and only small specimens should be moved from the open ground.

Morus alba 'Pendula'
VS-S Weeping
A most effective weeping tree with long, densely packed, greyish branches, often forming a curtain, and clothed with large, heart-shaped, pale green leaves which turn yellow in autumn. The "White Mulberry", of which this is a form, is the tree upon whose leaves the silkworm is fed. Young trees require training up a tall stake or cane to obtain a high crown.

Morus nigra

Morus nigra

S Spreading to Rounded AGM 1993
The widespreading, heavily branched
"Black Mulberry" is a familiar tree in old
college and cathedral gardens. It lives to a
great age, in time becoming gnarled,
picturesque, and of great architectural
value. Its dark green, heart-shaped leaves
are rough to the touch above, and late in
appearing, whilst the dark purplish-red
fruits in autumn are edible and agreeable
to the taste. They also stain mouths and
hands like blackberries. In the wild it is a
native of western Asia, but is known to
have been cultivated in England since the
early sixteenth century.

†MYRTUS
Myrtaceae

*Evergreen trees and shrubs, most of which are too
tender for outside cultivation in Britain.*

Myrtus lechleriana

S Broadly columnar to Dome-shaped
An evergreen tree of dense bushy nature
unless trained to a single stem. The hairy
pale brown branchlets are clothed with
dark green leathery leaves to 2.5cm long,
attractively copper-coloured when young.
The small creamy-white flowers are
borne in clusters from the upper leaf axils
in May, followed by small red, changing
to black, fruits. A native of Chile, this
uncommon evergreen is similar in
hardiness and requirements to *M. luma*,
differing most notably from that species
in its earlier flowering and duller bark. It
is often grown as a hedge or screen in
mild areas.

†Myrtus luma

S-M Broadly columnar to Dome-shaped
AGM 1993
A handsome evergreen tree, dense and
bushy when young with small polished
dark green leathery leaves. The whole
canopy is crowded in late summer with
small white flowers attractive to bees. As
if this were not enough, the bark of the
stem and larger branches is cinnamon-red
and mealy in texture, peeling in patches
to reveal the whitish new bark. In the
mild south-western areas of Britain and
Ireland, this is a well-known tree where
its patchwork bark and its late flowering
are much appreciated. In some gardens
with the help of birds it seeds around, the
seedlings commonly forming clumps and
thickets. It prefers a moist lime-free soil
and will tolerate shade, flowering most
freely, however, in full sun.

†Myrtus luma
'Glanleam Gold'

S Broadly columnar to Dome-shaped
This attractive variegated form was
raised in the garden of Glanleam on the
island of Valentia, Co. Kerry, Ireland. It is
slower-growing, smaller and hardier than
the type, the leaves irregularly margined
pale yellow at first, changing to cream
later, pink-tinged in winter.

Myrtus luma

NOTHOFAGUS
Fagaceae

Sometimes referred to as "Southern Beech", the members of this small but ornamental genus are related to Fagus, *differing, among other things, in their normally smaller evergreen or deciduous leaves. Most species are evergreen and most are fast-growing; but, unlike the "Common Beech", they are not very wind-resistant and are not suitable as screens or shelterbelts. They prefer a deep, moist but well-drained soil, and will not tolerate shallow chalk soils. Though relatively hardy, they seem best suited to the southern and western areas of Britain and the milder eastern and south-western areas of Ireland.*

Nothofagus antarctica
M Conical to Spreading
Native to the temperate regions of South America this is a deciduous tree of open habit, with irregular tiers of fan-shaped branches bearing small, diamond-shaped, crinkly-margined shining green leaves which often turn yellow or orange-yellow in autumn. A free-growing, elegantly branched tree, it is one of the hardiest of the deciduous species. Curiously, considering its merits, it is still uncommon in general cultivation. It requires an open sunny situation.

Nothofagus betuloides
M Conical to Spreading
An evergreen tree of dense compact habit, the small leathery, toothed, dark shining green leaves densely arranged on the spreading branches. These are borne in horizontally flattened sprays ascending from the main stem. It is a dark-crowned tree easily recognised by its regular conical habit, especially when young. It grows best in a position sheltered from cold drying winds. It is a native of Chile and Argentina.

Nothofagus dombeyi
M-L Conical to Spreading
A fast-growing evergreen tree from Chile and Argentina, similar to *N. betuloides* in some respects but more vigorous and openly branched, while the leaves are slightly longer and narrower. It requires similar conditions and is of similar hardiness.

†*Nothofagus menziesii*
M-L Conical to Spreading
Unlike the previously described species this evergreen tree is native to New Zealand where it is a tall tree of the forest. In Britain and Ireland it is only suited to warm sheltered gardens where its smooth cherry-like bark, dense habit (especially when young), and its small neatly toothed leaves, bronzed when young, are characteristic.

Nothofagus betuloides

Nothofagus obliqua

L Conical to Spreading
The "Roblé" is one of the fastest-growing and most elegant of hardy deciduous trees, its branches often gracefully drooping at their tips. The leaves are larger than in most species and are uneven at the base. It quickly develops into a beautiful specimen and is an ideal tree for a large lawn. It is a native of Chile.

Nothofagus procera

L Conical to Dome-shaped
Easily the most vigorous species and one of the fastest-growing of all deciduous trees, developing a conical habit at first, eventually with a handsome domed crown. Just as impressive are the leaves, large and boldly veined like those of a hornbeam, orange in colour when young and often giving rich tints in autumn. It requires space, shelter (but not competition) and a deep soil to reach its full potential. Possibly more tolerant of alkaline soils than most species, at least when young, it is native to Chile and Argentina.

Nothofagus pumilio

M Conical to Spreading
A strong-growing deciduous tree related to *N. antarctica* but developing a stronger, straight leader and a taller, more regular crown. Its leaves are, if anything, more ornamental, whilst it is said to be hardier. Rarely seen though represented in British cultivation, this fine tree from the temperate areas of South America has great potential and is worth searching for among specialist nurserymen.

Nothofagus solandri

M Conical to Vase-shaped
A fast-growing evergreen tree with smooth bark and ascending branches. These give way to fan-like sprays of wiry twigs crowded with tiny leathery oval leaves, glossy green above and without teeth. The "Black Beech" is a native of New Zealand and is best suited to a sheltered position such as in a woodland glade. The variety *cliffortioides* is very similar in general appearance.

NYSSA
Nyssaceae

This small genus contains two of the finest trees grown for autumn colour. Both flowers and fruit are insignificant. They require a moist, lime-free soil and, once established, resent disturbance; they should be planted, therefore, as young as possible.

Nyssa sinensis

S-M Conical to Dome-shaped AGM 1993
Like its American cousin (*N. sylvatica*) a deciduous tree, this Chinese species of relatively recent introduction is grown principally for its brilliant orange and scarlet autumn colour with purple tints. It differs most markedly from the "Tupelo", however, in its long pointed leaves which are reddish-purple when young.

Nyssa sylvatica

M-L Conical to Dome-shaped AGM 1993
The mound-like or broadly columnar shapes of the "Tupelo" in autumn dress are the pride and joy of several gardens in the south and west of England. At this season the dark glossy leaves are drained of their summer green and the whole tree erupts into a colourful bonfire of yellow, orange and scarlet. In the wild it occurs throughout eastern North America.

Nyssa sinensis

†OLEA
Oleaceae

A small genus of evergreen trees, mainly represented in cultivation by the following well-known species.

Olea europaea
S-M Spreading
The "Olive" of commerce is perhaps the most familiar of all trees in the Mediterranean region, its narrow leaves lending a greyish cast to hillsides and plains. The tiny white fragrant flowers in summer are borne in axillary clusters and are followed by the typical ovoid, oily, one-seeded fruits. Despite its preferred climate, it is just possible to grow this tree outside in the warmest areas of Britain and in suitably warm and sheltered pockets elsewhere, especially given a sheltering wall. It has even been known to fruit in Britain, at the Chelsea Physic Garden in London, but its attraction here lies mainly in its grey, downy, silvery-backed leaves.

OSTRYA
Betulaceae

A small genus of hardy deciduous trees, closely related to and resembling the "Hornbeams" (Carpinus), differing in the inflated husks of the fruits creating a pendant cluster not unlike that of a Hop (Humulus). They are easy and adaptable trees of elegant habit, suitable for most soils and, like the hornbeams, fit in comfortably with the rural landscape.

Ostrya carpinifolia
M Spreading
The "Hop Hornbeam" is, perhaps, most pleasing in spring when its spreading branches are hung with the numerous long yellow male catkins. The sharply toothed leaves give attractive yellow tints in autumn when they are accompanied by the curiously attractive hop-like fruit clusters. The smooth greyish-brown bark becomes flaking and fissured with age. It is a native of southern Europe and western Asia. The Japanese *O. japonica* and the eastern American *O. virginiana* are trees of similar attributes, differing mainly in minor botanical characters.

OXYDENDRUM
Ericaceae

A genus of only one species from the eastern USA. It requires a moist, lime-free soil and performs best in full sun, though it will tolerate light shade. It is best planted when small.

Oxydendrum aboreum
S-M Conical to Spreading
The pleasant acid flavour of the leaves gives this species its common name of "Sorrel Tree". These same leaves, which are long and shining dark green above, especially in spring, turn to exquisite shades of yellow, crimson and purple in autumn. In July and August the long drooping racemes of small white bell-shaped fragrant flowers emerge in clusters from the ends of the shoots, remaining effective for several weeks.

Ostrya carpinifolia

Oxydendrum arboreum

†PALMS
Palmae

Among the most distinct and easily recognised of all woody plants. The palm family is a very large one, encompassing a wide variety of types, from trees with single or multiple stems, shrubby species with little or no main stem, and climbers. The vast majority are tropical and rarely, if ever, seen outside in the cool temperate regions. A number, however, are suited to the warmer areas of Europe, principally the Mediterranean region where they are an important and familiar feature of gardens, parks and boulevards. Only one species, Trachycarpus fortunei, *is commonly seen in Britain and then principally in the warmer south and west; whilst there are several others which survive, and sometimes flourish, in scattered gardens where a warm microclimate has encouraged their establishment and growth. Alternatively, they make excellent tub specimens for summer effect, as long as they are given indoor protection in winter. Even the larger-growing species can be enjoyed this way when young and manageable.*

Although in ideal conditions, palms produce large and often spectacular spreading or drooping yellow or whitish flower-heads followed by often colourful fruits, it is their large evergreen leaves which are their principal ornamental attraction, and they can be divided into two main groups depending on their shape:

Fan palms – leaf blades rounded or fan-shaped in outline, with finger-like projections or lobes. Feather palms – leaves feather-shaped with numerous long, narrow leaflets either side of a long stalk or rachis.

With few exceptions, the following palms require full sun, warmth and a well-drained soil if they are to survive. They seem equally happy on acid or alkaline soils. They are also typically single-stemmed with a terminal head of stalked leaves, so the symbols denoting habit do not apply.

†*Chamaerops humilis*
VS-S AGM 1993
One of only two palms native to Europe, the "Dwarf Fan Palm" grows painfully slowly, eventually developing one or more stems up to 5m tall, depending on growing conditions. These support a head of long-stalked fan-shaped leaves with long, stiff, finger-like lobes. Often grown in large tubs or raised beds in courtyards, it is the only commonly cultivated palm suitable for small gardens, but only then in the mildest areas of Britain and Ireland. The fibre of its leaf bases has been used in some Mediterranean countries as stuffing for furniture and mattresses. The large-stalked clusters of yellowish flowers are followed in a hot summer by bunches of rounded brown or orange-yellow fruits. Commonly seen on the hillsides of coastal southern Spain and on the Rock of Gibraltar.

†*Erythea armata*
S
Known as the "Big Blue Hesper Palm" in its native California, this magnificent fan palm is easily recognised by the blue-grey waxy upper surface of the deeply fingered leaves. These are borne on long stalks densely armed with strong white curved teeth. The greyish-white flowers are borne in arching and drooping plumes up to 5m long. The fruits are black. It is only suitable outside in Mediterranean areas.

†Jubaea chilensis

M

The "Chilean Wine Palm", so called because of the sugary sap which in the wild has long been collected and boiled down by Chileans to make "miel de palma" or palm honey. Older specimens develop swollen stems of remarkable girth, topped with a great tuft of feathered green leaves up to 4m long. The heavy bunches of yellowish fingered flowers give way to yellowish fruits. If one raps the trunk of a large wine palm it produces a sound similar to that of a wine-filled cask or barrel. It is only suitable for the Mediterranean region and the mildest gardens in south-west Britain and in Ireland.

†Livistona australis

M

A tall, comparatively slender-stemmed, fan palm supporting a shapely crown of long-stalked, glossy green leaves which are circular in outline but deeply divided into long finger-like segments with characteristically drooping tips. Flowers are yellow, eventually long-stalked and hanging from the crown, fruits being reddish-brown. It is a native of eastern Australia and suitable only for the Mediterranean region and similarly warm areas.

†Phoenix canariensis

M

The "Canary Island Date Palm" is commonly seen in the Mediterranean region, and elsewhere in southern Europe where summers are warm and winters mild. It has even grown with conspicuous success in south-west Britain, especially on Tresco in the Isles of Scilly. It is a robust palm, the stout stems rough, with the old leaf bases supporting a very large dense crown of exotic arching feather-shaped leaves up to 6m long. The flowers are yellow in branched heads, male and female borne on separate trees, those of the female when pollinated producing heavy clusters of orange fruits. It is still found wild as well as being commonly planted in the Canary Isles.

top: Phoenix canariensis
bottom: Trachycarpus fortunei

107

Trachycarpus fortunei
S-M AGM 1993

The only palm hardy enough for general cultivation in Britain and only then in the warmer southern and western areas and in warm sheltered gardens elsewhere. Known as the "Chusan Palm" or "Chinese Windmill Palm", this familiar tree was first introduced into Britain from China by Robert Fortune. It is a shaggy-stemmed species owing to the persistent fibrous remains of the old leaf bases. The leaves themselves are long-stalked and circular in outline with numerous long stiff finger-like segments. The rich yellow fragrant flowers are borne in large dense clusters on a short stout stalk while the fruits ripen to blue. In parts of China the fibre of the stems is used to stuff mattresses or woven into waterproof cloaks or ponchos.

†*Washingtonia filifera*
S-M

A distinct and handsome fan palm suitable only for the Mediterranean region and similarly favoured areas of Europe. The large leaves are deeply divided into long finger-like, grey-green segments which droop at their slender tips and are mingled with long hanging threads. When old, the leaves hang down to form in time, and when allowed, a characteristic dense, thick, pale cloak, or skirt, around the stem. The white flowers are produced in crowded plumes up to 4m long, erect at first, hanging when in fruit.

PARROTIA
Hamamelidaceae

Rich autumn colour is the main feature of this interesting genus of which only a single species is known. It is a member of the same family as the "Witch Hazel" (Hamamelis) and is surprisingly lime-tolerant, although it thrives and colours best in a moist but well-drained soil, preferably in full sun.

top: Parrotia persica
bottom: Parrotia persica (bark detail)

Parrotia persica

S-M Spreading to Wide-spreading
AGM 1993
In cultivation this hardy deciduous tree
normally forms a mound of wide-
spreading branches on a short, thick,
piebald trunk. It therefore requires plenty
of elbow-room in which to develop. In
autumn the deep green leaves change to
fiery scarlet and gold, when a big
specimen presents a breathtaking sight.
The tiny reddish flower clusters in late
winter often create a warm haze when
seen from a distance. It is a native of
northern Iran and the Caucasus. On the
wet hillsides above the Caspian Sea,
Parrotia is plentiful and forms forests
together with hornbeam. In these forests,
trees are erect, often over 20m high, and
are late in colouring, usually December or
January.

Parrotia persica 'Pendula'

VS-S Weeping
A distinct form with weeping branches
closely packed, eventually forming a
dense mound. For the most spectacular
effect, young plants should be encouraged
to form a high crown by training a
leading shoot to a tall cane or stake. If a
very tall stake is used, or two or more 2m
canes are tied together, then a crown in
excess of 4m or more should be possible.

PAULOWNIA
Scrophulariaceae

*A small genus of deciduous trees thriving in most
soils so long as they are reasonably well-drained.
They flower best in a warm sunny position
sheltered from cold winds and, if possible, late
frosts.*

Paulownia tomentosa

M Spreading AGM 1993
A fast-growing, openly branched tree
bearing stout downy shoots and
oppositely arranged leaves which are
large, usually five-lobed, and downy
beneath. The beautiful heliotrope-blue
flowers, shaped like those of a foxglove,
are 3.5–5cm long. They are borne in
terminal panicles and, though formed in
autumn, do not open until the following
May. Young sucker shoots grow
prodigiously and produce leaves up to
60cm or more across. Large leaves may be
encouraged by hard pruning of the
previous year's shoots in March. It is a
native of China, giving the best results in
regions where both summer and winter
climates are consistent. Two other species
P. fortunei and *P. forgesii* are sometimes
offered by specialist nurserymen.

PHELLODENDRON
Rutaceae

*A small genus of hardy deciduous trees suitable for
most soils, preferably in an open situation. Male
and female flowers are borne on separate trees and
both sexes should be planted if fruits are required.*

Paulownia tomentosa

Phellodendron amurense

M Spreading

A relatively tough tree adaptable to a wide range of situations. The bark is greyish-brown and oak-like, becoming corky on older specimens, hence the

English name "Amur Cork Tree". The pinnate ash-like leaves are a glossy dark green above, turning yellow in autumn, and give off a pungent aroma when bruised. Small white flowers are produced in terminal branched heads followed on female trees by green, ripening to shining black, berry-like fruits which persist into winter. A good looking tree in summer and winter, it flourishes particularly well in countries enjoying a continental climate. It is native to north-east Asia.

PHILLYREA
Oleaceae

A small genus of evergreen trees with opposite leaves. They are hardy, tolerant of most soils and situations, including polluted atmosphere and coastal blasts.

Phillyrea latifolia

S Spreading to Rounded

For those who admire the billowy, dark green foliage of the "Evergreen Oak" (*Quercus ilex*) but cannot find the necessary space, this tree is a passable substitute. It is a native of southern Europe and western Asia and develops a dense rounded head with small, toothed leaves. The flowers are tiny and of no ornamental significance.

PHOTINIA
Rosaceae

An important genus of both evergreen and deciduous trees and shrubs, many of which are possessed of great ornamental merit. They are adaptable to most soils except waterlogged situations.

Photinia beauverdiana

S Spreading AGM 1993

A most desirable deciduous Chinese tree of graceful habit, producing clusters of hawthorn-like white flowers in May and June which give way to loose bunches of small orange, ripening to dark red, fruits

top: *Phillyrea latifolia*
bottom: *Photinea beauverdiana notabilis*

which often last into winter. Equally attractive are the richly tinted leaves in autumn. The variety *notabilis* differs in its somewhat taller habit, larger leaves and larger flower and fruiting-heads.

Photinia x fraseri

S Spreading to Rounded
Although this popular hybrid is bushy when young, developing into a large shrub of dense habit, it can be trained if so desired to form a main stem and produce a bold evergreen tree suitable for small gardens where it gives excellent value. The glossy dark green leathery leaves are coppery-red when young, whilst the tiny pink-budded flowers are borne in dense flat heads in April and May. There are several selections available, among which 'Robusta' AGM 1993 is the most satisfactory in British cultivation. It is certainly the hardiest. Equally spectacular if not more so is 'Red Robin' AGM 1993, in which the young growths are a brilliant red. *P. x fraseri* is the result of a cross between *P. serratifolia* and *P. glabra*. All are lime-tolerant.

Photinia serratifolia

S Rounded
A parent of the hybrid *P. x fraseri*, this handsome evergreen, better known though incorrectly as *P. serrulata*, will grow slowly into a small bold-foliaged tree, and with a little careful pruning in the early years will develop a strong main stem. The large leathery glossy green leaves are almost prickly-toothed and emerge in spring a cheerful coppery-red whatever the weather. The white flowers in dense heads are produced in April and May, followed in a warm year by red hair-like fruits. Like *P. x fraseri*, this tree is particularly tolerant of shallow soils over chalk.

Photinia villosa

S Spreading
A deciduous species which can be grown as a large shrub or a small tree with a wide-spreading head. The clusters of white hawthorn-like flowers in May are followed in autumn by small bright red fruits; when, at the same time, the slender pointed leaves give brilliant orange, scarlet and gold tints. It performs best in a moist but well-drained lime-free soil in sun or half shade.

†PITTOSPORUM
Pittosporaceae

A large genus of evergreen trees and shrubs best suited to the milder areas of Britain and Ireland and to southern Europe, especially the Mediteranean region. Although some have attractive fragrant flowers, they are chiefly grown for their ornamental foliage. Most of those cultivated are native to New Zealand. They are not entirely happy on dry chalk soils.

Pittosporum bicolor

S Broadly columnar
A densely twigged tree of compact growth, bushy in habit initially but slowly increasing in height to form a pleasing column of small, narrow leathery leaves, dark green above, white-felted beneath, darkening to brown with age. The small dark maroon-crimson flowers are at their best in spring. They are borne singly or in clusters from the leaf axils and are pleasantly fragrant.

Pittosporum eugenioides

S-M Rounded to Spreading
The "Tarata" of New Zealand is easily distinguished by its combination of dark twigs and dark glossy green, wavy-margined leaves up to 12.5cm long, which are fragrant when bruised. Even more fragrant are the small yellow flowers borne in dense clusters in spring. The fragrance is like that of honey and can be detected at some distance when conditions are favourable.

Pittosporum eugenioides 'Variegatum'

S Rounded to Spreading AGM 1993
A beautiful tree, the leaves boldy margined creamy-white. Unfortunately, it is for the mildest areas only and even there best in a sheltered situation.

Pittosporum 'Garnettii'

S Broadly columnar AGM 1993
One of the most striking and most
satisfactory of the variegated
pittosporums. A hybrid of *P. tenuifolium*,
the leathery leaves up to 4cm long are
greyish-green with a bold creamy-white
margin which becomes pink-tinged in
winter. Its numerous branches are dark
and slender, giving a bushy habit when
young. Hardier than most, it is not
suitable, however, for cold inland areas,
especially in the north and east of Britain.

Pittosporum tenuifolium

S-M Broadly columnar to Rounded or
Spreading AGM 1993
A densely branched tree, columnar at
first, broadening with age. The slender
twigs are almost black in colour and
densely crowded with small, leathery,
pale shining green, wavy-margined leaves
which are popular as cut material with
florists. The small chocolate-purple
flowers are not easily noticed, being
partially concealed among the leaves, but
their sweet honey-like fragrance is
unmistakable, especially in the evening,
and detectable from a distance. It is the
most commonly planted species in Britain
and Ireland and one of the hardiest, but
most suited to the milder southern and
western areas and warm pockets inland.
There are many named forms of this
species, most of which are less hardy.

Pittosporum tenuifolium 'Eila Keightley'

S Broadly columnar to Rounded or
Spreading
Leaves with a central splash of yellow and
yellowish-green, whilst the midrib and
veins are cream-coloured. It is sometimes
incorrectly offered as 'Sunburst'.

Pittosporum tenuifolium 'Irene Paterson'

S Broadly columnar to Rounded or
Spreading AGM 1993
An attractive and relatively hardy form in
which the leaves are white at first,
becoming speckled with green and
grey-green.

Pittosporum tenuifolium 'James Stirling'

S Broadly columnar to Rounded or
Spreading
Leaves smaller than in the type and
rounded giving a neat and delicate effect.

Pittosporum tenuifolium 'Purpureum'

S Broadly columnar to Rounded or
Spreading
Leaves coloured a burnished purple,
holding well through winter.

Pittosporum tenuifolium 'Silver Queen'

S-M Broadly columnar to Rounded or
Spreading AGM 1993
A well known and lovely form with leaves
suffused silvery-grey and with an
irregular creamy-white margin.

Pittosporum tenuifolium 'Warnham Gold'

S Broadly columnar to Rounded or
Spreading AGM 1993
Leaves greenish-yellow maturing to
golden-yellow, especially attractive in
autumn and winter. 'Abbotsbury Gold'
and 'Golden King' are similar.

Pittosporum undulatum

S Rounded to Spreading
A vigorous tree in the right conditions, its
leaves up to 10–15cm long, dark shining
green above with wavy margins. The
relatively large fragrant creamy-white
flowers are borne in loose clusters in May
and July. It is only suitable for the mildest
areas of Britain and Ireland, mainly in the
woodland gardens of the south-west, but
is not uncommon in parts of southern
Europe where it is a popular street and
garden tree.

PLATANUS
Platanaceae

A very distinct and highly ornamental genus of deciduous trees, resembling the "Maples" (Acer) in their palmately-lobed leaves which, however, are arranged alternately on the shoots. They are fast-growing when young and tolerant of most soils, though slower and least happy on shallow chalk soils.

Platanus x acerifolia

L Spreading AGM 1993
The "London Plane" is well known to most people, even to non-gardeners, and is one of the most commonly planted and most successful hardy shade trees in our towns and cities. No tree suffers pollution, mutilation and lack of care so well as this; and yet if it were to suffer the same fate as the "English Elm", the people of London and Paris, not to mention a thousand-and-one other cities and towns in the northern temperate regions, would be up in arms. Its familiar flaking piebald trunk and branches are especially effective in winter when, at the same time, the branches are hung with the curious strings of bauble-like fruits. Its origin is a long-standing source of debate among botanists and others, but it is generally considered to be a hybrid between the "Oriental Plane" (P. orientalis) and the "American Buttonwood" (P. occidentalis). It is sometimes catalogued under the name P. x hispanica.

Platanus x acerifolia 'Suttneri'

L Spreading
A striking tree in which the leaves are boldly splashed and streaked creamy-white and pink-tinged when young, turning green as they mature.

Platanus orientalis

L Spreading AGM 1993
Equally large and requiring as much, if not more, space as the "London Plane" is the "Oriental Plane". Just as handsome, this species differs from the other mainly in its deeper-lobed leaves. It is said to be

top: *Platanus orientalis insularis*
bottom: *Pittosporum* 'Garnettii'

Poliothyrsis sinensis

very long-lived; and in south-eastern Europe and western Asia where it occurs wild, there are many trees claimed to be of great antiquity. In northern Iran and elsewhere it withstands long hot summers followed by cold winters. It is best suited to large gardens, parks and estates where it can develop to its full and magnificent effect.

Platanus orientalis insularis
M Conical to Spreading
A fast-growing tree, conical when young, differing from the typical tree in its deeply-lobed leaves with narrower finger-like lobes. This is without doubt one of the most handsome of all hardy trees grown for foliage effect. Its bark is just as ornamental as that of the type.

POLIOTHYRSIS
Flacourtiaceae

A monotypic genus, the only species a small tree found mainly in botanic gardens and specialist collections, but deserving of wider planting as it is quite hardy and decidedly ornamental.

Poliothyrsis sinensis
S Spreading
A rare and desirable deciduous Chinese tree with attractive linden-like leaves which are downy and red-tinted when young. The tiny white and yellow fragrant flowers are carried in large, loose panicles in late summer, especially after hot weather but not on young trees.

POPULUS
Salicaceae

The "Poplars" are a large and varied genus of easy cultivation. The majority are hardy deciduous trees, growing well in most soils except shallow chalk soils. They are especially useful for planting in wet areas and are often found in the wild by rivers and streams. Very fast-growing, with rapidly expanding crowns and vigorous greedy roots, they should not be planted near buildings, or underground water or drainage pipes or, indeed, wherever water is not freely available. Catkins are produced, male and female on separate trees, those of the latter, when ripe, scattering cotton-woolly seeds which sometimes cause annoyance and frustration to city people.

Populus alba

M Spreading

A suckering species, the "White Poplar" bears white woolly-backed leaves which are three- to five-lobed on vigorous shoots and toothed elsewhere. These are effective when blowing in a wind, and turn yellow in autumn. In this country the smooth bark is greyish in colour, whilst in countries like Iran, where the atmosphere is drier, the bark gleams silvery-white and is quite outstanding. It is a native of Europe and western Asia, occasionally naturalised but not wild in the British Isles. The true species is less common in British cultivation than the hybrid *P. x canescens*, which makes a far better specimen tree for large gardens and estates. Typical *P. alba* suckers to the point of invasion and is perhaps best suited to seaside locations where it is helpful in controlling erosion.

Populus alba 'Pyramidalis'

M-L Columnar to Conical

A columnar tree when young, gradually broadening to conical, then vase-shaped with age. Sometimes catalogued as 'Bolleana' or "Bolle's Poplar", it is worth growing for its initially dense columnar habit and white-backed leaves.

Populus alba 'Raket'

M-L Columnar

A male form of slender columnar growth, ultimately not unlike a Lombardy poplar in habit and superior in this respect to 'Pyramidalis'. 'Raket' incidentally, is the Dutch for 'Rocket'.

Populus alba 'Richardii'

M Spreading

A distinct and attractive form in which the upper surface of many of the leaves is yellow contrasting effectively with the white felted lower surface. Slower-growing and a smaller tree ultimately

top: Populas 'Serotina Aurea'
bottom: Populas lasiocarpa

115

than the type, this poplar responds well to hard pruning; and if so desired, it can be maintained as a large bush or small bushy-headed tree when it is quite striking in its golden foliage, especially when seen at a distance against a darker background. It does, however, possess the suckering propensities of the type – so beware.

Populus 'Balsam Spire'

L Columnar to Broadly columnar
AGM 1993
An extremely vigorous balsam poplar hybrid between *P. trichocarpa* and *P. balsamifera* '32' from eastern and western North America respectively. Its narrow habit makes it ideally suited to restricted spaces whilst its foliage has all the merit of the parents. Sometimes offered under the name *P.* 'Tacatricho 32'.

Populus candicans 'Aurora'

M Spreading
This striking form of the "Balm of Gilead Poplar" produces stout angled shoots and broad heart-shaped leaves which are strongly balsam-scented when unfolding, scenting the air around. In colour they are boldly variegated creamy-white and pink-tinged when young, gradually turning green as they mature. It is a poplar counterpart to *Platanus x acerifolia* 'Suttneri' and is perhaps best hard pruned each or every other year in February to encourage the coloured young foliage. It is not entirely satisfactory on chalk soils.

Populus x canescens

L Spreading
The "Grey Poplar" is considered by many authorities to be a hybrid between the "White Poplar" (*P. alba*) and the "Aspen" (*P. tremula*). It is a large fast-growing tree, handsome in maturity with smooth grey bark, yellowish-grey on the younger branches. The leaves are mostly rounded and toothed, grey downy beneath and up to 5cm long, much larger and lobed on strong leading shoots, turning yellow in autumn. As a specimen tree this is superior to *P. alba*, suckering with less abandon and developing a more balanced crown, though the leaf undersurfaces are

less striking. It is not suitable to acid sands or dry shallow chalk soils, nor does it flourish in industrial or city situations.

Populus lasiocarpa
M Spreading AGM 1993
The stout hairy twigs of this spectacular Chinese poplar carry bold heart-shaped, red-stalked leaves which may be as much as 30cm long or more on young trees. It is a noble tree when well grown and suitable for planting in a large lawn.

Populus nigra 'Golden Lombardy'
L Columnar
A branch sport of the "Lombardy Poplar" *P. nigra* 'Italica' found in the English village of Normandy, Surrey, in 1974. It possesses the columnar habit, but with leaves golden yellow in spring maintaining the colour through summer. It colours best in full sun and is an ideal tree for restricted areas.

Populus nigra 'Italica'
L Columnar AGM 1993
Whether planted singly, in groups or in rows, the "Lombardy Poplar" is an easily recognised tree in the landscape and few other trees match it for its sentinel-like effect. As its English name suggests, it is Italian in origin and is mainly represented in cultivation by a male tree. Before planting this tree it should be remembered that its great height is matched by its vigorous root system.

Populus nigra 'Plantierensis'
L Columnar to Broadly columnar
A robust tree of tall columnar habit, broader than the "Lombardy Poplar", of which it is thought to be a hybrid. It is of French origin.

Populus 'Robusta'
L Conical
Probably the most satisfactory of the hybrid black poplars or cottonwoods for general planting. This is a bold, handsome, healthy looking tree at all times, having a tall straight leader into maturity with regular branching to produce a broad conical crown. It bears

luxuriant glossy green heart-shaped leaves, and is especially attractive in spring when the bright red male catkins drape the branches followed by the coppery-red young foliage. It is commonly used for screening purposes but is well worth considering either alone or in groups in larger gardens and estates.

Populus 'Serotina Aurea'
L Spreading AGM 1993
The "Golden Black Poplar" or "Van Geert's Poplar" is a most effective tree of vigorous growth. The heart-shaped leaves are bright yellow in spring and early summer, fading to yellow-green in summer and brightening to golden yellow before they fall in autumn. It is a male tree with a strong, openly branched head. If so desired, young trees may be hard pruned each or every other year in February to encourage the coloured young foliage and to control the size of the crown.

opposite top: Populus tremula 'Pendula'
opposite bottom: Populus 'Robusta'
below: Populus tremula (bark detail)

Populus tremula

S-M Broadly columnar to Spreading
AGM 1993
The "Aspen' is mainly known for its
smooth grey bark and its rounded,
prettily scalloped grey-green leaves
which, because of their slender flattened
stalks, tremble in the slightest breeze. It
is a suckering tree, often forming a
thicket if allowed and draping its
branches in February with delightful long
grey catkins. The leaves turn to butter-
yellow in autumn. In the wild it is
distributed throughout Europe to
western Asia and North Africa. Similar
species are found in North America and
north-east Asia, especially China.

Populus tremula 'Erecta'

M Columnar to Broadly columnar
A most useful aspen of narrow habit
contrasting well with both the type and
'Pendula'. It is sometimes offered under
the name 'Fastigiata'.

Populus tremula 'Pendula'

S Weeping
The "Weeping Aspen" forms a
mushroom-shaped head of gracefully
weeping branches and makes an
attractive tree for grass areas where its
suckering habit can be controlled by
frequent close mowing. Young plants
require training to a tall stake or cane to
produce a high crown.

Populus trichocarpa

L Broadly columnar to Spreading
Known as the "Black Cottonwood" or
"Western Balsam Poplar", this western
North American tree is known for its
extreme vigour especially in damp soils,
and for its large leaves which are whitish
beneath and balsam scented, especially
when emerging in spring. Unfortunately,
it is often of untidy habit with sprouts on
the main stem and is rapidly invasive,
often sending up masses of suckers from
the roots. Superior in every way are the
selections 'Fritzi Pauley' and 'Scott Pauley'
which are more shapely and apparently
disease free.

PRUNUS
Rosaceae

*Members of this large genus are, perhaps, the most
commonly planted of all ornamental trees. Indeed,
it would be difficult to find a single row of gardens
in which at least one flowering cherry, plum or
almond, was not represented. The popularity of
Prunus lies in the presence of so many hardy, easy-
to-grow trees suitable for small gardens. They are
a varied throng and include several distinct groups
such as cherries, plums, almonds, peaches and
laurels. Collectively, they are unfussy as to soil
provided it is not waterlogged; although it is
apparent that many of them, especially the
"Japanese Cherries", actually thrive on shallow
chalk soils, in which situations they often flower
magnificently. They demand full sun for flowering
but several are quite tolerant of some shade. These
include the laurels, which are among the best
evergreen subjects for such situations. Apart from
their floral attributes, many of the cherries also
give rich autumn leaf tints. Unless otherwise
indicated, the trees here described are deciduous.*

*Most trees of this genus are propagated by
budding or grafting onto stocks of common species,
e.g. "Japanese Cherries" onto stocks of the Gean P.
avium. This sometimes results in suckers arising
from the point of union. These must be removed as
soon as they appear, otherwise the stock will
prevail.*

*With few exceptions, the ever popular "Japanese
Cherries" are mainly planted for their blossoms
which are freely borne, being of little ornamental
merit otherwise though some do give autumn tints
of leaf. Flowering takes place over a limited period
and after 40–50 years, most cultivars in average
growing conditions become exhausted, flowering
less abundantly as they deteriorate.*

*The Prunus which follow, most especially the
cherries, are not amenable to hard purning and the
temptation to remove large branches should be
resisted until professional advice can be taken.*

Prunus 'Accolade'

S Spreading AGM 1993
One of the prettiest and most reliable of
cherries for small gardens. The wide-
spreading branches are crowded in late
March into April with rose-pink, paling to
blush-pink, semi-double blossoms which
have a charming fringed effect. The

leaves in autumn often give orange or red tints. Its origin is uncertain but probably *P. sargentii* x *P. x subhirtella*.

Prunus 'Amanogawa'

S Columnar to Broadly columnar
AGM 1993
One of the best of the "Japanese Cherries" for small gardens: a column of flower is a splendid sight on a sunny spring day. The large erect clusters of fragrant, single or semi-double, shell-pink flowers appear in late April or early May among the greenish-bronze young foliage. In autumn the leaves turn to yellow. It is normally grown feathered with branches to the base.

Prunus avium

M-L Spreading AGM 1993
The "Wild Cherry" or "Gean" is the commonest of our two native cherries, although in many areas it has been planted and become naturalised. It is conspicuous during late April or early May when the clusters of white cup-shaped flowers hang along the boughs. The leaves often turn red in autumn. It is a strong-growing tree and apt to sucker; not suitable where space is restricted.

Prunus avium 'Plena'

M Spreading AGM 1993
This splendid tree has all the qualities of the type but the white flowers are double and longer lasting. A favourite cherry for parks and roadsides. Superb as an avenue tree.

Prunus x blireana

S Spreading AGM 1993
Wherever this tree is planted it never fails to cause comment when, in late March or early April, the slender branches are wreathed in double rose-pink flowers which are slightly fragrant and 2.5cm or more across. The effect is of a striking pink cloud, highlighted by the emergence of coppery-purple foliage. It is an ideal tree for the small garden, and originated in France as a hybrid between the familiar "Purple-leaved Plum" *Prunus cerasifera*, 'Pissardii' and *P. mume* 'Alphandii'. 'Moseri'

top: Prunus 'Kanzan'
bottom: Prunus serrula

top: Prunus dulcis
middle: Prunus 'Kursar'
bottom: Prunus 'Kiku-shidare'

is another seedling of this parentage differing from the above in its darker foliage and smaller, paler flowers.

Prunus cerasifera 'Nigra'

S Spreading AGM 1993
For lovers of purple foliage this is probably one of the best sources. The leaves and stem are a blackish-purple, a very dark background for the small but abundantly produced pink flowers in March and early April. Its pink flowers and its shoots, which are seen to be purple stained when cut, readily differentiate this cultivar from 'Pissardii'.

Prunus cerasifera 'Pissardii'

S Spreading
"Purple-leaved Plum". Probably the commonest purple-leaved tree in cultivation, this was originally found sometime before 1880 by a M. Pissard, gardener to the Shah of Persia. The small pink-budded white flowers appear in profusion along the slender branches in March and early April, when they are effectively backed by the emerging dark red, turning to purple, foliage.

Prunis dulcis

S Spreading
The "Almond", formerly *P. amygdalus*, is one of the hardiest, earliest and most reliable of spring-flowering trees. Though rather open in branching, its clear pink flowers, 2.5–5cm across, seen against a blue March or early April sky are unforgettable. The fruits when produced are rarely as satisfactory as those sold in shops, which are mainly imported from southern Europe. In the wild it occurs from North Africa to western Asia, but is extensively naturalised in the Mediterranean region.

Prunus 'Hally Jolivette'

S Spreading
Not often seen in British or European gardens but well worth searching for, this hybrid of *P. x subhirtella* is ideally suited to small gardens. Its graceful slender branches are flooded in early spring with small semi-double blush-white flowers, which continue over a long period.

Prunus 'Hillieri'

S Spreading
A hybrid of *P. incisa* with *P. sargentii*, this lovely cherry combines the best qualities of both parents. The soft pink flowers flood the slender branches in April, whilst autumn brings rich foliage tints of orange and red.

Prunus incisa

S Broadly columnar to Spreading
The "Fuji Cherry" is a densely branched tree with small, jaggedly toothed leaves often providing rich autumn tints. In late March or early April the slender branches are inundated with small pink-budded white flowers creating a pink haze from a distance. It is a tough, hardy cherry and has been used as a hedge as well as for bonsai culture. It is native to Japan. 'Praecox' AGM 1993 is a selected clone flowering from January onwards, while 'February Pink' has deeper coloured flowers. There are numerous other forms, especially in Japan.

Prunus 'Kanzan'

S Vase-shaped to Spreading AGM 1993
This must be just about the most commonly planted of all flowering cherries; and while some people regard it as vulgar and overplanted, its popularity continues. The stiffly ascending branches are characteristic of its early years, becoming spreading later. In late April and early May, specimens of this tree become immediately noticeable when the branches are smothered by rich, hanging bunches of large double flowers which are a distinctive purplish-pink in colour at first, becoming pink later. It is a colour and effect which some people find garish but others see as the epitome of a flowering tree. It is sometimes grown under the name 'Sekiyama'.

Prunus cerasifera 'Pissardii'

Prunus 'Kiku-shidare'

VS Weeping AGM 1993
Perhaps the best weeping cherry for small gardens, its branches wreathed during April with double rose-pink flowers, like the pink button chrysanthemums. The leaves are bronze-green on emerging, becoming glossy green later. It makes an ideal specimen for the lawn and is especially effective when planted by a stream or pool, though it will not tolerate wet soils.

Prunus 'Kursar'

S Spreading AGM 1993
One of the best early-flowering cherries for the garden. Some would claim it to be the best. Compact in habit with ascending branches when young, it slowly broadens with age, the numerous branchlets flooded from March into April, earlier in a mild winter, with bright rich pink single flowers with red calyces. The latter are retained for some time after petal fall, further extending the display. Added to this, the leaves which emerge reddish-bronze often colour richly in autumn. It is probably the finest of the many hybrid plants produced by the late Captain Collingwood (Cherry) Ingram. It is the result of a cross between the Japanese *P. nipponica* var. *kurilensis* and the Formosan *P. campanulata*, inheriting the flowers of the latter and the habit and hardiness of the former. 'Okame' AGM 1993 is very similar in ornamental merit.

Prunus lusitanica

S-M Conical to Spreading AGM 1993
The "Portugal Laurel" is one of the very few evergreen species of Prunus, and to the casual eye bears no resemblance to the cherries or plums except when in flower or fruit. The leaves are dark glossy green with red stalks and, though dark in effect, are brightened in June by the numerous slender racemes of small hawthorn-scented white flowers. These are replaced by juicy red, turning to shining black, small, cherry-like fruits. A native of Spain and Portugal, this hardy tree is amenable to most soils and situations, including shallow chalk soils and dense shade.

Prunus lusitanica 'Variegata'

S Conical to Spreading
A pretty form with attractive though irregularly creamy-white margined leaves, often pink-tinged during winter. Unfortunately, it is less hardy than the type and should be given shelter from cold winds.

Prunus maackii

S-M Vase-shaped to Spreading
The "Manchurian Bird-cherry" is one of the most underrated small ornamental trees in Britain. It is especially suited to cold northerly climates where its crowded clusters of small white flowers are welcome in April. It is principally grown, however, for its shining amber-coloured peeling bark. Like the "Tibetan cherry", the beauty of the bark can be spoiled by algae in the warmer, wetter areas of Britain, although an annual scrubbing with warm water fully restores the effect.

Prunus 'Mount Fuji'

S Wide Spreading AGM 1993
Known as the "Mount Fuji Cherry" in reference to its snow-white flowers, this beautiful tree develops a comparatively low, wide habit with long horizontally spreading branches which become lax with age, their extremities often touching the ground. The very large fragrant flowers are semi-double or sometimes single, especially on young trees. In colour they are a dazzling snow-white and hang in long-stalked clusters from the branches in late April, when they are backed by the soft green, heavily fringed leaves. In a good autumn the leaves turn golden yellow. It was previously grown under the name 'Shirotae' which belongs to another cherry rare or absent from British cultivation.

Prunus padus

M Spreading
The "Bird Cherry" is a native tree but widely distributed in the northern hemisphere. The small white almond-scented flowers are borne in long, cylindrical, drooping tassel-like racemes after leaf flush in May, followed by shining black fruits bitter to the taste.

Prunus padus 'Colorata'

S-M Spreading AGM 1993
An unusual form with leaves coppery-purple when young, ideal backing for the pale pink flower tassels.

Prunus padus 'Watereri'

M Spreading
A free-growing tree with flower tassels up to 20cm long. A most striking tree in flower, it is suitable for a special position.

Prunus 'Pandora'

S Conical to Vase-shaped AGM 1993
An early-flowering cherry with ascending branches flooded in late March or early April with pale shell-pink blossoms. The young leaves are an attractive bronze-red and often colour richly in autumn. It is ideal for small gardens or restricted sites. It is a multiple hybrid between P. x subhirtella and P. yedoensis.

Prunus pendula 'Pendula Rosea'

S Weeping AGM 1993
A graceful mushroom-headed tree, ideal for the small garden. Its long, weeping, wand-like branches are sprinkled, during late March or early April, with small, single flowers which are pink in bud opening pale blush. The leaves often colour richly in autumn. 'Pendula Rubra' AGM 1993 is an even more striking tree with flowers carmine in bud opening deep rose. The leaves are characteristically lance-shaped. The flowers of 'Pendula Plena Rosea' are similar in colour to the last but double. All three were formerly thought to belong to the hybrid P. x subhirtella under which name they are commonly found.

Prunus persica

S Spreading
Flowering in April two to three weeks later than the "Almond", the "Peach" possesses similar but smaller pink single flowers borne in clusters along the naked stems. The young shoots are typically green, conspicuous in winter, and the flowers are followed by juicy fruits which, however, do not compare with those sold in shops: these are produced by selected fruiting clones. As a native tree it probably originated from China, although it has been cultivated from time immemorial and is naturalised in many regions of southern Europe and Asia. There are now available many named cultivars, varying mainly in flower colour.

top: Prunus persica 'Klara Mayer'
bottom: Prunus pendula 'Pendula Rubra'

Young trees have ascending branches which become more spreading with age. Leaves are often infected with peach-leaf-curl disease, for which a fungicide Bordeaux mixture is available; otherwise leaves should be picked off and burned.

Prunus persica 'Cardinal'

S Spreading

A charming tree with semi-double rosette-like flowers of a glowing red. 'Russell's Red' is an old cultivar with double crimson flowers and is still the best of its colour.

Prunus persica 'Iceberg'

S Spreading

A free-flowering form with exquisite, large semi-double flowers of pure white. 'Alba Plena' is an older cultivar with flowers of similar form and colour.

Prunus persica 'Klara Mayer'

S Spreading AGM 1993

This is perhaps the best double peach for general cultivation. Its flowers are a beautiful peach-pink and crowd the branches. 'Prince Charming' has double rose-red flowers.

Prunus 'Pink Perfection'

S Spreading AGM 1993

A first-class free-blooming cherry, a cross between 'Shogetsu' and 'Kanzan', flowering in May when the last named is on the wane. From bright red buds the fully double flowers open bright pink and fade to white. They are relatively large and borne in substantial clusters, hanging on long stalks from the pale bronzy-green young foliage. In some ways it is better than 'Kanzan', though later flowering.

Prunus 'Pink Shell'

S Spreading AGM 1993

A beautiful hybrid of *P. subhirtella*, an elegant tree, the slender branches drooping beneath the weight of countless cup-shaped delicate pink blossoms which blend with the pale green of the emerging leaves in early April.

Prunus sargentii

S-M Vase-shaped to Spreading
AGM 1993

Without doubt this is the one of the finest of all trees grown for autumn colour. In late March or early April, the spreading branches become crowded with single bright pink flowers which are later joined by the coppery-red young foliage. As autumn approaches this is one of the first trees, and certainly the first cherry, to colour, usually in mid to late September. Not only is its autumn display rich in orange and crimson tints, but it is reliable and regular, whatever the weather. Native to Japan, Sakhalin and Korea. It is longer lived than most "Japanese Cherries" and ultimately larger.

Prunus sargentii 'Rancho'

S-M Vase-shaped

An American selection of narrower habit with larger, deeper pink flowers than the type. Its autumn foliage is just as richly coloured and it is an ideal choice for gardens too small to accommodate *P. sargentii* itself.

Prunus serrula

S Spreading AGM 1993

A native of western China, the "Tibetan Cherry" is one of the most distinctive and easily recognised trees in cultivation. Unlike most other cherries, this species is not planted for its flowers but for its bark. The white flowers are not only small, but appear with and are virtually concealed by the narrow willow-like leaves in April. The bark on the trunk and branches, however, more than makes up for the lack of floral beauty. In colour it is dark shining coppery-brown and peels prettily to reveal the highly polished mahogany-red new bark. This is highly effective and attractive at all times, especially so during winter when the garden offers few, if any, counter attractions. The brilliance and shine of the trunk is encouraged by constant rubbing, and I once knew a gardener who always invited visitors to give his tree a vigorous patting and smoothing with their hands to help achieve this.

Prunus 'Shirofugen'

S Wide-spreading AGM 1993
One of the best "Japanese Cherries" for general planting, being attractive in habit and generous in its flowering which is late and long-lasting. The Japanese name for this tree means "White God" and is certainly most appropriate. It is a vigorous tree with wide-spreading branches, the lower ones often pendulous with age. The large double flowers are pink in bud, opening white and fading to pink. They are produced in long-stalked clusters during May, hanging from the branches and contrasting effectively with the coppery-bronze young foliage. The leaves in autumn turn to deep orange and coppery-brown.

Prunus 'Shogetsu'

S Wide-spreading AGM 1993
A lovely cherry of distinct habit, forming a low, wide-spreading head of branches, in later life becoming rather flat-topped with the long branches gracefully drooping at the tips. As such it is a most effective lawn tree for the medium-sized or large garden. During May the large, fringed, double flowers hang in long-stalked clusters all along the boughs. They are pink flushed in bud, opening pure white, and resemble ballet-girls' skirts in their frilled effect. The young leaves are green and appear with the flowers, turning orange and red before falling in autumn. It was previously, though incorrectly, known as 'Shimidsu-zakura'.

Prunus 'Spire'

S Columnar to Broadly columnar AGM 1993
Probably one of the best small trees raised this century. Its shape makes it ideally suited to small gardens and confined spaces. The soft pink flowers crowd the branches in April, while in autumn the leaves turn a rich red. This tree is just as effective with its branches retained to the base as it is trained to a single stem.

Prunus x subhirtella 'Autumnalis'

S Spreading AGM 1993
During the normally dreary months from late autumn to early spring there exists a small nucleus of woody plants which dare to flower and bring colour into the garden. The "Autumn Cherry" is one of them. The small semi-double and frilled blossoms are pale pink in bud, opening white – a charming contrast. They first appear in October and continue to open during mild spells until the end of March. Most days during winter will find the slender, wand-like branches of this cherry clustered with flowers and, like most winter-blooming plants, it is useful for cutting and bringing a few sprigs into the home. In autumn the leaves often turn a rich red and bronze. 'Autumnalis Rosea' AGM 1993 has flowers of a deeper pink, less effective than the type, while 'Fukubana' AGM 1993 is perhaps the most colourful, with flowers of rose-madder. Recent research suggests that *P. x subhirtella* is the result of a hybrid between *P. pendula ascendens* and *P. incisa*.

Prunus sargentii

Prunus 'Tai Haku'

M Vase-shaped to Spreading AGM 1993
The name "Great White Cherry" aptly
describes this Japanese tree which has the
distinction of having the largest flowers
of any cherry, up to 6cm across. These
are borne in April, and though pinkish in
bud, open to a dazzling white, contrasting
superbly with the rich coppery-red young
foliage. It is a strong-growing tree and
one of the best cherries for general
planting. The leaves turn yellow and
orange in autumn.

Prunus 'Ukon'

S Spreading AGM 1993
The unusual colour of the flowers of this
robust cherry makes it a popular choice
for special effects and a favourite with
flower arrangers. They are semi-double
and pale yellowish in colour with a tinge
of green, ageing to white with a pink or
reddish eye. Borne in large clusters in late
April and early May, they show up well
against the brownish-bronze young
foliage. In autumn the leaves turn rusty-
red, bronze and purplish.

Prunus virginiana 'Shubert'

S-M Conical to Spreading
A free-growing tree, an American Bird
Cherry, erect when young, becoming
more openly branched and spreading
later. The broad leaves are a rich green
when young, gradually changing to a rich
purple. By mid-summer, all but the
terminal leaves are the colour of a
"Purple-leaved Plum". By contrast, the
tassels of small white flowers in April are
of little merit.

Prunus x yedoensis

S Spreading to Wide-spreading
AGM 1993
Unknown in the wild, the "Yoshino
Cherry" originated in Japan and is
generally thought to be a hybrid between
P. lannesiana var. *speciosa* and *P. x subhirtella*.
It is particularly valued for the profusion
of its almond-scented white or blush-
white flowers before the leaves in late
March or early April. The foliage often
colours attractively in autumn. It should
not, however, be planted where
bullfinches occur.

PTELEA
Rutaceae

*The Hop trees, of which there are several, are
perfectly hardy deciduous trees, easy of cultivation
and adaptable to most soils, saving those ill-
drained. Native to North America and Mexico,
they are generally bushy in habit and may require
initial training to encourage a single stem.*

Ptelea trifoliata

S Spreading AGM 1993
A most useful tree, surprisingly little
known and little planted in British
gardens. The handsome bright glossy
green leaves, composed of three leaflets,
are aromatic when bruised and turn a
clear yellow in autumn. The small yellow-
green flowers are borne in dense terminal
clusters during summer, and are notable
for their strong perfume similar to that of
orange blossom. They are replaced by
pale green winged disc-like fruits which
have a bitter taste and often hang on the
branches long after leaf fall. It prefers an
open, sunny situation.

Ptelea trifoliata 'Aurea'

S Spreading AGM 1993
A lovely form with leaves of a glistening
soft yellow, ideal for contrasting with
purple or dark green foliaged subjects. It
brings the warmth of the sun to the
garden on a dull day.

PTEROCARYA
Juglandaceae

*Only a few species represent this handsome and
useful genus of hardy deciduous trees. They belong
to the "Walnut" family and, like these trees, have
long pinnate leaves with numerous leaflets; the
fruits, however, are winged and are borne in
pendulous strings. They are suitable for most soils
and are tolerant of damp situations, but their often
shallow roots and suckering habit makes them
unsuitable for planting in lawns.*

Pterocarya fraxinifolia

L Spreading AGM 1993
A handsome suckering tree, generally
developing a wide-spreading head when
isolated, taller when growing with other
trees. It is effective enough when in leaf
and is even more so during summer when
the long greenish catkins drape the
branches. These are replaced by unusual
and decorative green winged fruits. Once
established, it is a fast-growing tree,
tolerant of damp sites, and requires
plenty of room in which to spread. In the
river valleys south of the Caspian Sea I
have seen this tree forming thickets and
groves by the water's edge. It is native
from the Caucasus to northern Iran. The
Chinese and Japanese wingnuts *P.
stenoptera* and *P. rhoifolia*, while similar in
many ways, are not the equal of this tree.

Pterocarya x rehderiana

L Spreading
A hybrid between *P. fraxinifolia* and the
Chinese *P. stenoptera*, equal to the former
in ornamental merit and even more
vigorous. If plenty of space is available
this tree is worth searching for.

PTEROSTYRAX
Styracaceae

*A small genus of deciduous trees from China,
mainly grown for their styrax-like flowers in
spring. They thrive best in a rich well-drained soil
and are not suitable for shallow chalk soils,
flowering best in an open sunny situation.*

Pterostyrax hispida

S-M Conical to Spreading AGM 1993
A handsome hardy tree with grey and
brown striated bark, especially attractive
in summer with its bold foliage and
drooping tassels of fragrant white
flowers. These are replaced by grey
bristly fruits which are retained through
winter. Indeed, a tree in winter, its bare
branches draped with seed tassels
highlighted by a late afternoon sun, is
quite magical. In North America it is said
to be tolerant of wind and drought and is
particularly useful in city gardens there.

†PUNICA
Punicaceae

*A genus of only two species, of which the following
is the only one normally seen in cultivation.*

Punica granatum

VS Rounded to Spreading
The "Pomegranate" is most often seen as
a large densely branched shrub, but it can
be trained to a single stem by careful
pruning from an early age and then
makes an attractive small tree. It is,
however, best suited to regions enjoying
warm summers and is one of the most
drought tolerant of all woody plants. In
Britain it is most satisfactory in warm
southern areas, where it should be given
a sunny sheltered position and a well-
drained soil. It is deciduous, the narrow
glossy green leaves, copper-coloured
when young, turning yellow in autumn,
whilst the fleshy scarlet flowers with
crimson petals appear through summer.
The fruits are only normally developed
after a hot summer and are not a feature

Pterocarya fraxinifolia

top: Pyrus salicifolia 'Pendula'
bottom: Pyrus nivalis

in British cultivation. There are several named cultivars available of which 'Flore Pleno' with double orange-red flowers is the one most often seen, while 'Alba Plena' (creamy-white, double), 'Legrellei' (salmon-pink, variegated white, double) and 'Spanish Ruby' (ruby-red, double) are also grown.

PYRUS
Rosaceae

A small genus of hardy deciduous trees suitable for most soils and tolerant of drought, maritime exposure and industrial pollution. Considering these values, it is puzzling that the ornamental pears, save for the "Weeping Willow-leaved Pear", have never become more widely established in cultivation. All bear clusters of white flowers in April and several have attractive grey or silver foliage. Undoubtedly, a warm dry summer encourages freer flowering and in the green-leaved pears, commendable autumn colour.

Pyrus calleryana 'Bradford'
S-M Conical to Rounded
An extremely tough and hardy pear, erect-branched when young, becoming conical and eventually rounded. In April the branches are flooded with white blossoms which have the effect of a snow cloud from a distance. The broad, glossy green leaves, greyish when young, are capable of attractive scarlet and purple tints in autumn. In habit it is a first-rate tree, a pear version of *Carpinus betulus* 'Fastigiata'. The species is native to central and south China.

Pyrus calleryana 'Chanticleer'
S-M Conical AGM 1993
Without question one of the most ornamental of all pears for the garden, worth growing for its robust habit and compact crown alone. The snow white flowers preceding the leaves in spring are a bonus. The latter are silver-white on emerging, changing to green and often colouring richly in autumn. Its narrow crown makes this a more suitable tree than 'Bradford' where space is limited.

Pyrus communis 'Beech Hill'
S-M Conical
Erect-branched when young, this
attractive selection of the "Wild Pear" is
worth considering for its compact habit,
white flowers in spring and its glossy
green rounded leaves which often turn a
brilliant orange-yellow in autumn.

Pyrus nivalis
S Conical to Spreading
A most attractive silver-leaved tree.
Native of southern Europe, its stout
ascending branches are clothed in April
with clusters of white flowers. At the
same time the white, woolly young leaves
emerge, turning grey later. The rounded
greenish-brown fruits which follow are
very hard, only becoming soft and edible
when over-ripe. Eye-catching effects may
be had by planting and training into this
tree the "Purple-leaved Vine" (*Vitis vinifera*
'Purpurea').

Pyrus salicifolia 'Pendula'
S Weeping AGM 1993
"Weeping Willow-leaved Pear". The best
known and most commonly planted
ornamental pear, this popular tree forms
a dense mound of weeping branches
clothed with silvery-grey, downy,
narrow, willow-like leaves. Later in the
season, these become grey-green and
smooth above. Flowers are white, in mid-
April. The small fruits are top-shaped and
brown in colour. A most effective
combination may be achieved by planting
the "Purple-leaved Vine" (*Vitis vinifera*
'Purpurea') to grow through the branches
of this pear. Careful pruning is required
to prevent the crown from becoming too
crowded and untidy with age.

Pyrus ussuriensis
S-M Spreading
An elegant tree from north-eastern Asia,
with glossy green, slender pointed leaves
turning bronze-crimson in autumn. The
clusters of white flowers appear in early
April and are replaced by small, hard,
yellow-green fruits.

QUERCUS
Fagaceae

The "Oaks" are a large and variable genus of
deciduous and evergreen trees occurring in cold,
temperate and tropical regions. As ornamental
trees they have much to offer. Most are of noble
proportions when mature and many are long lived,
some gathering stories, true and false, by the score.
A number of the American oaks are known for
their autumn colours, while others bear large and
imposing leaves. The male and female flowers are
borne separately on the same tree. Neither are of
ornamental merit. Female flowers produce the well-
known fruits – acorns. Those described here are
relatively hardy and, unless indicated otherwise,
are suitable for most soils and situations. None is
really suitable for the small garden.

Quercus acutissima
M Conical to Spreading
A hardy deciduous oak from eastern Asia,
conical as a young tree, broadening with
age. The leaves, similar in shape to those
of a "Sweet Chestnut", are glossy green
above, parallel veined, and margined with
bristle-tipped teeth. It is a good looking
tree in foliage; and even in winter, when
older trees develop a greyish rugged bark,
it is not unattractive. In Britain it
flourishes best in warmer, drier areas.

Quercus canariensis
L Conical to Dome-shaped AGM 1993
Known as the "Algerian Oak", this fine,
hardy, fast-growing species develops in
time a rounded to dome-shaped head of
branches. The comparatively large, boldly
lobed, dark green leaves, paler beneath,
thickly clothe the twigs, giving the crown
a dense compact appearance. Even in
winter the leaves seem reluctant to fall,
and not until the New Year do they
finally succumb. This is a bold, good
looking oak, happy on most soils,
including those on chalk or heavy clay. It
is a native of North Africa, southern
Portugal and Spain.

Quercus castaneifolia
M-L Spreading
A native of north Iran and the Caucasus.

I have seen the "Chestnut-leaved Oak" in the former country, growing in the forests above the Caspian Sea and in the Elburz Mountains behind, its dying foliage in the late sun creating tall flames and mounds of copper and gold against the darkening hillside. It is a fast-growing tree resembling the "Turkey Oak" in general appearance, with oblong, coarsely-toothed sweet chestnut-like leaves, dark shining green above, grey and downy beneath.

Quercus castaneifolia 'Green Spire'

M Columnar to Broadly columnar
AGM 1993
An erect-branched tree like a 'Lombardy Poplar' initially, becoming more open in maturity.

Quercus cerris

L Spreading AGM 1993
The "Turkey Oak", though a native of southern Europe and western Asia, is commonly planted in the British Isles and has become naturalised in some areas. Indeed, it fits quite happily into the rural landscape and is often mistaken for a native tree. It is one of the fastest-growing of all oaks and is an excellent screening tree, particularly in coastal areas. It is also excellent on dry chalk soils. The coarsely-toothed or lobed leaves are glossy green and rough to the touch above. The acorns have characteristic whiskery cups.

Quercus cerris 'Variegata'

M-L Spreading
An uncommon and desirable form of the "Turkey Oak" with leaves boldly but irregularly margined creamy-white. Well worth searching for and demanding of a special place such as a large lawn.

Quercus coccinea

L Spreading
One of the most spectacular large trees grown for autumn colour, the "Scarlet Oak" is a fast-growing tree when young, soon making a sizeable specimen of rather openly branched habit. The large, deeply and sharply-lobed leaves are glossy green

top: Quercus cerris 'Variegata'
bottom: Quercus canariensis

on both surfaces and in a good season turn a rich scarlet, the colour often developing in patches, almost branch by branch. It is a native of eastern North America and was introduced into cultivation as long ago as 1691. It is quite hardy and suitable for all soils except those of an alkaline nature.

Quercus coccinea 'Splendens'
L Spreading AGM 1993
Like all autumn-colouring trees grown from seed, the "Scarlet Oak" is variable in effect and this clone is generally considered to be the best selection. It is grafted on to stocks of the common kind. The leaves are larger than those of the type and colour brilliantly and consistently. It is also more vigorous than the type and makes a larger tree.

Quercus dentata
S-M Spreading
The "Daimyo Oak" of north-east Asia, especially Japan, is a relatively slow-growing bold-foliaged tree with stout downy shoots and handsome lobed leaves, which on a young tree may expand to as much as 30cm. It grows best where summers are warm and winters cold.

Quercus ellipsoidalis
M Conical to Spreading
A handsome North American Black Oak, similar in some respects to the "Pin Oak" *Q. palustris* to which it is related, but in cultivation of shapelier habit. The glossy green deeply-lobed leaves are capable of outstanding autumn colour, a rich scarlet in Britain. In the wild it is more tolerant of dry soils than others of its group.

Quercus frainetto
L Conical to Spreading
Bold foliage is the chief attraction of the "Hungarian Oak". It is a relatively fast-growing tree, older specimens displaying a handsome, rugged, fissured bark. The large leaves are broad at the top, narrowing to the stalk, and are deeply-lobed with characteristic oblong lobes. It is hardy, and is excellent on all soils except those which are excessively wet. It is native to south-eastern Europe. Also known as *Q. conferta* which is a synonym.

top: Quercus coccinea 'Splendens'
bottom: Quercus ilex

131

Quercus frainetto
'Hungarian Crown'

L Conical AGM 1993
A selected form equal in every way to the
type, but distinct in its upright habit
developing a compact conical or oval
crown.

Quercus x hispanica
'Lucombeana'

L Spreading AGM 1993
The "Lucombe Oak" is a hybrid between
the "Cork Oak" Q. *suber* and the "Turkey
Oak" Q. *cerris*, old trees having the corky
bark and evergreen nature of the former
and the leaf character of the latter.
Seedlings from the original tree,
however, have produced trees varying in
character, some resembling more the one
parent and some the other. Most are
ultimately large, heavy-limbed, dense
foliaged trees and suitable only for a large
lawn or similarly spacious area. Like *Q.
ilex*, they cast a deep shade.

Quercus x hispanica
'Wageningen'

L Spreading
A Dutch selection from the University of
Wageningen. Popular on the Continent.
It is hardy even in Holland and its leaves
last until spring, turning brown only in
cold winters.

Quercus ilex

L Spreading AGM 1993
Although growing to a large size, few
trees match the "Evergreen Oak" or
"Holm Oak" for its lush evergreen
foliage, which is especially effective in
winter when all around is grey and bare.
It is variable in leaf and those of young
saplings can look very different from
those of a mature specimen. Older trees
develop a picturesque chequered grey
bark, while the leathery leaves are
generally narrow, dark glossy green
above and grey downy beneath. In June
the whole canopy is transformed by the
emergence of white, woolly young shoots
and clusters of pendulous yellow male
catkins. Native of the Mediterranean
region and south-western Europe, this
majestic tree is suitable for most soils and
situations, even tolerating shade and
coastal gales. It is, however, subject to
damage by frost in cold inland districts of
the north.

Quercus macranthera

L Spreading
A native of the Caucasus and the
mountains of northern Iran, this is a
strong-growing deciduous oak with stout,
densely hairy shoots and bold leaves
similar in shape to those of the "English
Oak", *Q. robur*, but larger and densely
hairy beneath. It is easy and hardy in
most soils, blending well with the rural
landscape.

Quercus palustris

L Spreading AGM 1993
A handsome and cheerful looking tree,
the "Pin Oak" of eastern North America
belongs to the same group – the Black
Oaks – as *Q. coccinea* and *Q. rubra*. It is a
strong, fast-growing tree, older
specimens with a pale smooth bark and
somewhat pendant lower branches. The
deeply and sharply-lobed leaves with
bristle-tipped teeth are a bright polished
green on both surfaces, the lower surface
with tufts of down in the vein axils. In
autumn these turn a rich scarlet and
crimson, starting with the outermost
leaves then moving in. One of the most
satisfactory of the Black Oaks, in Britain
it does best in the south and east
whenever summers are drier. Like others
of its group it is not at its best on alkaline
soils.

Quercus petraea

L Spreading to Dome-shaped AGM 1993
Although less known and planted, the
"Sessile Oak" or "Durmast Oak" is every
bit as ornamental and desirable as its
more well known relative the "English
Oak" – *Q. robur*. With its often tall,
powerful trunk and dome-shaped crown
of straight branches, a mature tree is an
outstanding feature in the landscape. In
Ireland it is commonest in the south and
west, whilst in Britain it prefers the hills
of the north and west. In cultivation it
thrives best in a moist but well-drained
soil.

Quercus phellos

M Spreading AGM 1993
The "Willow Oak" of eastern North
America is so called because of its narrow
strap-shaped leaves which emerge yellow
and colour equally attractively in autumn.
The branches too are large and slender. It
is of easy cultivation, but does best where
summers are warm and dry.

Quercus pontica

S Conical to Spreading
The "Armenian Oak" is without doubt
one of the most handsome and easily
recognised of its clan. A deciduous
species, its large broad-ended leaves are
boldy ribbed and rich glossy green above
with a yellowish midrib, sometimes
turning gold in autumn. The stout
branches are draped with yellowish male
catkins in spring. Although not always
available, this is an oak worth waiting for.
It makes a striking specimen tree in a
lawn or bed. A hybrid between this
species and the "Daimyo Oak", (*Q. dentata*)
known as *Q.* 'Pondaim', is sometimes
available from specialist nurseries. It is
similar to *Q. pontica* in habit and foliage.

Quercus robur

L Spreading AGM 1993
One cannot praise too highly the merits
of our native "English Oak" which,
despite its common name, is also found in
the wild throughout Europe, the
Caucasus, south-western Asia and North
Africa. There is a danger that many
people, with the necessary garden space,
might disregard this oak as being
ordinary and not exotic or exciting
enough to be considered for planting. If
this attitude were to become widely
accepted it would be a sad day. Its habit
and growth are perhaps too familiar to
need describing, but I must add that few
trees inspire so much feeling in people as
this. It is a strong and unshakable part of
our history and development, and there
are many ancient specimens up and down
the country, witnesses to the time when
oak forests were more dominant in the
land. The oak is one of several trees
planted for posterity, and I only hope that
in this often selfish epoch we can, when

top: Quercus robur 'Fastigiata'
bottom: Quercus x turneri

circumstances permit, forget our preoccupation with short-term values, long enough to permit the planting of trees such as this. Hardy and happy in most soils and situations, the "English Oak" has given rise to numerous unusual, as well as attractive, variations.

Quercus robur 'Concordia'

S Spreading to Rounded
Slower-growing than the type, maddeningly so if you start as is normally the case with a small specimen, the "Golden Oak" is, when well developed, one of the most effective coloured-foliage trees. The leaves of this round-headed tree are golden-yellow throughout spring and summer. Like the equally effective but faster-growing and larger "Golden Poplar" (*Populus* 'Serotina Aurea'), it was raised at Van Geert's nursery at Ghent in about 1843.

Quercus robur fastigiata

L Broadly columnar AGM 1993
Known as the "Cypress Oak", this very useful tree is fastigiate in youth, broadening out and becoming broadly columnar as it matures. In time it reaches a considerable height, and is an ideal tree for formal effects or to give height to otherwise low or horizontal plantings. There are several named selections now available including 'Koster' and 'Kassel'. These are claimed to be of narrower, more compact habit.

Quercus rubra

L Spreading AGM 1993
The "Red Oak" of eastern North America is easily one of the most vigorous and impressive of all hardy large trees. Given a lime-free soil it soon develops into a fine specimen with bold, sharply-lobed leaves. These are normally dull green beneath and are capable of superb colouring in autumn. However, as most trees are normally seed-grown by the nurseryman, autumn colour is variable; and whilst the leaves of some trees turn a rich red, those of other trees may turn yellow, or brown before falling. It is a most adaptable tree and thrives in most situations, even in industrial areas.

Quercus rubra 'Aurea'

S-M Spreading
This unusual form of the "Red Oak" is mainly grown for its striking effect in spring when the emerging leaves appear a bright yellow, gradually turning to green as summer arrives. Although rare in cultivation, it is one of the finest trees for spring effect.

Quercus shumardii

M-L Spreading
An American Black Oak similar in many respects to *Q. coccinea* and like that species capable of brilliant autumn colours. In Britain it thrives best in southern and eastern areas. In North America it has proved tolerant of adverse sites and has even shown a tolerance of alkaline clay soils, unusual for a black oak.

Quercus suber

M Spreading
The "Cork Oak" is native to south-west Europe, especially Portugal where it is commonly cultivated for its characteristic thick, rugged bark which provides the cork of commerce. Naturally, it thrives best in a Mediterranean climate but can be grown in the warmer southern and south-western areas of Britain, and in the drier south-east where it is capable of reaching a large size. One of the best specimens I have seen grows in the University Botanic Garden Cambridge where it thrives despite foliage scorch and shoot damage in severe winters. The leathery evergreen leaves provide a dense canopy and a heavy shade. It is suitable for a warm sunny position, preferably sheltered from cold winds.

Quercus x turneri

S-M Spreading to Rounded
Known as "Turner's Oak", after the nurseryman who raised it at the end of the eighteenth century, this dense round-headed tree is a hybrid between the "Evergreen Oak" (*Q. ilex*) and the "English Oak" (*Q. robur*). Its long, broadly-toothed leaves are dark green above and thickly clothe the stems, creating an almost black-green effect from a distance. Though deciduous, the leaves remain on the branches until well in the New Year.

It is a very hardy, tolerant and adaptable tree, especially good on shallow chalk soils.

Quercus variabilis

M Spreading

A distinguished oak from north-east Asia where it occurs over a wide area in the wild. As the stem matures it develops a handsome, thick corky bark giving rise to its English name "Chinese Cork Oak". The cork, however, is inferior to that of the European "Cork Oak" – *Q. suber*. The leaves are similar in shape to those of a "Sweet Chestnut", parallel veined, the margins set with bristle-tipped teeth. Dark green above, they are covered beneath with a close, pale grey or whitish felt. The acorn cups too, are densely set with long whiskers. This is an extremely hardy tree in countries enjoying hot summers, whilst in Britain it is seen at its best in the south and east.

RHUS
Anacardiaceae

A large genus of deciduous trees, shrubs and climbers. Those trees in general cultivation are hardy and grown mainly for their handsome leaves which are pinnately divided into numerous leaflets, colouring richly in autumn. The male and female flowers are normally borne on separate trees. They are easily cultivated and generally unfussy as to soil. They are also tolerant of atmospheric pollution and are, therefore, good town and city trees. The sap, of some species certainly, is poisonous, causing dermatitis or even blistering on sensitive skins, and care must be taken when pruning or even handling them.

Rhus trichocarpa

VS-S Spreading

A most attractive Japanese tree or shrub of pleasing habit with long downy ash-like leaves mainly gathered towards the ends of the branches. These are coppery-pink when emerging, becoming rich green in summer and turning to a fiery scarlet or orange in autumn. A tree in early autumn contains some striking effects, with some leaves colouring and others

top: Rhus trichocarpa
bottom: Rhus typhina 'Dissecta'

still green. For the best results in autumn, this sumach should be grown in an open situation preferably in full sun.

Rhus typhina

VS-S Spreading AGM 1993
The "Stag's-horn Sumach" is one of the most frequently planted of all small trees in cities and town gardens, which is not surprising as it is "bone" hardy and easy to grow. In fact, it is almost impossible not to succeed with this tree. Its broadly domed or flat-headed shape is a common feature in suburban gardens, particularly noticeable in autumn when the handsome leaves turn to red, scarlet orange and yellow. Even in winter the gaunt, densely brown-felted stems are not without interest, especially those of female trees which retain tight terminal cones of dark crimson, bristly fruits. It is prone to suckering, which need not to be a bad thing, providing, as it does, ideal gift plants for friends. The previous year's shoots may be pruned hard back each or every other year in February to encourage strong young shoots bearing extra large leaves. Care should be taken when pruning to prevent the sap from making contact with the skin.

Rhus typhina 'Dissecta'

VS-S Spreading AGM 1993
A handsome female form with leaflets deeply cut and divided producing a fern-like effect, which is even more beautiful in autumn when the foliage colours brilliantly. It was previously grown as 'Laciniata' which name correctly belongs to another, inferior and rarely grown, form.

ROBINIA
Leguminosae

A small genus of deciduous trees and shrubs all native to North America. They are members of the "Pea" family and are closely related to Gleditsia, the "Honey Locusts". Their leaves are divided into numerous leaflets like those of an ash, and their stems are often armed with hooked thorns. All are hardy and fast-growing, suitable for most soils and

top: *Robinia x slavinii 'Hillieri'*
bottom: *Robinia pseudoacacia 'Frisia'*

especially useful for dry or sandy soils. They are tolerant of atmospheric pollution and coastal conditions, but are not the best trees for windswept situations where they are prone to broken branches. Ideally they require a position in full sun for flowering. Any pruning necessary is best carried out in late summer as Robinias "bleed" if pruned in spring.

Robinia x ambigua 'Decaisneana'

S-M Spreading
A hybrid between the "False Acacia" (*R. pseudoacacia*) and the "Clammy Locust" (*R. viscosa*), this easy-to-grow and attractive tree was raised in France over a hundred years ago and is still very popular there, particularly as a street tree. In June the large pendulous clusters of pink flowers thrust their way through the foliage, creating a most pleasant effect.

Robinia pseudoacacia

M-L Spreading AGM 1993
Known as the "Common Acacia" or "False Acacia", this is one of the most vigorous and easiest to grow of all hardy trees. Once established, it suckers prodigiously and will, if allowed, form dense thickets of thorny stems, hence its use as a soil binder in sandy areas. As a specimen tree it bears an impressive grooved and fissured bark, and old trees often develop a picturesque gnarled and ancient appearance. The drooping clusters of white, slightly scented flowers appear along the branches in June and are very attractive to bees. Native to the Appalachians in the eastern United States, it is now widely planted and naturalised in cool temperate regions of the world, especially in China where its tolerance of compaction, pollution and lopping, as well as its shade and nitrogen fixing capacities, are much admired.

Robinia pseudoacacia 'Frisia'

S-M Spreading AGM 1993
Raised in a Dutch nursery in 1935, this splendidly colourful-foliage tree has become one of the most popular and desirable of all ornamental trees. Its foliage remains a striking golden yellow right through from spring until autumn.

Robinia pseudoacacia 'Rozynskiana'

S Spreading
Under this resounding name we find a most elegant tree. The spreading branches droop at the tips, but it is the large drooping leaves which give this tree its almost weeping effect. The usual clusters of white flowers are produced in June. It was raised in the nursery of the Polish Count Zamoyski around 1900.

Robinia pseudoacacia 'Umbraculifera'

S Rounded
An easily recognised tree with its densely rounded head of spineless branches giving it the common name "Mop-head Acacia". It is rather formal in effect and is commonly planted as a street tree, particularly in France. It is liable to breakages in exposed or windy situations. Sometimes catalogued under its synonym 'Inermis'.

Robinia x slavinii 'Hillieri'

S Spreading AGM 1993
One of the most satisfactory of the small tree robinias, developing a rounded head of slender branches and elegant leaves. The lilac-pink flowers are slightly fragrant and appear in nodding clusters in June. Like all Robinias, its branches are brittle and are easily broken when exposed to strong winds. It is a hybrid between *R. kelseyi* and *R. pseudoacacia*.

SALIX
Salicaceae

The "Willows" are a very large and diverse genus of deciduous trees and shrubs, most of which are hardy and of the easiest cultivation. Indeed, some species, in common with the poplar, are extremely vigorous and rapidly develop into a large size: they should not, therefore, be planted near buildings or underground drains. Others, however, do not reach a great size and are quite suitable for the smaller garden. Apart from their vigour and ability to grow on a variety of soils, particularly those of a wet nature, many of the willows are

top: *Salix alba argentea*
bottom: *Salix caprea* 'Kilmarnock'

notable for their display of male catkins in late winter or early spring, whilst others have attractive coloured twigs in winter. In connection with the production of catkins, it should be remembered that male and female catkins are borne on separate trees, and when buying for attractive catkins a male clone must be asked for.

Salix acutifolia

S Spreading
A very hardy willow widely distributed in the wild through Russia, as far east as Siberia and north-east China. It is closely related to *S. daphnoides*, differing principally in its more slender branches, somewhat pendulous at tips, and in its narrower leaves. It has similarly bloomy young shoots and is most attractive. An excellent selection with blue bloomy shoots is known as 'Blue Streak' AGM 1993.

Salix aegyptiaca

S Spreading
In February and March the stout grey felted shoots of this willow are decorated in the male form with conspicuous yellow catkins, creating a cloud of welcome colour at the end of winter. Once cultivated from Egypt to Kashmir for its male catkins which were sugared and eaten as a sweetmeat by Muslims, or else used as a perfumed drink and for perfuming linen, the "Musk Willow" is truly native of the eastern Caucasus region and northern Iran. In the latter country I have seen it crowding the rivers which flow through the rugged Elburz Mountains, lighting the dark gulleys where all above was cold rock and snow.

Salix alba

L Spreading
The "White Willow" is one of the most familiar and easily recognised of our large native trees. It occurs in water meadows, by river, etc, and presents a great mound of narrow silver-backed leaves shimmering and flashing in the wind. It is an excellent tree for maritime exposure and is often used as a windbreak in coastal areas. It is found wild through Europe to northern Asia and North Africa.

Salix alba argentea

M Rounded AGM 1993
A slower-growing, smaller version of the type, with leaves of an intense silvery hue, very striking, especially from a distance. It is sometimes catalogued under the name 'Sericea'.

Salix alba 'Britzensis'

M-L Conical AGM 1993
Although its summer foliage is pleasant enough, this male willow is essentially a tree for winter effect, when its bright red young stems lend warmth and much-needed colour to the bleak garden landscape. If allowed to develop unchecked it will soon make a tall tree, when the coloured twigs have to be admired from afar. Alternatively, as a young tree, it may be hard pruned each or every other year in April in order to encourage stronger and brighter new shoots enjoyable nearer eye-level. Often grown and sold incorrectly under the name 'Chermesina'. See also 'Chrysostela'.

Salix alba caerulea

L Conical
The famous "Cricket-bat Willow" is a greener tree in foliage than the type, due to the leaves becoming smooth in late summer. It is known for its rapid growth, erect branching and, of course, its wood which from the female tree is prized more than any other by cricket-bat makers.

Salix alba 'Chrysostela'

M-L Conical to Broadly columnar
A vigorous tree of erect habit which is mainly noted for its coloured young shoots in winter. These are orange-red maturing to yellow at the base. Like 'Britzensis', this willow makes a colourful winter feature when pollarded. It is sometimes grown wrongly as 'Chermesina'.

Salix alba 'Liempde'

L Conical
A Dutch selection commonly planted in Holland for its well developed central leader and narrowly ovoid to conical crown.

Salix alba vitellina

M Conical AGM 1993
In general effect, a golden-twigged version of 'Britzensis'. The young shoots are a yolk-of-egg yellow, sometimes orange flushed, brightest from autumn to spring. Left alone it develops a tall conical crown with ascending branches; but, like 'Britzensis', it can be hard pruned each or every other year in April to encourage a fresh crop of brightly coloured shoots. Its leaves are less silky and silvery than the type.

Salix caprea 'Kilmarnock'

VS Weeping AGM 1993
Known as the "Kilmarnock Willow", this neat, umbrella-shaped tree is a weeping form of our native "Goat Willow" or "Pussy Willow", beloved by children for its silky "pussies" and its golden male catkins known as "Palm" in early spring. The true plant of this name is a male clone, its branches in late winter studded with golden-yellow catkins. The female version, which is broader and less ornamental, is known as "Weeping Sally".

Salix daphnoides

S-M Spreading
The "Violet Willow" is a justly popular choice with gardeners. Its vigorous upright shoots are deep purple in colour, and are covered by a blue-white plum-like bloom which can be rubbed off with the finger. In order to enhance the winter display, the branches may be hard pruned each or every other year in February or March thereby encouraging the production of strong, heavily bloomed, young shoots. Its leaves are a handsome polished dark green above, blue-white below. In the wild it ranges from northern Europe to central Asia. If a male clone, such as 'Aglaia' AGM 1993, is acquired, one can also enjoy the large yellow catkins which appear before the leaves in late winter or early spring.

Salix 'Eugenii'

S Conical
A fine willow of slender conical habit with very narrow sea-green leaves. It is a male clone and the pink-flushed grey

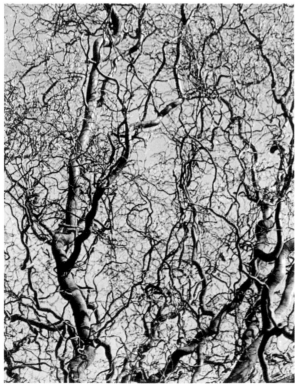

top: *Salix x sepulcralis* 'Chrysocoma'
bottom: *Salix matsudana* 'Tortuosa'

catkins appearing all along the erect branches in early spring add just that extra touch of charm. Most usually catalogued as a form of *S. purpurea* which it most closely resembles, it is thought to be a hybrid between the above species and *S. viminalis*.

Salix magnifica

VS-S Spreading AGM 1993
An extraordinary willow in its stout ascending dark purplish stems and large grey-green entire leaves, which bear a superficial resemblance to those of certain magnolias. It is a Chinese tree or large shrub suitable for a special position, preferably one sheltered from exposure. Its purple, changing to red, young growths are subject to damage by late spring frost but it is otherwise quite hardy and never fails to attract comment.

Salix matsudana

M Conical to Spreading
A graceful tree of pleasingly neat habit, the slender stems clothed with narrow leaves, green above, grey beneath. Known as the "Pekin Willow", it is native to northern China, Manchuria and Korea, and is an excellent willow for dry soils and difficult situations.

Salix matsudana 'Pendula'

S-M Weeping
If a beautiful, not-too-large weeping willow is required for the garden, none can better this tree. Its long, slender branches arch and weep in a most graceful fashion, and apppear even more ethereal in spring when spattered with the bright green tufts of the emerging leaves. Though less spectacular than *S. x sepulcralis* 'Chrysocoma', it has the advantage of being scab and canker resistant.

Salix matsudana 'Tortuosa'

M Conical to Vase-shaped AGM 1993
One of the most striking and easily recognised willows because of the curious twisting and spiralling of its branches and shoots. It provides one of the best talking-points in any garden, especially during winter when its strange growth is seen to best advantage. In old age the crown more vase-shaped or spreading.

Salix pentandra

S-M Spreading
The "Bay Willow" is one of the most handsome of our native willows, it is also one of the most neglected by gardeners, which is surprising considering its ornamental merit. Its shining brownish-green shoots are clothed with bold polished, brilliant green leaves which are aromatic when bruised and when flushing in spring. Male clones have attractive yellow catkins in late spring.

Salix purpurea

S Spreading
Occurring in the wild throughout Europe and into central Asia, the "Purple Osier" is one of our more graceful native species. Often shrubby in habit, it may be trained up to a single stem, and its long, slender branches allowed to arch and splay out in all directions. In April the slender, often paired, catkins appear all along the stems and are later replaced by the narrow blue-green leaves. If the bark of the young shoots is scraped with the finger-nail the wood revealed will be a bright yellow. It is one of the most adaptable willows, being as good on dry soils as on wet; its strong flexible stems are used in basket making.

Salix purpurea 'Pendula'

VS Weeping AGM 1993
The best weeping willow for small gardens, reproducing all the charm and elegance of the larger weepers on a miniature scale. It is normally grafted onto a tall stock.

Salix x rubens 'Basfordiana'

M Conical to Spreading AGM 1993
Less often seen than its merit deserves, this vigorous willow has young shoots of a polished orange-yellow colour quite as effective as those of S. alba vitellina or S. alba 'Chrysostela', if not more so, especially when hard pruned. Its leaves are narrow and a bright polished green. It was raised in the 1860's at Basford in Nottinghamshire by William Sealing, a basket maker, and is the result of a cross between S. fragilis and S. alba var. vitellina. Both male and female trees are in cultivation.

Salix x sepulcralis 'Chrysocoma'

M-L Weeping AGM 1993
The "Golden Weeping Willow" is perhaps the most popular and commonly planted of all weeping trees. It is usually the one most people think of when they picture a weeping tree, the strongly arching branches splaying out long, slender, golden-yellow shoots which eventually hang down to touch the ground, forming attractive curtains. The effect is best seen during winter when the tree is naked; but even in summer, when clothed with slender, bright green leaves, it presents an unforgettable picture. Its origin is obscure though some authorities believe it is the result of a hybrid between S. babylonica (not best suited to the British climate) and S. alba var. vitellina. Like most willows it is fast-growing and forms a wide-spreading head. It is, therefore, mainly suitable for large gardens and parks; and the temptation to plant it in small gardens, where it is all too frequently seen, should be resisted. One shadow lies over this willow and that is its susceptibility to scab and canker, a disfiguring disease which is only practicably controlled on a small, young tree. The large limbs of old trees are subject to fracture in strong winds and this should be borne in mind when choosing a suitable planting site.

†SAPIUM
Euphorbiaceae

A large genus of trees and shrubs from the tropical and subtropical regions. The following are the only species normally encountered in Europe, and then only in the warmer areas of the south and south-east. Their sap is milky white and poisonous.

Sapium japonicum

S Spreading
Although hardier than the next species, this is a rare tree in cultivation, in Britain certainly, where it is mainly found in specialist collections and arboreta in southern, warmer areas. It is native to

eastern Asia especially Japan, China and Korea and is notable for its large, toothless deciduous leaves 7.5–15cm long, glaucous beneath which often turn a rich red before falling in autumn. The erect catkin-like flowerheads appear in June, and after a warm summer are followed by three-lobed fruits.

Sapium sebiferum

S-M Spreading

Known as the "Chinese Tallow Tree" because of the use put to the waxy seed coat in candle and soap making. A native of China, this attractive deciduous tree is valued for its neat appearance and its long-stalked, long pointed leaves which, at a glance, may be mistaken for those of a small-leaved poplar. They often turn a rich crimson in autumn. Neither the tiny creamy-white flowers, which occur in dense terminal spikes, nor the fruits are of significant ornamental value. It makes a charming specimen tree for the lawn but only in consistently warm areas, especially the Mediterranean region. It is drought tolerant.

SASSAFRAS
Lauraceae

A small genus of deciduous trees, of which only the following is in general cultivation. It requires a lime-free, moist but well-drained soil, preferably in the shelter of other trees.

Sassafras albidum

M Spreading

A hardy tree producing suckers when happily established. Its flowers are insignificant, though its dark blue fruits on red stalks, borne only after a warm summer, are attractive close to. The chief ornamental value of this tree, however, lies in its leaves which exhibit a startling range of shapes. They may be oval and entire or from two- to three-lobed, all variations appearing on the one tree. In colour they are bright green above and blue-green below, turning a lovely butter-yellow in autumn. Even when leafless in winter, the tree displays a rugged fissured bark and wavy twigs and branches.

top: Sassafras albidum
bottom: Schima argentea

Belonging to the "Bay" family, all parts of the tree are aromatic, and in its native eastern North America the bark of the roots is sometimes used to make Sassafras tea. Not always easily obtainable in Britain, it is well worth searching for.

†SCHIMA
Theaceae

A small genus of evergreen trees and shrubs from subtropical and warm temperate regions of south-east Asia and the Himalaya. The following species is the only one normally seen out of doors in Britain and Ireland, though others are occasionally found in specialist collections, often under glass.

Schima argentea

S-M Conical to Spreading
A handsome Chinese evergreen of dense bushy habit with slender pointed, leathery leaves which are a deep glossy green above and glaucous beneath, conspicuous when ruffled by the wind. The small, creamy-white flowers are borne on slender stalks in autumn. Although easily the hardiest of the species this attractive, late-flowering subject is best suited to a sheltered, especially woodland, site in the milder, moister areas of Britain and Ireland.

†SCHINUS
Anacardiaceae

A small genus of evergreen trees and shrubs with ornamental foliage, only suitable for subtropical and Mediterranean climates.

Schinus molle

S Weeping
The "Pepper Tree" or "Peruvian Mastic Tree" is one of the most commonly planted trees in Mediterranean regions. This is not surprising, considering its elegant weeping habit and its tolerance of heat and drought. Its evergreen attractively divided leaves are daintily poised on the long slender branchlets, and

the small yellow flowers are borne male and female on separate trees. Female trees when pollinated produce coral-red fruits the size of small peas in summer and autumn. A native of South America, this is a popular avenue tree in cities and towns of southern Europe, eventually reaching 10m or more high. It casts a light shade, ever changing, as its branches are blown in the wind.

SOPHORA
Leguminosae

Both evergreen and deciduous trees and shrubs are found in this interesting genus, though only the following species makes anything like a large tree in the British Isles.

Sophora japonica

M-L Spreading to Dome-shaped
AGM 1993
The "Pagoda Tree", although native of China, has long been cultivated in Japan and is very common there. It is a spectacular tree when mature, of bold rounded appearance with rugged bark, and with leaves divided into numerous leaflets like those of an ash. The tiny creamy-white pea-flowers are borne in large terminal branched heads during late summer and autumn and, when finished, shower the ground below. Unfortunately, trees do not normally flower until at least 30 years of age. It thrives best in the drier eastern regions of the British Isles, and requires a well-drained soil and plenty of sun to be seen at its best.

Sophora japonica 'Pendula'

VS-S Weeping
The "Weeping Pagoda Tree" is normally grafted on a tall stem when it will make in time a perfect parasol or mushroom head of arching and hanging branches, eventually reaching to the ground. It is, however, a non-flowering tree, or virtually so, and is normally grown solely for its weeping habit and its shade. It is best suited to a lawn, large patio or even a courtyard.

Sophora japonica 'Violacea'
M-L Spreading
This Chinese selection has flowers stained rose-violet appearing later than those of the type. It is just as free-flowering and, more importantly, flowers at an earlier age.

SORBUS
Rosaceae

Second only to the "Cherries" (Prunus) and "Crabs" (Malus) as the most popular small garden trees, the many members of this large genus present a wide range of ornamental effects. Botanically they fall into two main groups, the "Whitebeams" and the "Mountain Ashes". The former are grown mainly for their attractive, often large, oval or rounded, greyish-green leaves which are covered in white down in spring. The mountain ashes, by far the larger group, bring rich autumn colouring of leaves and fruits, the former of which are divided like those of an ash. All species are hardy and deciduous, growing in a wide variety of soils and situations, and are tolerant of atmospheric pollution as well as coastal blasts. Some members of the mountain ash group are not ideally suited to dry, sandy or shallow chalk soils, flourishing best where summer moisture is available. Unless indicated otherwise, all have white flowers in dense flattened or slightly domed heads (corymbs) in May. Compared with other, larger trees, they are not long lived but amply repay their keep with some of the most reliable and satisfying attractions in the gardening year. With few exceptions, the trees here described are erect-branched or vase-shaped in habit, gradually broadening in maturity. Sorbus, being members of the family Rosaceae, are susceptible to fire-blight, some species more so than others. In areas where this debilitating bacterial disease is common, it is worth seeking local advice as to which species and cultivars are best suited. Sorbus species may be grown from seed or vegetatively by budding or grafting. Named selections are vegetatively propagated.

top: *Sophora japonica* 'Pendula'
bottom: *Sophora japonica*

Sorbus alnifolia

S-M Conical to Spreading
This uncommon but desirable species from north-east Asia is quite hardy and easy of cultivation. It develops a neat compact head of ascending branches, densely clothed with sharply-toothed leaves somewhat resembling those of "Hornbeam". These turn to a warm orange and scarlet in autumn when they are accompanied by small, oval, red or orange-red fruits.

Sorbus aria

S-M Spreading
Our native "Whitebeam", a familiar tree of chalk downs in the south of England where it often jostles for space with the yew. It is an extremely tough, round-headed tree and is one of the few trees which is able to withstand fierce coastal winds as well as atmospheric pollution. Its rounded, toothed leaves are covered by a startling white down on emerging in spring, becoming grey-green and white-backed in summer, then turning to russet and gold in autumn when they are joined by bunches of large deep crimson, brown-speckled fruits. The creamy-white flowers are produced in May. It is found as a native throughout Europe.

Sorbus aria 'Lutescens'

S-M Conical to Spreading AGM 1993
Only in spring is this tree distinguishable from the common "Whitebeam". Then the emerging leaves are coated in a dense creamy-white tomentum which renders the tree most conspicuous at a distance; soon after, the leaves become the normal grey-green.

Sorbus aria 'Majestica'

S-M Spreading AGM 1993
A distinct and impressive form of the "Whitebeam", of upright habit when young and bearing large leaves often 10–15cm long. Even the deep crimson fruits in autumn are larger and more conspicuous. It is sometimes catalogued under the name 'Decaisneana' which is a synonym.

Sorbus aucuparia

S-M Spreading
The "Mountain Ash" or "Rowan" is one of the most ornamental of our native trees. The leaves are divided into numerous sharply-toothed leaflets and, in late May or early June, are joined by flattened heads of creamy-white flowers. It is usually the first of the Sorbus to ripen its fruit when, in late August or September, they turn a bright orange-red, the heavy bunches filling the branches, lighting the early autumn days until, inevitably, the blackbirds take their toll. Although common and easy to grow, this is one of the most reliable of small trees and is adaptable to almost any soil and situation, although on shallow chalk soils it is shorter-lived than *S. aria*. It is distributed in the wild throughout Europe and has given rise to many different forms, most of which bear similar fruits. Seedlings are used as stocks for grafting the selected clones of this and related species.

Sorbus aucuparia 'Beissneri'

S Conical to Rounded
A superb tree when seen at its best. Its crown is often rather thin initially, gradually filling out to an ovoid or rounded head in maturity. The bark of both the trunk and the erect branches is a warm coppery-orange in colour which glows when wet and develops a thin whitish bloom on drying. This effect is best developed on trees growing in the drier eastern regions of the British Isles. Like several other coloured-bark trees, specimens growing in moister western areas often have the ornamental effect diminished by the tendency for algae or lichen to form on the bark. Even without the coloured bark, this tree is worth growing for its attractive leaves, which are yellow-green, when young, carried on red petioles, and have deeply cut or divided leaflets creating a fern-like effect.

Sorbus aucuparia 'Fructu Luteo'

S Spreading AGM 1993
Similar in habit to the type but with amber-yellow fruits freely born. A fine tree when heavily fruited in autumn.

Sorbus aucuparia
'Sheerwater Seedling'
S-M Conical to Spreading AGM 1993
A fine selection of the "Rowan", narrowly
conical in habit at first, broadening in
maturity. The fruits are freely borne in
larger bunches than the type. It is
frequently planted as a street tree.

Sorbus cashmiriana
S Spreading AGM 1993
This rather openly branched tree bears
pinnate leaves that can turn a rich yellow
in autumn, and pale pink flower clusters
in May. These are replaced by
comparatively large, glistening white,
marble-like fruits which hang in loose
clusters from the branches. Like most
white or yellow-fruited trees, this is
spared the attentions of birds who seem
averse to eating its fruit which, as a
result, remain on the branches until the
leaves have fallen in late autumn. As the
name implies, it is a native of Kashmir.

Sorbus commixta
S-M Vase-shaped to Spreading
A free-growing mountain ash with a
distinct vase-shaped habit when young,
the ascending branches spreading in later
life. The pinnate leaves are capable of
brilliant tints in autumn while at the
same time the polished bright red fruits
hang in ample bunches. Widely
distributed in the wild in Japan and
Korea, this is a tree of easy cultivation.
'Embley' AGM 1993 is a fine selection, its
leaves colouring reliably, later than most
and quite as brilliant. Suitable for all but
the smallest gardens.

Sorbus domestica
M-L Spreading
A strong-growing tree distinguished from
all others by its ultimate size, rough scaly
bark, and the combination of both pinnate
leaves and relatively large white flowers
in dense globose or conical panicles. It is
also distinct on account of its relatively
large rounded or pear-shaped, greenish-
brown, red-tinted fruits which are edible
when bletted (ripe). The round-fruited
form is distinguished as *pomifera* and the
pear-shaped form as *pyrifera*. Known as

top: Sorbus alnifolia
bottom: Sorbus meliosmifolia

the "Service Tree", this handsome species is native to southern and eastern Europe, western Asia and North Africa, thriving and fruiting most satisfactorily where summers are warm and dry, though it is hardy enough and long lived in Britain given a moist but well-drained loamy soil.

Sorbus forrestii

S Spreading
A first-class tree for the small garden introduced, from south-west China by the plant hunter George Forrest. It is allied to *S. hupehensis*, but is a smaller tree with larger and more conspicuous white fruits from October to December. The leaves also have more numerous leaflets.

Sorbus hupehensis

S Spreading AGM 1993
A distinct species recognisable, even from a distance, by the blue-green colour of its bold, deeply divided leaves. It is a strong-growing tree with purplish-brown branches, ascending on a young specimen. The fruits in autumn are white or pink-tinged and borne in loose drooping clusters lasting well into winter. A tree so laden is a welcome spectacle at Christmas time. It is a native of south-west China. The pink fruited forms are botanically referred to var. *obtusa* AGM 1993. There are available several named selections including 'Rosea', 'Rufus' and more recently, 'Pink Pagoda' which was selected in the University of British Columbia Botanic Garden in 1972.

Sorbus hybrida 'Gibbsii'

S-M Rounded to Spreading AGM 1993
A dense, round-headed tree with broad leaves deeply-lobed at the base, dark green above and grey-felted below. The bright red fruits are produced in large bunches in autumn, standing out from the dark foliage. This is a really tough and adaptable tree for all situations. *S. hybrida* is now considered to be the result of an ancient hybrid between *S. aucuparia* and *S. rupicola*, a rare member of the whitebeam group.

Sorbus intermedia

S-M Rounded to Spreading
The "Swedish Whitebeam" is a most adaptable tree, particularly suitable for town and city gardens where its dense, normally rounded dark crown is conspicuous from afar. The leaves are strongly-toothed and shallowly-lobed, being dark glossy green above and grey-felted below. The orange-red fruits in autumn occur in bunches along the branches. It is native to north-western Europe. 'Browers' AGM 1993 is a selected form, its ascending branches making a more ovoid crown and it is better suited to smaller gardens and street plantings.

Sorbus 'Joseph Rock'

S Vase-shaped to Spreading AGM 1993
Commemorating a famous American plant collector and explorer in western China, this superb tree richly deserves the praise it has received and the popularity it enjoys. As with most other Sorbus of this group, young trees possess upswept branches forming a vase-shaped head arching at the extremeties, spreading in maturity. The deeply divided leaves are made up of numerous toothed leaflets which turn from a bright summer green to a fiery combination of orange, red, copper and purple in autumn. At the same time, the clusters of fruit deepen from creamy-yellow to amber-yellow, glistening amid the rosetted foliage. These remain untouched by the birds and hang from the branches until well after the leaves have fallen. In some areas this rowan has been badly affected by fire-blight making its further cultivation impossible, while elsewhere it continues healthy.

Sorbus meliosmifolia

S Conical to Vase-shaped
One of the many Sorbus from western China, this uncommon but highly ornamental tree is notable for its compact head of upright branches and its strongly and conspicuously veined, oval leaves, which taper to a slender point. The clusters of white flowers appear with the young leaves in April, and are later

replaced by small brown fruits which hang in bunches from the branches and persist until long after leaf fall. A distinguished and unusual species, its compact habit makes it an ideal candidate for a small bed or border or as a lawn specimen.

Sorbus x kewensis

S Spreading AGM 1993
This is, perhaps, the heaviest-cropping of all the mountain ashes, the branches bending under the weight of its large dense bunches of orange-red berries. Its berries colour early, in September, and there is no greater autumn spectacle than a mature tree fully laden, before the birds have gone to work. As the name suggests, this tree originated in Kew Gardens. It is a hybrid between *S. aucuparia* and *S. pohuashanensis*.

Sorbus latifolia

M Rounded to Spreading
The "Service Tree of Fontainbleau" is not commonly seen in British gardens, though why this is so is hard to ascertain. It is a handsome species with rounded leaves margined with sharp teeth and shallow lobes. These are glossy dark green above, grey-felted beneath, ideal backing for the relatively large white flowers which are followed by rounded, brownish-red, pale-speckled fruits.

Sorbus sargentiana

S-M Conical to Spreading AGM 1993
A handsome, bold-foliaged Chinese rowan of distinct conical habit at first, becoming less so in maturity. The large pinnate leaves are often 30cm long on reddish stalks. These tend to form bold ruffs towards the ends of the stout shoots, providing a striking backing for the large flowerheads and equally large flattened bunches of small orange-scarlet fruits which follow. The leaves in autumn exhibit rich orange and red tints while even in winter this species is recognisable by its large red sticky terminal buds. Given space it makes a notable specimen tree.
top: Sorbus hupehensis
centre: Sorbus scalaris
bottom: Sorbus 'Joseph Rock'

Sorbus scalaris

S Spreading AGM 1993
If one has space in the garden for a small but wide-spreading Sorbus of handsome and elegant appearance, then this is probably the best choice. Its long branches arch outwards, eventually curving gently towards the ground. The leaves, which are dark glossy green and divided into numerous narrow leaflets, are gathered into delightful rosette-like clusters all along the boughs. Amid the leaves appear large, flattened, white flower-heads in spring, to be replaced by equally large clusters of small, late-ripening, bright red berries. The berries are generally ripening when the leaves are donning their autumn hues of red and purple. A native of western China, this is altogether a first-class all-round tree for any garden, space permitting.

Sorbus thibetica
'John Mitchell'

M Spreading AGM 1993
A handsome whitebeam, erect-branched when young, noted for its vigorous growth and its large rounded white-backed leaves. It has claims to being the largest leaved of its group and is easily the most handsome. Some leaves produced are almost circular like a small plate. The fruits are green at first, ripening to brown. It grows well on most soils, acid or alkaline. It was known at one time as *S. 'Mitchellii'*.

Sorbus x thuringiaca
'Fastigiata'

S-M Conical to Ovoid
In effect, the crown of this tree is more ovoid or lollipop-shaped than conical. The branches are stifly ascending, and so closely packed that the head is dense and impenetrable. The leaves are divided to the midrib at the base and shallowly-lobed elsewhere, whilst the clusters of white flowers in spring are replaced in autumn by bunches of glossy red berries. A hybrid between the "Whitebeam" (*S. aria*) and the "Rowan" (*S. aucuparia*), this easily recognisable tree possesses all the qualities of its parents, being very hardy and adaptable, particularly suitable for town and city gardens and those where space is restricted.

Sorbus torminalis

M-L Spreading
The "Wild Service Tree" is native to much of Europe (including England) as well as North Africa and western Asia. It is free-growing and distinguished by its relatively large, sharply and deeply-lobed maple-like leaves which are a shining dark green above, often turning yellow or red in autumn. The flowers are produced in June to be followed by relatively large brownish fruits, which in south-east England are known as "chequers". It is happy with most soils apart from those of strong acid nature, and is particularly good in chalk or limestone areas.

Sorbus vestita

M Conical to Spreading
The "Himalayan Whitebeam" presents a distinct erect habit as a young tree, broadening in maturity. It is mainly notable for its large, bold, often rounded leaves up to 25cm long. These are covered in a white down when emerging, becoming greyish-green above, silver-white beneath later. The creamy-white flower-clusters in May are followed, in autumn, by globular or pear-shaped brown and green fruits resembling small russet "crabs". This handsome tree is a native of the Himalayas and is quite hardy and vigorous in the British Isles, happy on most soils. Previously known as *S. cuspidata*.

Sorbus vilmorinii

VS-S Spreading AGM 1993
A charming tree of graceful habit, highly suitable for the small garden. The slender arching branches bear clusters of small fern-like leaves, each made up of numerous, small, prettily-toothed leaflets. These turn to shades of purple and red in autumn. The drooping clusters of small, rounded berries in autumn are glossy red at first, slowly changing to pink and finally white with a pink flush. They are long-lasting and decorate the naked branches after leaf fall. This is another desirable native of western China.

Sorbus wardii

S Broadly columnar to Conical
A rare Himalayan whitebeam introduced from the Burma-Tibetan border by the plant hunter Kingdon Ward. In early life it is remarkably columnar, gradually swelling out to an ovoid or conical crown. Its broad, boldly veined leaves are greyish-green at first becoming green later, when they are an ideal foil for the clusters of relatively large yellow fruits which ripen to orange-yellow and finally brown. It is still rare in cultivation but well worth seeking out. Its compact crown makes it an ideal candidate for the smaller garden where it makes an excellent lawn specimen.

STUARTIA
Theaceae

A small genus of deciduous trees and shrubs notable for late summer flowering, autumn colour and ornamental bark. None is very large in cultivation and all appreciate a moist but well-drained, lime-free soil and a sheltered site. They resent disturbance and are best planted small in a position where their shallow root system is shaded from the direct rays of the summer sun. Sometimes catalogued under the alternative spelling STEWARTIA.

Stuartia malacodendron

S Spreading
A choice American species with rich brown bark and dark green leaves 5–10cm long. The blue and purple stamens give a striking dark "eye" to the white flowers, which are 6–8cm across and produced singly from the leaf axils in July and August. Its habit tends to be shrubby but with careful initial pruning it can be encouraged to develop a central stem. It flowers best in the warmer areas of Britain, preferably in a sunny but sheltered site.

Stuartia pseudocamellia

S-M Vase-shaped to Spreading
AGM 1993
This attractive long-flowering Japanese tree is free-growing when once established. The slender spreading or arching branches each carry numerous cup-shaped, yellow-anthered, white flowers which rapidly open and fall to be replaced by others over several weeks. Thus, throughout July and August this tree is never out of bloom. In a good autumn the leaves turn to shades of yellow, red or purple, finally succumbing to the cold fingers of winter, when, leafless and alone, a large specimen shows off its flaking bark for all to see.

Stuartia pseudocamellia koreana

S-M Conical to Spreading AGM 1993
A beautiful Korean tree of elegant growth, often conical when young. The slender pointed leaves often give warm orange-brown or orange-red tints in autumn, whilst the white flowers with silky-backed spreading petals and a central tuft of yellow stamens occur singly in the leaf axils at intervals along the branches, opening in continual succession from July to August. The bark, especially on older trees, is attractively flaking, creating a striking effect.

Stuartia sinensis

S-M Spreading AGM 1993
One of the best trees cultivated for ornamental bark, this handsome Chinese species makes a striking lawn or border specimen in full sun. Its thin smooth bark changes from a reddish shade in summer, to purple and finally brown when it peels away to reveal the pale young bark. The solitary white fragrant cup-shaped flowers up to 5cm across are borne in the leaf axils in late summer.

STYRAX
Stryracaceae

A large genus of deciduous trees and shrubs grown mainly for their flowers and often attractive foliage which turns yellow in autumn. Like the Stuartias they thrive best in a moist but well-drained lime-free loam, in sun or semi-shade. They also resent disturbance when once established and are best

*planted when small, straight into their permanent
position, which should be carefully prepared
beforehand.*

Styrax hemsleyana
S-M Spreading AGM 1993
A handsome bold-foliaged Chinese tree
similar in some respects to *S. obassia*,
differing principally in the chocolate-
coloured winter buds which are exposed
during summer, and in the less rounded,
more finely-toothed leaves which are
smoother beneath. These turn yellow in
autumn. The beautiful white, yellow-
beaked flowers are borne in downy
racemes or panicles from the tips of the
shoots in June, when a tree in full bloom
is a lovely sight.

Stryax japonica
S Spreading AGM 1993
To see a large flowering specimen of this
beautiful tree is a most satisfying
experience. Its slender fan-like branches
are wide-spreading and are piled layer
upon layer to form a dense mound. The
small white star-like flowers have a
central yellow cluster of stamens and
appear, often in prodigious numbers,
along the slender branchlets in June.
Because they are pendulous, the flowers
tend to be obscured by the dense but
elegant foliage, and the branches
therefore need to be lifted or viewed from
below in order to appreciate fully the
display. In order to facilitate viewing it is
sometimes planted on a convenient bank.
It is a native of China, Japan and Korea.

Styrax japonica 'Benibana'
S Spreading
A charming variation of the type in which
the flowers are a pale almond pink. 'Pink
Chimes' is very similar if not the same.

Styrax obassia
S-M Rounded to Spreading AGM 1993
Very different in appearance from *S.
japonica*, this choice Japanese species
develops a conical or rounded head of
branches, with large handsome rounded
leaves which are softly felted beneath.
The bark of the previous year's shoots is
chestnut-brown in colour, curling and

top: Stuartia pseudocamellia koreana
bottom: Styrax japonica

151

flaking in a pleasing manner. In June the fragrant white bell-shaped flowers appear in long, lax racemes from the tips of the branches, but not on young trees. In order to grow this tree well it is important to give it a good start, adding to the planting hole a nice leaf-mould or similar. It also appreciates the company and shelter of other trees or large shrubs. It is most closely related to *S. hemsleyana*, differing in its larger, more rounded leaves, felted beneath, and in its paler winter buds which are concealed during summer in the swollen base of the leaf stalks.

SYRINGA
Oleaceae

Many lilacs will naturally develop into a very small tree in time or they can be encouraged to do so by careful pruning. The following, however, is the one most often seen as such in British gardens though it is nowhere common

Syringa reticulata
S Spreading
Although uncommon in British cultivation, this strong-growing Japanese lilac is extremely hardy and tolerant of most soils including those on chalk. Its neat heart-shaped, slender pointed leaves and reddish-brown cherry-like bark distinguish it from most others of its clan, as do the fragrant creamy-white flowers borne in large terminal heads in late June. The fragrance is heavy and to some noses cloying, like that of privet. In North America it is considered the toughest of all lilacs, although it has to be said that it performs best where summers are warm and dry.

TETRACENTRON
Tetracentraceae

A rare monotypic genus normally only represented in specialist collections. It is native to China and the eastern Himalaya.

Tetracentron sinense
S-M Spreading to Wide-spreading
A deciduous commonly multi-stemmed tree with an aspect and leafage not unlike a *Cercidiphyllum*. The ovate or heart-shaped leaves however are alternate (not opposite). Minute yellowish flowers are born in pendulous slender catkin-like spikes from the leaf axils in summer.

TETRADIUM
Rutaceae

A small genus of deciduous and evergreen trees and shrubs off the Rue family. The following species, previously included in the genus Euodia, *are hardy and deciduous trees suitable for most soils. Male and female flowers are often but not always borne on separate trees. Not suitable for exposed sites but reasonably tolerant of city conditions where, given space, they grow into handsome specimens.*

Tetradium daniellii
S-M Spreading
A handsome tree from Korea and China, with large shining opposite ash-like leaves sometimes turning yellow in autumn. The small white pungently scented flowers beloved of bees are borne in terminal branched heads in July to August or later, followed on female trees by reddish-purple fruits containing shining blackish seeds.

Tetradium hupehensis
S-M Spreading
Similar in ornamental merit to the last, it is especially tolerant of poor or shallow chalk soils. Like *T. daniellii*, this distinguished foliage tree is at its most ornamental when in fruit which can be spectacular after a warm summer. These ripen from bright orange-red to red.

TILIA
Tiliaceae

The 'Limes' or 'Lindens' ('Basswoods' in North America), are a large genus of hardy deciduous trees occurring in the wild throughout the northern temperate regions. None are grown for their flowers, which, though scented and produced in abundance, are small and greenish yellow in colour. Several have attractive leaves, and the majority make stately specimens ideal for large gardens and parks. They are easily grown on almost all soils and are tolerant of atmospheric pollution as well as hard pruning. They may be recognised in summer by their alternately arranged heart-shaped leaves, and in winter by their wavy twigs.

The apparent toxic effect on bees shown by the nectar of some limes, especially Tilia 'Petiolaris', *is not as simple as it was once believed. Like all nectars, that of limes is a mixture of various sugars. According to Andrew Halstead of the Royal Horticultural Society, the nectar of* T. *'Petiolaris' contains significant quantities of a sugar called mannose. Bees are unable to metabolize this fully and some of their digestive enzymes become irreversibly bound up wih the sugar. They soon run out of enzymes capable of digesting other sugars and, as a result, they starve, even though their stomachs may be full of nectar. In the early stages of this type of poisoning the bee lacks co-ordination and crawls around drunkedly underneath the tree. In Britain certainly, the bees most commonly affected often fatally so are bumble bees.*

Tilia americana

L Conical to Spreading
The "American Linden" or "Basswood" is a handsome foliage tree of vigorous growth, especially when young, with striking rich deep olive-green heart-shaped leaves with prominent yellow veins on shining green young shoots. The flowers are green rather than the typical cream colour. It develops a conical habit at first, the lower branches drooping, then curving upwards in maturity. There are several excellent selections.

Tilia americana 'Nova'

L Conical to Spreading
A strong-growing selection of German origin with ovoid crown at first and large bold long-lasting leaves. Suitable for parks and large estates.

Tilia cordata

M-L Spreading to Rounded AGM 1993
The "Small-leaved Lime" is one of our two native species, the other being T. *platyphyllos*. It develops a handsome rounded head of branches, with small, neatly heart-shaped, rather leathery leaves of a glossy dark green above. The tiny ivory-coloured flowers in July are sweetly scented and beloved by bees. It occurs in the wild throughout Europe. 'Winter Orange' is a recent selection with orange-red shoots in winter. It is not commonly available in Britain but worth searching for.

Tilia x europaea 'Wratislaviensis'

153

Tilia cordata 'Greenspire'

M-L Conical AGM 1993
A selection of more upright growth with a strong main leader and attractive branching habit. This is more suitable for the garden than the type.

Tilia x euchlora

M Spreading AGM 1993
An elegant tree when young, with olive-green shoots in winter, becoming rather dense and twiggy, with pendulous lower branches, when older. The comparatively large, handsome leaves are rounded and of a bright glossy green above. This tree is said to be a hybrid between the "Small-leaved Lime" (*T. cordata*) and the uncommon *T. dasystyla*. It is especially noted for its healthy appearance and does not suffer from the sticky attentions of aphids in the same way as does the "Common Lime" (*T. x europaea*). Its nectar however is toxic to bees, bumble bees certainly.

Tilia x euchlora

Tilia x europaea

L Spreading
Although the "Common Lime" has been planted extensively formerly, particularly as an avenue tree, its dense and unsightly suckering habit, early leaf fall and attraction to aphids has caused it to be relegated in favour of more desirable limes. The following cultivars, however, are worth consideration.

Tilia x europaea 'Pallida'

L Conical to Spreading
A far more desirable tree than the type, developing a more conical crown. Its leaves also differ in being a distinct yellowish-green beneath. It is suitable for large parks and other open spaces, being fairly wind resistant.

Tilia x europaea 'Wratislaviensis'

L Spreading AGM 1993
An uncommon and unusual form of the "Common Lime" in which the leaves are a bright golden yellow when young, becoming green as they mature. This is a most attractive large tree in the same mould as the "Golden Poplar" (*Populus* 'Serotina Aurea').

Tilia henryana

S-M Spreading
A rare Chinese lime distinct on account of its large, heart-shaped leaves which are margined with conspicuous bristle-tipped teeth. Dark green and glossy-topped when mature they are a characteristic coppery-red on first emerging. In the wild in Hubei province this species is known to reach a large size, but it is rarely more than 10m in cultivation.

Tilia maximowicziana

M-L Spreading
A handsome "Silver Lime" from northern Japan with large greyish-white backed leaves and creamy-white, fragrant flowers in June. Suitable for a large garden or park. Like *T. oliveri* it is rarely offered by the nursery trade. More's the pity, for it is a splendid hardy tree.

Tilia 'Moltkei'

L Weeping
A vigorous handsome tree in maturity, resulting from a cross between *T. americana* and *T.* 'Petiolaris'. It bears large rounded leaves, dark green above and silvery-grey beneath, borne on pendulous shoots. Young trees are upright in habit.

Tilia mongolica

M Spreading AGM 1993
The "Mongolian Lime" is one of the few species suitable for relatively small gardens, although in a good soil it grows vigorously. It develops a neat, compact, rounded head of branches and is easily recognised by its small leaves which are sharply three-lobed (at least on young trees) and strongly-toothed. In fact, they resemble more those of certain thorns (*Crataegus*) and would puzzle all bar the experts on first being seen. They are a glossy green during summer, turning butter-yellow in autumn. It is native to Mongolia and northern China.

Tilia oliveri

L Spreading
One of the most beautiful of all limes: a Chinese species noted for the silvery-white downy underside to the leaf which is especially effective when the leaves are ruffled by a wind. The creamy-white flowers are fragrant and well displayed. It remains rare in cultivation.

Tilia 'Petiolaris'

L Spreading and Weeping AGM 1993
Along with *Salix x sepulcralis* 'Chrysocoma', the "Weeping Silver Lime" is perhaps the most spectacular of large weeping trees. The leaves are dark green above and white-felted beneath, rustling and turning in the wind. The tiny flowers, though sweetly fragrant, are toxic to bees, bumble bees certainly. It is of unknown origin though very close to *T. tomentosa*. 'Chelsea Sentinel' is a selected form of 'Petiolaris' raised in the grounds of the Royal Hospital at Chelsea, home of the Chelsea Flower Show. The original tree of broadly columnar habit with weeping extremeties sadly blew down in the Great Gale of October 1987.

Tilia platyphyllos

L Conical to Spreading
This is a large vigorous tree in the manner of *T. x europaea*. It differs from the "Common Lime", however, in its downy young twigs and leaves and in its relatively clean, non-suckering habit. The larger flowers are fragrant and the first among limes to open. In common with other "green leaved" limes, with the possible exception of *T. x euchlora*, the nectar they produce is not toxic to bees. Its leaves, however, are subject to aphid infestations. It is found in the wild in Europe, including the British Isles, and is commonly represented in cultivation by the cultivar 'Rubra'.

Tilia platyphyllos 'Laciniata'

S-M Conical to Spreading
A most effective tree of dense habit with leaves which are deeply and variously cut and toothed, often with tail-like points. It is an excellent tree to plant where the type would be too large.

Tilia mongolica

Tilia platyphyllos 'Rubra'

L Conical to Spreading AGM 1993
The "Reg-twigged Lime" is very popular as a roadside tree particularly in industrial areas. In habit it is more compact and erect than the type and the bright reddish young twigs are conspicuous during winter. A most attractive large tree for towns and cities, wherever space is available. Most suitable as an avenue tree.

Tilia tomentosa

L Conical to Spreading
Conical as a young tree, the strongly ascending branches of the "Silver Lime" gradually open up at the tips with age to present one of the most stately of all trees. The large rounded leaves are dark green above, white-felted beneath and are very effective when ruffled by a breeze. The nectar produced by the fragrant flowers has proved toxic to bees, bumble bees certainly. It is a native of south-eastern and east-central Europe and is commonly planted as a park tree in many countries.

Toona sinensis

Tilia tomentosa 'Brabant'

L Conical to Spreading AGM 1993
A Dutch selection of vigorous, erect growth at first, later broadening. Highly thought of in Holland where it is planted on large estates and in parks. It is recommended as being particularly adaptable to sea winds and industrial pollution although its young growths are susceptible to late spring frosts.

TOONA
Meliaceae

A small genus of trees belonging to the Mahogany family. The following is the only species hardy in the northern temperate zone.

Toona sinensis

M-L Spreading
A tall tree eventually: hardy, deciduous and possessed of large handsome pinnate leaves which tend to form bold ruffs towards the ends of the branches. They are similar in some respects to those of the "Tree of Heaven" (*Ailanthus altissima*) but the leaflets lack teeth and have a distinct oniony smell and taste when young. Indeed, in its native North China the leaves are cooked and eaten. The tiny white fragrant flowers are produced in large pendulous panicles from the tips of the branches in June but only on mature trees. It flowers best and certainly more reliably in countries and regions enjoying regular warm summers. In Britain this distinguished tree is often capable of a good height. It is generally found catalogued under the name *Cedrela sinensis*.

Toona sinensis 'Flamingo'

M Spreading
In this remarkable selection, the young leaves, which in the typical tree are reddish-bronze, are coloured a striking shrimp pink. It needs protection, however, from cold winds and spring frosts.

TROCHODENDRON
Trochodendraceae

A genus of a single species native to Japan, Korea and Taiwan. It will thrive in most soils except those on shallow chalk, and is tolerant of light shade. Although relatively hardy it does not enjoy positions exposed to cold winds.

Trochodendron aralioides

S Spreading

An extremely handsome evergreen capable of reaching a large size in the wild but normally a small tree in Britain. The young stems and the long-stalked leaves are a rich green, the latter leathery, pointed and typically glossy above. They are borne in ruffs towards the ends of the branches, above which from April to June rise domed clusters of vivid green flowers. Indeed, this curious and uncommon tree is green in all its parts and well merits a place in all but the smallest or exposed garden.

ULMUS
Ulmaceae

Some of the stateliest of deciduous trees are found among the 'Elms'. They are hardy, fast-growing trees adaptable to most soils and situations, withstanding strong winds and atmospheric pollution equally well. Their flowers are rather small and of no great ornamental merit, appearing in most species, before the leaves in early spring. The leaves are usually peculiarly uneven at the base and turn a clear yellow in autumn. Dutch Elm Disease (Ceratocystis ulmi) has all but wiped out the elm populations, wild and cultivated, in many parts of Britain though some species, notably U. glabra and its hybrids, are holding out in isolated areas especially in the north. While the disease continues to spread there is clearly no point in recommending elms which may only be grown in limited areas. There are, however, two species from north-east Asia, U. parvifolia and U. pumila, plus a hybrid, which have demonstrated a resistance to the disease and are therefore included here.

There are in addition, several relatively new elms of Dutch origin notably 'Clusius', 'Dodoens', 'Lobel' and 'Plantijn', (all hybrids of the Himalyan species U. wallichiana) which are giving cause for hope in Holland and have recently been introduced into Britain. Only time will tell if they possess the ultimate immunity, although Dutch growers speak very favourably of them.

Ulmus parvifolia

S-M Spreading

A small-leaved often elegant elm native to China, Korea and Japan where it is tolerant of drought and cold as well as air pollution and compaction of the soil. The stems on some trees are attractively dappled as the older bark turns grey and flakes to reveal the reddish-brown young bark, hence the English name "Lacebark Elm". In warmer climates than ours the bark effect is paler and beautifully marbled. This characteristic, however, is most usually seen on trees growing in a continental climate of cold dry winters and hot summers. It is unusual in being one of the few elms that flower in late summer or autumn while the leaves are still green. The small neatly-toothed leaves remain on the slender branches until December or the New Year. Several clones are becoming available in Britain including 'Geisha' and 'Hokkaido'.

Ulmus pumila

S-M Spreading

Although far less ornamental than the last, the Siberian elm is just as tough and adaptable. Its bark is grey and ridged and its leaves usually slightly longer, less glossy above and, unusual for an elm, equal-sided at the base. Its flowers appear in spring though these are of no ornamental merit. Like *U. parvifolia* it is said to be resistant to Dutch Elm Disease. Its main fault lies in its brittle branches which are liable to break in strong winds, and it should not therefore be planted in exposed sites. Several selections have been made including 'Coolshade', a slower growing clone with less brittle branches, and 'Den Haag' with a loose open crown to 20m high eventually, and resistant to wind damage.

Ulmus
'Sapporo Autumn Gold'
S-M Spreading
A Japanese bred hybrid between *U. pumila* and *U. japonica* which is upright in habit at first, later spreading. The lush dark green leaves are capable of turning a rich golden yellow in autumn. As yet this elm is in limited supply and has mainly been planted experimentally in collections and parks, but hopefully it will soon become more widely available.

†UMBELLULARIA
Lauraceae

A monotypic genus native to Oregon and California where it is found in the coastal ranges and the Sierra Nevada.

Umbellularia californica
S-M Spreading
The "California Laurel" is an evergreen tree of dense bushy habit suitable only for warmer areas of the British Isles. Its narrow leathery leaves give off a pungent aroma when crushed, and when deeply inhaled is claimed by some to bring on a headache: hence the alternative name "Headache Tree". Although related to the "Bay" (*Laurus nobilis*), its leaves lack the sweetness of that tree, nor are they quite so ornamental.

ZELKOVA
Ulmaceae

Related to the 'Elms', the zelkovas are a small genus of hardy, deciduous trees and occasionally shrubs. Their ornamental value rests in their attractive leafage and sometimes stately habit. They thrive best on a deep well-drained loam and are tolerant of both shade and atmospheric pollution.

Although neither of the following species is entirely immune to Dutch Elm Disease, they have shown enough resistance to make their planting a fairly safe recommendation: though it would be prudent perhaps not to consider them for important or critical sites, especially in cities or towns.

Zelkova carpinifolia
L Vase-shaped
This is definitely a tree to plant for posterity; for, although its boldly-toothed leaves, turning golden in autumn, are effective enough, it isn't until a tree is maturing that its full beauty is appreciated. Large specimens may be seen in several parts of the British Isles, usually in parks or on large estates, although I have seen a fine specimen on a street in one of the London boroughs and another in a vicarage garden in Hampshire. Slow-growing, it gradually develops its characteristic short-trunked, erect and densely branched habit to form a dome-shaped head in maturity, with long upswept branches somewhat like a monstrous besom. The bark is grey, similar to that of a beech, on older trees flaking attractively to create a piebald effect. It is native to the Caucasus and northern Iran, where, in the latter region, I have seen it growing with oak trees on the northern slopes of the Elburz Mountains, above the Caspian Sea.

Zelkova serrata
M Vase-shaped to Dome-shaped
AGM 1993
Quite unlike the previous species in habit, the present tree although vase-shaped for a time forms a rounded or dome-shaped head of graceful widespreading branches. The bark is grey and smooth, flaking on older trees, while the slender pointed, boldly toothed leaves turn to yellow, bronze or reddish-brown in autumn. It is a native of China and Korea as well as Japan, in which countries it is commonly planted by temples and shrines. A selection called 'Village Green' is occasionally available. It is said to have a more symmetrical habit and superior autumn colour, and to be highly resistant to Dutch Elm Disease.

page 160: Cornus nuttallii

INDEX OF COMMON NAMES